Spring 2003   Vol. XXIII, n
ISSN: 0276-0045   ISBN: 1-564

D0450874

THE REVIEW OF
CONTEMPORARY FICTION

Editor

JOHN O'BRIEN
Illinois State University

Senior Editor

ROBERT L. MCLAUGHLIN
Illinois State University

Book Review Editor

TIM FEENEY

Guest Editor

DAVID ANDREWS

Production & Design

N. J. FURL

Editorial Assistant

ADAM JONES

Cover Illustration

SAMUEL BERKES

www.centerforbookculture.org
www.dalkeyarchive.com

The Review of Contemporary Fiction is published three times a year (January, June, September) by the Center for Book Culture, a nonprofit organization located at ISU Campus Box 8905, Normal, IL 61790-8905. ISSN 0276-0045. Subscription prices are as follows:

Single volume (three issues):
      Individuals: $17.00; foreign, add $3.50;
      Institutions: $26.00; foreign, add $3.50.

DISTRIBUTION. Bookstores should send orders to:

Review of Contemporary Fiction, ISU Campus Box 8905, Normal, IL 61790-8905. Phone 309-438-7555; fax 309-438-7422.

This issue is partially supported by a grant from the Illinois Arts Council, a state agency.

Indexed in *American Humanities Index, International Bibliography of Periodical Literature, International Bibliography of Book Reviews, MLA Bibliography,* and *Book Review Index.* Abstracted in *Abstracts of English Studies.*

The Review of Contemporary Fiction is also available on 16mm microfilm, 35mm microfilm, and 105mm microfiche from University Microfilms International, 300 North Zeeb Road, Ann Arbor, MI 48106-1346.

www.centerforbookculture.org

THE REVIEW OF CONTEMPORARY FICTION

BACK ISSUES AVAILABLE

Back issues are still available for the following numbers of the *Review of Contemporary Fiction* ($8 each unless otherwise noted):

DOUGLAS WOOLF / WALLACE MARKFIELD
WILLIAM EASTLAKE / AIDAN HIGGINS
ALEXANDER THEROUX / PAUL WEST
CAMILO JOSÉ CELA
CLAUDE SIMON ($15)
CHANDLER BROSSARD
SAMUEL BECKETT
CLAUDE OLLIER / CARLOS FUENTES
JOHN BARTH / DAVID MARKSON
DONALD BARTHELME / TOBY OLSON
PAUL BOWLES / COLEMAN DOWELL
BRIGID BROPHY / ROBERT CREELEY /
    OSMAN LINS
WILLIAM T. VOLLMANN / SUSAN DAITCH /
    DAVID FOSTER WALLACE
WILLIAM H. GASS / MANUEL PUIG
ROBERT WALSER
JOSÉ DONOSO / JEROME CHARYN
GEORGES PEREC / FELIPE ALFAU
JOSEPH MCELROY
DJUNA BARNES

ANGELA CARTER / TADEUSZ KONWICKI
STANLEY ELKIN / ALASDAIR GRAY
EDMUND WHITE / SAMUEL R. DELANY
MARIO VARGAS LLOSA / JOSEF
    ŠKVORECKÝ
WILSON HARRIS / ALAN BURNS
RAYMOND QUENEAU / CAROLE MASO
RICHARD POWERS / RIKKI DUCORNET
EDWARD SANDERS
WRITERS ON WRITING: THE BEST OF *THE*
    REVIEW OF CONTEMPORARY FICTION
BRADFORD MORROW
JEAN RHYS / JOHN HAWKES /
    PAUL BOWLES / MARGUERITE YOUNG
HENRY GREEN / JAMES KELMAN /
    ARIEL DORFMAN
JANICE GALLOWAY / THOMAS BERNHARD /
    ROBERT STEINER / ELIZABETH BOWEN
GILBERT SORRENTINO / WILLIAM GADDIS /
    MARY CAPONEGRO / MARGERY LATIMER

NOVELIST AS CRITIC: Essays by Garrett, Barth, Sorrentino, Wallace, Ollier, Brooke-Rose, Creeley, Mathews, Kelly, Abbott, West, McCourt, McGonigle, and McCarthy

NEW FINNISH FICTION: Fiction by Eskelinen, Jäntti, Kontio, Krohn, Paltto, Sairanen, Selo, Siekkinen, Sund, Valkeapää

NEW ITALIAN FICTION: Interviews and fiction by Malerba, Tabucchi, Zanotto, Ferrucci, Busi, Corti, Rasy, Cherchi, Balduino, Ceresa, Capriolo, Carrera, Valesio, and Gramigna

GROVE PRESS NUMBER: Contributions by Allen, Beckett, Corso, Ferlinghetti, Jordan, McClure, Rechy, Rosset, Selby, Sorrentino, and others

NEW DANISH FICTION: Fiction by Brøgger, Høeg, Andersen, Grøndahl, Holst, Jensen, Thorup, Michael, Sibast, Ryum, Lynggaard, Grønfeldt, Willumsen, and Holm

THE FUTURE OF FICTION: Essays by Birkerts, Caponegro, Franzen, Galloway, Maso, Morrow, Vollmann, White, and others

Individuals receive a 10% discount on orders of one issue and a 20% discount on orders of two or more issues. To place an order, use the form on the last page of this issue.

www.centerforbookculture.org/review

The Review of Contemporary Fiction is seeking contributors to write overview essays on the following writers:

Felipe Alfau, Chandler Brossard, Gabrielle Burton, Michel Butor, Julieta Campos, Jerome Charyn, Emily Coleman, Stanley Crawford, Eva Figgs, William H. Gass, Karen Elizabeth Gordon, Carol De Chellis Hill, Jennifer Johnston, Gert Jonke, Violette Le Duc, Wallace Markfield, Ollive Moore, Julián Ríos, Esther Tusquets.

The essays must:

- be 50 double-spaced pages;
- cover the subject's biography;
- summarize the critical reception of the subject's works;
- discuss the course of the subject's career, including each major work;
- provide interpretive strategies for new readers to apply to the subject's work;
- provide a bibliographic checklist of each of the subject's works (initial and latest printings) and the most;
- be written for a general, intelligent reader, who does not know the subject's work;
- avoid jargon, theoretical digressions, and excessive endnotes;
- be intelligent, interesting, and readable;
- be documented in MLA style.

Authors will be paid $250.00 when the essay is published. All essays will be subject to editorial review, and the editors reserve the right to request revisions and to reject unacceptable essays.

Applicants should send a CV and a brief writing sample. In your cover letter, be sure to address your qualifications

Send applications to:

Robert L. McLaughlin
Dalkey Archive Press, Illinois State University, Campus Box 8905, Normal, IL 61790-8905

Inquiries: rmclaugh@ilstu.edu

Contents

Editor's Note

This special issue of the *Review of Contemporary Fiction* offers a casebook on Gilbert Sorrentino's 1971 novel *Imaginative Qualities of Actual Things.* Guest editor David Andrews has gathered a group of essays that offer different interpretive strategies for approaching the novel, and he has provided an introduction to the novel, its critical reception, and the interpretive challenges it offers, as well as his own response to some of those challenges. We hope this casebook will be a resource for instructors interested in teaching the novel, students studying it, and all readers devoted to innovative fiction.

We also offer the casebook as one example of what can be found on the Center for Book Culture web site <www.centerforbookculture.org/casebooks/index.html>: casebooks on William H. Gass's *The Tunnel,* Carole Maso's *AVA,* Flann O'Brien's *At Swim-Two-Birds,* Gert Jonke's *Geometric Regional Novel,* and Stanley Elkin's *The Dick Gibson Show,* with other titles forthcoming.

This issue also presents Miriam Fuchs's interview with Marguerite Young, author of *Miss MacIntosh, My Darling.* Fuchs spoke to Young two years before her death, not long before the publication of her last book, *Harp Song for a Radical.*

Jacket front panel:

      Title: Imaginative Qualities of Actual Things

      Author: Gilbert Sorrentino

      Copy: A Novel

Jacket spine:

      Title: Imaginative Qualities of Actual Things

      Author: Gilbert Sorrentino

      Imprint: Pantheon

Binding die:

      Title: Imaginative Qualities of Actual Things

      Author: Gilbert Sorrentino

      Imprint: Pantheon

OK 7/15

First edition, Pantheon 1971

Of Love, Scorn, and Contradiction: An Interpretive Overview of Gilbert Sorrentino's Imaginative Qualities of Actual Things

David Andrews

Gilbert Sorrentino has said that Edward Dahlberg "exists as an enormous, stubborn giant of American letters," who, because of his obstinacy, is "largely unread" (*Something* 99). He might, of course, have said the same of himself, and, more particularly, of his third novel, *Imaginative Qualities of Actual Things* (1971). Though Dalkey Archive Press has, since 1991, made sure that *Imaginative Qualities* remains in print, the book remains relatively unread despite its virtues, which include an acerbic aesthete narrator and an inventive send-up of the New York City artworld of the 1950s and 1960s. Part of this neglect owes to the misunderstandings evinced by the novel's reviews. Reacting, for instance, primarily to its sharp satire, the novel's reviewers have typically complained of the author's "malicious" wit, as if *Imaginative Qualities* were no more than a droll effusion of literary bile—a view that has subtly infected the criticism as well. This, I believe, is an unfortunate simplification—though not a surprising one, given that the novel is far more complicated than it first appears, an avant-garde metafiction characterized by its tensions, qualifications, and apparent contradictions.

Take the novel's central paradox. Judging from intrinsic and extrinsic evidence, *Imaginative Qualities* is meant to be a useless work of art, one whose aesthetic value, in Sorrentino's aesthete opinion, transcends "mere" referentiality. On the other hand, the author has admitted the book's satirical intentions. Satire is one of the most use-oriented forms; it depends not only on realistic linguistic assumptions to convey its didactic point but also on realistic literary conventions to make its caricatures recognizable. How can any work be at once antireferential and referential, a useless work of art and a use-oriented satire? Still, this is but one of the text's many knots. The novel is also "about" a romantic form of aestheticism, one that sacralizes art as Art, even as the book focuses on trash (or Trash). Similarly, the novel pits an ideal, Platonic form of love against adultery, a sexual form of love that is presented as corrupt, joyless, and use-oriented. I could continue—on a more theoretical plane, for example, the novel puts epistemological antiessentialism at the service of aesthetic essentialism—but for now it is best to stop.

To put it plainly: though often misconstrued as *primarily* sneering and cynical, *Imaginative Qualities* is an idealistic text that, in a complex way, is "about" love; it is also the product of a defiantly romantic aestheticism. To understand this, one must first understand that *Imaginative Qualities* presents its reader with a web of interdependent, value-laden binaries wherein all the negative terms may be viewed as subordinate to their positive opposites; indeed, it is not too much to say that the intense emphasis the novel's author places on each positive term (love, art, uselessness, etc.) in a sense determines the often cynical emphasis his primary narrator places on the negative. Though abstract, this view of the book has its benefits. For one, it suggests that the author views the art/satire dichotomy in a hierarchical way that makes it unproblematic: the useless work of art is the author's end, while the satire, a component of the whole and a direct product of the narrative voice, is his means. This view also allows one to escape a related dilemma involving the "wise guy" narrator, whose opinions often resemble Sorrentino's own. If the narrator's implacable opinions are too simplistically linked to Sorrentino, *Imaginative Qualities* may, beyond seeming cynical, seem overtly hateful, given another resemblance: its characters have been viewed as satirical reconstructions of the author's acquaintances. Put this together and it may seem that Sorrentino has disguised a personal attack on former friends and acquaintances via ostensibly impersonal literary devices.

This view, though tempting and understandable, is a more egregious misreading than the one noted earlier. For one thing, it fails to trust Sorrentino on two key modernist issues on which he has *never,* over the course of a long, unswerving career, equivocated: his critical belief that works of art are autonomous (and, by extension, "useless") and his primary artistic imperative to make such works of art. Obviously, Sorrentino has always known that his characters and his narrator bear resemblances to his acquaintances and to himself, respectively. Consequently, if he is taken at his word apropos his critical beliefs and aesthetic intentions, one can only surmise that the novel is his attempt to manipulate those similarities to artistic ends. Perhaps, in accord with critic and publishing ally John O'Brien's suggestion, Sorrentino injects self-referential allusions and opinions into *Imaginative Qualities* so as "to treat this subject formally, finally showing that the 'I' is not *I*" ("Every" 75). This idea might in turn be applied to the seemingly transparent characters. Sorrentino, it seems, has chosen self-referential, even hortative material so as to present himself with an apparently insoluble problem: How does one "transfigure" potentially didactic subject matter into useless artistic content?

Predictably, his solution to this problem involves the processes of complication and contradiction noted above. These procedures—which I will refer to as an art of "mixed signifiers"—are designed to neutralize the text's referential codes, making it an autonomous, useless, modernist artwork. And whether or not one agrees that Sorrentino has transformed self-referential satire into Art, one may still agree that the failure of readers to discern *Imaginative Qualities*'s complex intention has inspired him to create increasingly artificial works—works whose ideas and voices cannot be confused with reality or even, for that matter, with realistic illusion. I say this because *Imaginative Qualities* is clearly a transitional text (a point, incidentally, that Stacey Olster also makes in this issue). Though Sorrentino revisits many of the same themes and devices in *Splendide-Hôtel* (1973) and *Mulligan Stew* (1979), these fictions are artificialized and depersonalized to greater extents, an accelerating modernist process that eventuates in the unprecedented artifice of *Pack of Lies,* a trilogy of novels written during the 1980s and published in tandem in 1997. That is, it is possible the aforementioned misreadings of *Imaginative Qualities*—and the personal attacks on the author they inspired—have played a role in determining the shape of his oeuvre as a whole.

Before limning this interpretive path, it helps, first, to provide a descriptive and historical overview of the book and its reception. As noted at the outset, *Imaginative Qualities* is framed as a satirical treatment of the New York artworld of the 1950s and 1960s. The narrative divides into eight chapters roughly equal in length. Each is devoted to a single character: Sheila Henry, Lou Henry, Guy Lewis, Bunny Lewis, Leo Kaufman, Anton Harley, Bart Kahane, and Dick Detective, respectively. According to the narrator, *Imaginative Qualities* "is a book about destruction" (191), in fine, the destruction of art and talent, so it is apt that all of these characters except one, Bunny, comprise a list of artists manqués on the one hand and legitimate talents compromised by alcoholism, cheap notions of success, and arty clichés on the other. Though interconnected, these eight sections never coalesce into a conventional narrative. *Imaginative Qualities* contains no protagonist in the usual sense and, despite its narrative vignettes, it features no unitary plot. Instead, the sketches coalesce into a mordant, highly particularized depiction of the New York artworld. Like the sad, Brooklyn setting of *Steelwork* (1970), Sorrentino's second novel, this arty urban milieu fulfills the unifying function typically filled by a protagonist-oriented plot structure—as if the author, by scrambling and fragmenting the book's temporal structure, intends to emphasize the spatial and the tactile, creating a narrative that functions more like a collage than a traditional novel.

Imaginative Qualities's chapters also function in collagelike ways, suggesting that the novel's structure is hardly its only salient innovation. Each chapter is a comic bricolage containing idiosyncratic features, including letters, inept poems and songs, catalogs of names and things (Kevin Boon's discussion of the novel's catalogs is quite helpful in this regard), footnotes and marginalia, question-and-answer sections, essay fragments, and quotations. The "poems" are riotously funny, their vitriolic comedy sharpening their thematic significance. Indeed, such "samples" may be the author's most incisive way of lampooning his false poets, for each poem parodies a historically discrete species of corruption. Sheila's and Lou's poems may be equally terrible, but readers familiar with contemporary American poetry will perceive their poems as referring to subtly distinct forms of ineptitude.[1] Like other features of the book, the poems also establish a kind of hierarchy. Poets like Sheila and Anton have neither talent nor skill; others, like Lou and Dick, have a bit of skill but no talent; still others, like Leo and Guy, have talent and skill but nevertheless manage to compromise their art.[2]

Plainly, even if *Imaginative Qualities* cannot, in the end, be reduced to a "mere" historical document, its satirical components have much to say about the New York artworld. Beyond the main characters, some of whom are apparently modeled on aspects of significant historical personages like the poet Joel Oppenheimer, the artist and writer Fielding Dawson, and the sculptor John Chamberlain, the reader will encounter a vast number of influential figures. Many of these allusions are, to be sure, derisive. The narrator's sarcastic invective typically makes it clear which (then) current figures he finds lacking—ethically, aesthetically, or both. Into this group fall popular musicians like Donovan and Bob Dylan, jazz musicians like Oscar Peterson, journalists like Jimmy Breslin and Truman Capote, writers like Terry Southern and Saul Bellow, poets like John Berryman and Tom Clark, and painters like Larry Poons and Larry Rivers, to name a few. The implication is that the processes that have corrupted the main characters are at work throughout the artworld. Consequently, these allusions provide the narrator's critique with an illusion of cultural depth. Still, the novel also contains numerous positive historical references, a fact often overlooked by partial readings. The narrator's affection for his various art heroes—poets like Frank O'Hara, Ed Dorn, and Jack Spicer, musicians like Dexter Gordon and Ornette Coleman, and artists like Franz Kline, Philip Guston, and Willem de Kooning—is no less manifest than his hatred for his artists manqués. If my rough inventory is accurate, these positive references outstrip the negative. *Imaginative Qualities* provides, then, a balanced evaluation of the New York artworld, one in which references to corrupt figures are juxtaposed with references to art heroes who have resisted this corruption. Besides the impression of cultural depth, the narrator's allusions provide historical depth, and this, too, has celebratory aspects. References to Herman Melville, Arthur Rimbaud, Hart Crane, Charlie Parker, and especially Williams create a positive sense of the literary and artistic traditions. Thus *Imaginative Qualities* provides a balanced perspective that includes a contemporary foreground (the main characters), a contemporary background (the current cultural allusions), and a historical background (the historical literary allusions). Finally, the novel is valuable for its detailed treatment of legendary New York art haunts—including publishing houses, galleries, and famous bars like The Cedar Bar and Max's Kansas City—and of artists and writers hailing from common backgrounds, most notably Black Mountain College.

Another major element worth describing at this juncture is the novel's obsession with sex, and, more specifically, with its degradation through adultery or other means. Consider, for example, the novel's unforgettable opening, in which Sheila attempts to elicit poetic flattery[3] from an anonymous critic in return for sex:

> What if this young woman, who writes such bad poems, in competition with her husband, whose poems are equally bad, should stretch her remarkably long and well-made legs out before you, so that her skirt slips up to the tops of her stockings? It is an old story. Then she asks you what you think of the trash you have just read—her latest effort.... The most delicate equivocation about the poem, the most subtle relaxation of critical acumen, will hasten you to bed with her. (3)

The narrative does not resolve this deliciously Aristotelian subplot; it is not revealed whether the critic, the anonymous "you," will compromise his judgment or not.[4] Given, the extended adultery motif introduced by this scene, however, the suggestion is that he will. Several of the major characters engage in adultery, with Sheila and Dick engaging in one act of infidelity after another. Similarly, another narrative obsession involves, for lack of a better word, "quirky" sex, with Lou's and Leo's more inventive attempts at pleasing their respective mates serving as the main examples (e.g., 8, 134).

Overall, the sexual motif is an energetic source of mirth, yet it is clear that it forms a profoundly somber design. If nothing else, the connections between the novel's sexual motifs and its aesthetic motifs make this seriousness apparent. Such a connection is established at the outset, as when, in the above passage, corrupt, use-oriented art ("trash") is explicitly associated with corrupt, use-oriented sex, thus initiating one of the novel's basic patterns. (For an excellent discussion of this topic, see Tyrus Miller's essay.)

Perhaps the novel's most distinctive contribution to literature, however, is its narrative voice. In his classic interview with O'Brien in the inaugural issue of the *Review of Contemporary Fiction,* Sorrentino characterizes this voice as "a tone that reveals the brittleness, the cynicism, the depression, the waste, the loss, the futility, and the oddball sense of humor in that particular world" (16). Though the narrator of *Imaginative Qualities* may be a wise guy, he is also, as Jerome Klinkowitz notes, a raging Jeremiah, lamenting "fallen standards and ideals" (*Literary* 162). The corruption the narrator makes most obvious is aesthetic. Still, it would be a mistake to view the narrator's critique as narrowly aesthetic, for it is clear that he views the characters' artistic shortcomings as an extension of their more fundamental moral corruption. Take Anton Harley, whose colossal greed is equally manifest in his shoddy attempts at poesy (see, e.g., 162-63) and his shoddy treatment of his fellow characters—including his girlfriend, whom he locks in a bathroom as he eats, then rapes, a pizza (167). Ergo, if Sorrentino manipulates depraved straw men that his narrator can mock and vilify and otherwise comically humiliate, he does so with a deep moral-aesthetic seriousness of purpose.

Interestingly, Sorrentino argues that *all* authors manipulate their characters, and, more particularly, *all* satirists mock their characters (O'Brien, "Interview" 14). In his view, the virtue of his narrator is that the characters he attacks are parodies of people who are both difficult to mock and eminently worth mocking:

> the really terrible people in the world are not the people who read Irving Wallace and enjoy the films shown at Radio City Music Hall. They are simple, defeated at every turn. The really dangerous people are the ones who know everything, the people who know everything worthwhile to know; they do everything right. Those are the people who must be watched every minute of the time. (O'Brien, "Interview" 14)

As a satirist, then, Sorrentino has more in common with Wyndham Lewis than Sinclair Lewis.[5] He is not intent on satirizing politicians or middle-class Americans; he has no interest in Babbitts. Instead, his narrator focuses on the hipsters, on the knowing, self-styled radicals of the New York artworld—and the sheer energy with which this narrator lays waste to these arty emblems of waste is nothing short of arresting.

A final noteworthy aspect of the novel's voice is its intertextual self-reflexiveness. *Imaginative Qualities* is exemplary of the metafictional zeitgeist that characterized the 1960s and 1970s. Along with John Barth, Donald Barthelme, Robert Coover, Ronald Sukenick, Raymond Federman, Kurt Vonnegut, William Gaddis, William Gass, and many others, Sorrentino is intent on disrupting, to use Klinkowitz's term, the conventions of the novel, its illusionism in particular. One disruptive strategy employed by these authors is self-reflexiveness; i.e., they write fictions that openly comment on their own fictional status and that refer to other literary works, those of other writers as well as their own. Sorrentino does this in almost all his novels. In *Imaginative Qualities* his narrator engages in a running commentary on his own strategies, and misgivings, as a narrator. He consistently points out that his readers are seeing neither "reality" nor "people." They are, rather, seeing a text with its own special reality: "The reader will see that what I am driving at is that these words that he is reading—are words" (37). The narrator also mocks his audience's conditioned desire for "round" characters, for characters that, to use a signature Sorrentino phrase, "walk off the page":

> Now I have this character. This "character." You can think that he's real, i.e., representative of someone who is alive (outside of this book); you can think that he is real, that is, when I say "Anton walked" you think of some figure in your mind, representative of Anton, who walks. Or . . . you can think of the words. I mean, not in any dull way, but the words in relation to all the others in this book. Now, what if I were to tell you that Anton is a character in this book, based on a character in this book? That is, Anton is "really" Lou Henry. It seems complicated, but it isn't, because it wouldn't change the book at all. There is *no* character development whatsoever (I hope) to Lou Henry, so if Anton is Lou, it means nothing. But what is nice about making fiction is that I can do this. (169-70)

Imaginative Qualities attacks the rounded-character illusion perfected by writers like Forster and Henry James in two consistent ways. Not only does the novel contain characters like Anton who are "Totally unreal" (166)—and Anton is perhaps the most exaggerated and comic emblem of greed in American letters, the kind of character Sorrentino calls a "humour" in the Jonsonian sense—it also, as the above passage indicates, contains a narrator who often addresses the reader directly so as to talk about such literary practices openly. Clearly, innovators like Sorrentino have no necessary interest in obeying James's dictum about showing rather than telling.

That said, if Sorrentino is part of a general metafictional movement, his reasons for employing metafiction do not necessarily dovetail with those of Barth, Coover, Vonnegut, etc. Ideologically, the main reason he insists on the word, the signifier, as apart from the illusion, the signified, is that he is a modernist and an aesthete bent on creating useless, antireferential works of art, an incentive that sets him apart from his more obviously postmodern contemporaries. The narrator thus advises readers to think of his characters as words only to stipulate that they not do so in a "dull way." *By itself,* the revelation that characters are words is not, as it was for some of his peers, particularly revolutionary or interesting. The point of looking at characters as words is that it allows one to focus more clearly on "the words in relation to all the others in the book," which in turn puts the focus on design rather than on mimetic phantoms. On the other hand, Sorrentino's self-reflexive asides are often contradictory and illusionary in their own right. Though the narrator frequently asserts that his narrative's characters are flat and one-dimensional, this is not strictly true; some, like Sheila, Leo, and Guy, are brilliantly realized, inventively rounded illusions. Notice, also, that the narrator, by talking directly to the reader about his strategies as a novelist, "disrupts" one illusion only to form another, i.e., the illusion that this voice, this pure invention (a status that the narrator, in accord with the novel's spirit of contradiction, acknowledges (see, e.g., 216)) who is clearly not Sorrentino himself, is "behind" the novel, writing it. Finally, considering Sorrentino as part of a zeitgeist neglects that he views his own work as a late stage of modernism.[6] His metafictions have more affinities with the works of earlier modernists like James Joyce, Flann O'Brien, and Samuel Beckett, Irish writers with metafictional tendencies, than with those of his American contemporaries.

Completed in 1970, *Imaginative Qualities* was released by Pantheon in October 1971. Pantheon did little to promote and distribute the novel, so it did not sell well and was remaindered in 1973. Yet the novel did receive a fair number of reviews.[7] The initial reception was mixed. Positive notices were posted in significant forums, including *Antioch Review, Publishers Weekly,* and *Nation,* and by influential critics, including Klinkowitz and Robert Scholes, who both applauded the novel's fresh characterization (Klinkowitz, "Review" 27-28; Scholes 88)—a compliment that contradicts a complaint evinced by a number of reviews, i.e., the notion that Sorrentino's characters are made of cardboard and straw (e.g., "Review" 274). A more significant motif of the negative reviews, and one the criticism would extend, is the idea that its narrator, whom reviewers routinely if uncritically identify with Sorrentino, exhibits a "merely" malicious wit, which expresses itself through a snobbish, almost misanthropic invective (see, e.g., Graver 6-7; for a summary of the reviews, see McPheron 143-45).

Such judgments are not restricted to the reviews. Commentators familiar with the author have reported that the novel's main characters, artificialized, multiplex caricatures though they may be, seemed close enough to actual people that several acquaintances felt abused and betrayed. Indeed, Lyman Gilmore, Oppenheimer's biographer, claims that "Joel and his friends recognized the thinly disguised portraits as Fee [Fielding] Dawson, Joe and Anna Early, Tony Weinberger . . . Basil King, John Chamberlain, and Joel" (181). Perceiving himself as the inspiration for the fallen, drunken poet Leo Kaufman, Oppenheimer, a close friend of Sorrentino during the 1950s and 1960s, was spectacularly devastated by *Imaginative Qualities*. "Joel was so hurt and enraged by this portrayal," Gilmore writes, "that not only did he never speak with Sorrentino again (refusing to even acknowledge him as they passed each other in Westbeth halls and on neighborhood streets), he avoided even mentioning Sorrentino's name" (181).[8] Oppenheimer's autobiographical reading of *Imaginative Qualities* neglects the narrator's observation that people "who 'recognize' themselves in books are never in the books" (48). Still, this interpretation is not singular. In *The Dramaturgy of Style*, Michael Stephens reads *Imaginative Qualities* in an equally personal manner, concluding that Sorrentino is a brilliant but flawed writer, whose defect "is not political [like Pound's] but rather interpersonal, a wrathful judging of others" (86).[9] A similar notion is visible in Richard Elman's memoir *Namedropping*. According to Elman, Sorrentino "used to be very harsh on old friends in certain of his novels . . . such as *Imaginary* [sic] *Qualities*" (208). By contrast, another friend-cum-critic, Robert Creeley, turns this flaw into a virtue by arguing that Sorrentino's acerbic voice certifies his moral seriousness:

One can hardly *not* recognize how much this writer cares about the . . . human world he shares with others. *Imaginative Qualities of Actual Things* (the title itself a quotation from an equally moral writer, and a significant model for Mr. Sorrentino, William Carlos Williams) is an intensive judgement of the specific world of artists and writers of the New York Sixties, say, Max's Kansas City Before the Fall. It engages its various subjects most intentionally—real details from real lives—so that two thus, feeling themselves maliciously parodied, will not speak to him ever again, etc. But this is a risk the writer presumes to take, in this case with full responsibility. The necessity to make judgement, to define value, is *always* primary in this writer, no matter the formal means employed or the technical pattern. (157; Creeley's italics)

Unifying these writers is the fact that each takes it for granted that *Imaginative Qualities* is a roman à clef, a rather straightforward vehicle for self-expression through which Sorrentino makes "his" opinions plain. To judge from the criticism, this is the standard view of the matter.[10] Especially when they are *not* focused on issues of voice and narrative expression, critics tend to speak as if Sorrentino simply "is" his narrator (see Wright 62-63; Armstrong 65-68; Klinkowitz, *Literary* 218-24; Phelps 90-93; Emerson 86-87; Eilenberg 89; etc.). Naturally, more than a few critics have taken a more nuanced view of this issue (e.g., Olson 52-53; O'Brien, "Every" 75-76; Thielemans 122), but such critics are relatively rare — and unfortunately, *no* critic has taken the time to fully examine the narrator as a sophisticated and polymorphic literary construct.

This is not to suggest that critical discussions of the novel have focused solely on autobiographical issues, just that many have — in part because a large proportion of these critiques have been written by people with personal connections to the author. This has narrowed the conversation without utterly constraining it. Indeed, valuable pieces have been written that deal with *Imaginative Qualities,* including essays by (along with those authors noted above) William Bronk, Robert Caserio, Linda Hutcheon, Brian McHale, Kim McMullen, Nicholas Mosley, Toby Olson, Stephen Emerson, Maria Vittoria D'Amico, Doug Nufer, Louis Mackey, Peter Armstrong, Martin Wright, Barbara Jacobs, Paul Emmett, Anthony Miller, Eric Mottram, Bernard Share, Johan Thielemans, and Patricia Waugh, among others. These articles cover an array of issues, from aesthetics (D'Amico and McHale) and philosophy (Mackey and Thielemans) to psychology (Olson and Emmett) and various historicist concerns (Mottram and Nufer). Unfortunately, few critics have written essays that focus on *Imaginative Qualities* alone, and those that have have in the main written brief, undistinguished pieces.

In consequence, there is a dearth of serious scholarship devoted to *Imaginative Qualities* — even as compared to other Sorrentino works such as *Mulligan Stew* and *Aberration of Starlight,* which, relatively speaking, have been lavished with attention. This situation is aberrant, for by most accounts, the novel is an important work of contemporary literature, not to mention one of Sorrentino's finest comic efforts. For a book like *Imaginative Qualities,* one repeatedly accused of "mere" malice, this neglect has proved especially unfortunate, for it has allowed distortions of the book to flourish, misunderstandings that seem to reflect badly on the author himself. Sorrentino has for the most part remained above the fray, declining to defend a work of art that should provide its own defense. When he has spoken out, he has expressed dismay that anyone would view an artwork—which he considers a specialized phenomenon—as a historical document. "Sorrentino is still puzzled by [Oppenheimer's] reaction," Gilmore writes, "acknowledging that while the book was indeed sharp social criticism . . . it was a work of art, not a personal attack" (181). Sorrentino has also contended that his characters, including Leo, are composite figures modeled on various people, with liberal doses of pure artifice further "scrambling" each characterization—in part, no doubt, to defuse attempts at autobiographical interpretation.

Such arguments, it seems, have had little effect, as I know from firsthand experience. Consider that when soliciting essays for this issue, I was turned down by a well-known critic. This critic closed his E-mail by saying that he would look up this issue when it was published, for "perhaps" it would explain why *Imaginative Qualities* was "not quite the hateful book" he took it to be. It strikes me as characteristic of the omissions and confusions that have so persistently enmeshed *Imaginative Qualities* that this man refused the chance to take a second look at the novel—refused, that is, to challenge his assumptions about it—though I do hope this issue will perform the service he hoped it would.

Interestingly, Lewis's novel *The Apes of God* (1930) experienced a similar reception in the years following its introduction. As Paul Edwards observes,

> Lewis modelled many of his characters on aspects of people he knew who were prominent in the arts in England at the time. Because he did so, his satire was for many years seen as a purely personal attack on people he happened to dislike. No doubt this was, at the time of publication, a reasonable interpretation, though the element of scandalous gossip and its importance in the book was exaggerated even then. (634)

Ezra Pound, one of Sorrentino's modernist heroes, mocked this reaction, arguing that in "eighty years no one will care a kuss whether Mr X, Y or Z of the book was 'taken from' Mssrs Puffun, Guffin or Mungo. The colossal masks will remain with the fixed grins of colossi" (qtd. in Lewis 634). An aesthete concerned with artistic endurance rather than short-term fame—see, for example, his breathless remarks on the beauty of Thomas Nashe's poetry in his interview with O'Brien (7)—Sorrentino would surely be receptive to Pound's argument. If using aspects of actual people would allow his satire to achieve immortality, he would use them. Taking such a long view, however, ignores one small thing. Though Pound and T. S. Eliot once considered Lewis the most accomplished novelist of his time, he is now barely read, a situation partly attributable to reactions like those noted above. To avoid a similar fate, Sorrentino and *Imaginative Qualities* must attract readers, some of whom must be critics capable of imparting to other potential readers more varied and comprehensive views of the novel than those that currently exist.

No critic has yet noted in any systematic way that *Imaginative Qualities* has many positive (and, moreover, *positivist*) attributes. This is not altogether surprising, given that the novel's most memorable feature is the primary narrator's comic voice, which is etched in acid. Still, it stands to reason that if this narrator is attacking something—as he definitely is—he is most likely defending something as well. What critics have failed to articulate coherently is just what that "something" comprises.

For clarity's sake, I would first posit an assumption that I will complicate and problematize later on, i.e., the idea that the primary narrator's worldview, especially his aesthetic ideology, dovetails with Sorrentino's own. If this idea, which is not difficult to demonstrate, is granted, it becomes rather easy to discern what the narrator is implicitly defending through his explicit attacks: a worldview whose main feature is an aestheticism bearing romantic, modernist, and even postmodernist components. This worldview is not limited to the narrator's aestheticist ideology, but it is accurate to say that his aestheticism interpenetrates and organizes every other aspect of his worldview.

To understand this relationship between the worldviews of Sorrentino and his narrator, it helps to focus first on the author. Sorrentino is an aesthete. His interviews and essays are impassioned defenses of art, artist, and beauty, which he typically refers to in essentialist terms. To cite one example, in "The Act of Creation and Its Artifact" (1981), he characterizes the creative process as "ecstatic, mysterious, and sublime," with the artist figuring as the repository of a secret and ultimately unintelligible power (*Something* 5). These romantic notions are supported by a modernist principle, aesthetic autonomy. In Sorrentino's economy, the "true" artist is a free agent, and the artwork is an autonomous artifact—so much so that it is correct to call it "useless," as he often does (e.g., *Something* 253, 330, etc.). This notion of uselessness, an extreme extension of the concept of autonomy that recalls the aestheticism of Théophile Gautier and the theory of Maurice Blanchot, explains Sorrentino's insistence in his criticism and his art on the antireferential value of literature: if art's value is useless, it has nothing to do with expression or meaning or function. Indeed, Sorrentino's emphasis on autonomy may be seen as an elaborate defense of an essentialist notion of aesthetic value. It stands to reason that only if the artist and the artwork are autonomous, noncontingent entities can such people and things be defended as intrinsically valuable.

Curiously, this modernist notion of autonomy—along with the essentialist notion of value that it implicitly supports—also connects with those antiessentialist aspects of the author's worldview that seem postmodern. Sorrentino's antiessentialism recalls that of the late poet William Bronk, whose work Sorrentino admires. In Bronk's poetry there is the unstinting awareness that the external world is an uncaring rock that stands iron and aloof amid humanity's diverse projections of value, as shaped by hope, desire, and other subjective necessities. Throughout his own work, Sorrentino evokes the same awareness, albeit with a greater sense of passion, pain, and especially *play* than the serenely blunt Bronk. This existentialist view of the universe has a literary logic to it. Like the world in general, the word and the work are cold, autonomous entities that resist subjective and ultimately arbitrary projections of meaning. Indeed, such antiessentialist concepts are a major motif of the Sorrentino canon, including his poetry, prose fiction, and criticism.[11] Though this obsession with meaninglessness and "eroding signifiers" (*Under* 136) may at first glance imply Sorrentino's skeptical and even cynical theoretical kinship with the deconstructionists and various other postmodern theorists, such a view distorts the matter. Ironically, his linguistic antiessentialism is more accurately viewed as subordinate to his aesthetic *essentialism*; more specifically, it is a logical function of his antireferential and nonutilitarian notions of autonomy, uselessness, and intrinsic value.

I am suggesting that even those aspects of Sorrentino's worldview that seem negative or cynical are determined by his aesthetic positivism. This is also true of the worldview articulated by the narrator of *Imaginative Qualities*. Like his author, the narrator is an aesthete. From the opening scene, his attack is directed against the false art of false poets like Sheila who corrupt the artworld and betray "true" art—and it is crucial to remember that the narrator views art and language as reified and personified essences, which can be "harsh" (126), which can be insulted (159-60), etc. Like Sorrentino in "The Act of Creation and Its Artifact," the narrator evinces a romantic, mystical view of the creative act. This essentialist view is explicit in the scene in which Guy's painting is "opened by something inside it" (84). In response to this "demonic" revelation, the narrator asserts that "Art is magic, that is true" (85). Further, he believes that creation is a romantic mystery, not a "learned process" (45). Modernist autonomy and uselessness are also crucial aspects of his aestheticism. The artist is a free agent whose "particular devotion is the one thing that cannot be reached or tampered with" (42). He has no obligation to instruct, express, or remedy, for art is "not idea" (133); according to the narrator, the only "Duty of an Artist Is to Make Art" (189). Art is beyond the quotidian, beyond use, for "it is totally removed from the world" (175). Again, for satirical and comic reasons, the narrator often expresses these positivist beliefs via comic indictments, as when he observes that "in America . . . they either hate art or try to use it. I think of Horace Rosette. The poem as tool. Break open somebody's door with it, or unhook a brassiere" (137; see also 120). And again, the different aspects of the narrator's aesthetic ideology, especially the idea of autonomy, support the essentialist belief that artist and artwork are repositories of an objective, unchanging value.

Furthermore, the philosophical antiessentialism visible throughout Sorrentino's oeuvre is a visible component of the narrator's worldview, and it, too, is related to his aesthetic essentialism. The narrator typically expresses this antiessentialism through anti-interpretive, antimetaphorical assertions, which may be reduced to the following notion: things are what they are and not something else.[12] In *The Orangery* (1978), Sorrentino communicates this sentiment through poems like "To William Bronk," which contains the lines, "This cottony and juiceless orange is/this cottony and juiceless orange" (74). In *Imaginative Qualities* a similar idea is conveyed through the narrator's mockery of Lou's optimistic belief that the "world is what you want it to be" (37). Interestingly, the narrator's general point, that the world is what it is and not a subjective essence or idea, is almost always tied to some linguistic point. The conclusion he draws from his mockery of Lou is no exception: "The reader will see that what I am driving at is that these words that he is reading—are words" (37). This antiessentialist linguistic point has, in turn, literary implications that lead directly to aesthetic essentialism: "The difference between a good writer and a bad one—or, the difference between a writer . . . and an artist—is that the former thinks the words are pictures, and so on. He thinks they 'represent' things, and take their place. The artist is a slave to the fact . . . that they represent nothing, and that you pay homage to them on their terms" (169). The world is a discrete, autonomous thing, as are words and works; what value they have is fixed and objective rather than malleable and subjective. "True" artists understand this "fact"; artists manqués like Lou ignore it. That is to say, the narrator uses antiessentialist logic to rationalize an essentialist aestheticism. This also suggests an idea already noted, i.e., Sorrentino's self-reflexive, metafictional, intertextual, "disruptive" approach to words *qua* words (rather than words *qua* illusions) is stimulated by tendencies that are, finally, more romantic and modernist than postmodernist.[13]

The narrator's anti-interpretive stance also resembles Sorrentino's own insofar as it is crucial not only to his aesthetic posture but to his ethical posture as well. Goodness is a function of one's ability to perceive and respect difference, idiosyncrasy, etc. By contrast, evil is a function of abstraction, of solipsism, of careless ignorance—indeed, of any process that levels difference or imposes a foreign idea upon a sovereign thing. This is related to Sorrentino's poetic "attempt to destroy metaphor that conceals simile," which he abhors due to his disbelief "that anything is alike" (O'Brien, "Interview" 5). "I never try to compare anything because I don't think that anything can be compared," he asserts. "Comparisons make unclear the uniqueness of an object."

These ideas clarify why *Imaginative Qualities* so frequently relates art to love and trash to adultery. Art is a game of specifics, of idiosyncrasy, and of *full emotional involvement*, for the imagination refuses to "turn memory into sentiment" and insists "upon remembering the specific emotional responses that were once actual" (113).[14] Similarly, love is an irrepressible autotelic affection for a thing as *that* particular thing. Trash ignores specifics; it is a derivative, formulaic blob at once untrue to the world it pretends to represent and without any identity of its own. At best it has some use- or exchange-value; as a commodity, it can be translated into other terms. In a sense, then, the hack resembles the "careless and perennial adulterer," who is "a man who lacks imagination. In his orgasms is centered the energy that can generate the subtle differences that drive the poet to his obsession" (17). The hack, like the adulterer, responds to formula, to sentiment and similarity, and he is only marginally involved with his object; in the end, he is more interested in what he wants the world to be than in what it is. "Out of this sort of spastic adultery," the narrator notes, "come remarks like 'they're all the same upside down,' 'they're all the same in the dark' " (17). By contrast, the artist, like the lover, insists on the particular object, which is defined by its unyielding, irreducible uniqueness. For this reason, it might be said that true art, like true love, is "no comforter" but rather "a nail in the skull": "However read, that sits true. It *is* a nail in the skull. Or: rather to *have* a nail in the skull. What anodyne to ease that agony? While the body heaves and shudders the imagination staggers through the sweet wind off the ocean, straining to recall the precise contours of the youthful face its earlier acrobatics played over" (17; Sorrentino's italics). It is no wonder that the loveless relationships one finds throughout the Sorrentino canon involve people who translate their lovers into other terms, into other people. This is true of *Imaginative Qualities,* where an adulteress like Sheila trades sex for fawning comments about inelegant poetry and whose relationship with Lou is destroyed by her inability to be satisfied with him as he is. Her tendency to perceive Lou via cultural clichés (12-13) and "the mental paraphernalia of the erotic" eventuates in disappointment and adultery, for it becomes "clear that Sheila's husband can only satisfy or at the least intrigue her by being someone else" (8, 9). One final idea is worth noting. As Sorrentino argues in "The Act of Creation and Its Artifact," the artist values the creative process more highly than the physical product of that process; for the artist, art is primarily active and psychological. As the above makes clear, the same is true of the lover, whose love is incorporeal, manifesting itself not through sex, primarily, but through an imaginative act that insists on an object's idiosyncrasy. There is, then, an interesting Platonic twist to the text's hierarchical dichotomies, one that stands in ironic contrast to the text's explicitly anti-Platonic statements (e.g., 37). Trash is associated with adultery, a bodily process; art is associated with love, an imaginative process (see also 151).

Plainly, the narrator's worldview is not perfectly coherent, nor is it meant to be. Still, it is coherent enough to suggest a stable outlook dominated by interrelated and Manichaean binaries: uselessness/usefulness, art/craft, art/satire, art/trash, love/adultery, imagination/body, aestheticism/commercialism, essentialism/antiessentialism, etc. The narrator attacks the terms on the right of each pair largely by venerating the positive terms on the left — which indicates that *Imaginative Qualities* is at bottom "about" pure art, love, and modernist positivism more than false art, scorn, and postmodernist cynicism. This positivism is made the plainer through inventories of the narrator's hierarchical allusions. As noted, these allusions more often indicate a canon of cherished masterworks than an anticanon of false art — although the latter is registered as well. These positive allusions begin with the novel's dedication. According to William McPheron, Sorrentino dedicated *Imaginative Qualities* to Morton Lucks and Dan Rice, "because they were two legitimate painters who were outside the 'artistic feeding frenzy' that [the novel] satirizes" (16). In the body of the novel, the narrator refers in reverential tones to a variety of writers and artists. "The allegiance one has to Kline and Charlie Parker," he observes, "is secret and almost inarticulate. Certainly beyond aesthetics" (72).

The narrator makes this remark in reference to Guy, which leads me to another unrecognized feature: sympathetic characterization. Judging from the criticism, Sorrentino showers his main characters with nothing but contempt.[15] While this is true of Sheila, Anton, and Dick, it is untrue of Guy and Leo, both of whom possess talent. The narrator indicates that he has loved both men. In fact, as if to deflect the very criticisms that his narrative has since accumulated, the narrator stipulates that he "once deeply loved Leo Kaufman— oh, for many reasons. The reason that I state this here is so that as I investigate and reveal certain aspects of his character and life to you, such labor will not be mistaken for malicious zeal" (111). Though characterized as a solipsist (57-58, 61), Guy is treated with even more affection than Leo. Unlike Leo, he never sheds his integrity. Like Dahlberg, Guy is "holy, because he is not for sale" (*Something* 99). He remains autonomous and authentic, able to discern Leo's "surrender" even as he is himself falling apart due to alcoholism, impotence, and editorial butchery (146, 148).

The most telling emblem of the narrator's sympathy for Guy is the sample of his writing that the narrator shares with the reader. All the other sample writings are mocking parodies either subtly vulgar or obscenely trashy; indeed, though it is clear that Leo has written masterly poems (128, 149), the only poem shared with the reader is exemplary of his "later manner" (134-35), which the narrator considers corrupt. Only Guy's sample is above reproach. It appears at the end of Guy's chapter (85-86), but it is foreshadowed at the start, when the narrator describes a letter Guy once sent him:

> There is a paragraph at the end of it that has the sort of sweet clarity that presages a distinguished career. . . . It is, as a matter of fact, a photographic passage describing a photograph. I love writing of this sort, because I love photographs . . . the photo . . . is absolute revelation. The faces of those dead bourgeois, meaningful and famous only to the dead photographer—they are enough to wrench the heart. Absolute pictures of mortality. . . . To describe such a photograph in prose is a mark of excellence. (57-58)

As Sorrentino indicates in his fiction and criticism, he too adores such cold yet nostalgic description, as the lovely photographic opening of *Aberration of Starlight* demonstrates (3-4). Though love evades Guy, "excellence" does not. That this is the greatest sympathy Sorrentino and his narrator could bestow on Guy is suggested by the narrator's litany of compassionate hopes for Guy, which appears midway through his chapter—and which ends with the wish that Guy will "see that those particles of language, the bones of the very letters themselves, that are particularly his, in his imagination, can be marshaled, crafted, shaped, molded, urged and sweated into the absolute image of the old photograph. That lances the heart" (80). In a sense, the appearance of Guy's prose at the end of the chapter is an answer to the narrator's sympathetic prayer.

In sum, while it may be fair to characterize the aestheticism shared by Sorrentino and his narrator as elitist, exclusivist, dualistic, and at times intolerant, it is not at all fair to paint that aestheticism (as expressed in *Imaginative Qualities*) as "merely" malicious, misanthropic, uncompassionate, and so on. Not only is there direct evidence that the primary narrator is, morally and aesthetically, a romantic and a positivist, there is likewise a great deal of indirect evidence that his satirical (and hilarious) invective is fueled by this same romanticism and positivism. In regard to *The Apes of God,* Edwards notes that Lewis depicts "in detail the activities and conversations of a collection of characters who are completely worthless" (630). He then poses three sharp questions that critics have, more or less, posed apropos of *Imaginative Qualities*: "The effect is devastating, and however much we laugh, our laughter remains uneasy. Aren't we assisting at, and enjoying, a display of gratuitously inhuman mockery? Doesn't it damage us as human beings to do so? And isn't Lewis's colossal artistic energy being squandered in satirising such petty dilettantes?" (630). If "Sorrentino" is substituted for "Lewis," the answer to each question is "no." Indeed, it is possible to overstate *The Apes of God* connection. Sorrentino's characters are not equally "worthless," and his mockery of them, while uniformly entertaining, is tinged with eminently human characteristics, including sadness, sympathy, love, and even hope. I do not, of course, mean to suggest that *Imaginative Qualities* is a ray of sunshine, pure sweetness and light. Far from it. In any analysis, the novel is still a raging jeremiad, and comic scorn is still its major key. I would, however, suggest that critics who ignore the novel's "human" moments are much less likely to recognize that the source of the narrator's scorn is a complex and idiosyncratic form of positivism.

The picture I have drawn of the novel so far is admittedly riddled with knots and paradoxes. Fortunately, the most crucial knot is not difficult to unravel. Via his narrator and his own critical statements, Sorrentino has suggested that *Imaginative Qualities* is meant to be a "useless" work of art; at the same time, he has suggested in interviews that the novel is meant to be a satire of characters who "who want to be artists—not make art" (Andrews 62). But how, if art "is form in the service of . . . nothing" (Andrews 62), can a novel be at once art and satire, given that satire has obvious referential, didactic, and social functions? The answer to this quandary is rather simple. Nowhere does Sorrentino assert that his primary purpose in writing *Imaginative Qualities* is satirical. As always, his primary purpose is to create artistic form, which, to paraphrase Kant, he considers "purposeful without a purpose" (see 64-66). Its general function is to be artistic form—and as such, it has no specific functions. The satire is an element of the design, one means of creating a useless whole; the total design is the end and as such remains paramount. Even in his interview with O'Brien, where he notes that the people he wants "to deal with in *Imaginative Qualities* [are] the people who know everything," Sorrentino stipulates that writing "has always seemed to me an end in itself" (15). Ergo, in satirizing those "who write because they think writing is a tool . . . a way of changing the environment" (O'Brien, "Interview" 15), he must scrupulously prioritize design over satire so as to avoid becoming the very kind of writer his satire impugns.

The question that I would set aside for now is whether Sorrentino succeeded in transforming useful satire into useless form. Not only does such a question raise thorny and, in my view, ultimately arbitrary matters of taste, it also rests on assumptions that not all readers will be willing to grant, namely the black-and-white, modernist distinction that Sorrentino uses to divide useless art from useful craft.[16] What I would instead point out is that recognizing Sorrentino's stated intention allows one a clearer understanding of various other problems associated with the novel. Although Sorrentino and his narrator are identical in certain decontextualized, theoretical *particulars,* Sorrentino's aesthetic precludes his viewing his novel as a roman à clef or his narrator as a mouthpiece. Naturally, this raises questions: Why, if he does not identify with his narrator, does he stuff his narrator with opinions that resemble his own? Why, if he does not mean to attack actual people, does he construct characters like Leo who in many particulars resemble actual people?

The answer, I think, is that Sorrentino consciously chooses this subject matter to set himself a uniquely difficult formal problem: the transformation of clearly didactic, self-referential subject matter into useless artistic content. Indeed, if any didactic purpose informs the novel, it is an inadvertent, purely formal one: to prove once and for all that a narrator "is an invention of the voice" and that artistic form, regardless of the subject matter chosen for aesthetic treatment, is "totally removed from the world" (216, 175). If Sorrentino could take the subject matter handled in *Imaginative Qualities* and formalize it into a useless beauty, he would have performed a seemingly impossible aesthetic feat. Perceiving his purpose in this way makes sense because the alternative, i.e., viewing the final product of his work as intentionally didactic and autobiographical, would necessitate perceiving him as a hypocrite, for in his criticism he has *never* over five decades wavered in his support of nonutilitarian art. Perceiving Sorrentino's purpose as a problem-solving task also makes sense inasmuch as he has regularly noted his fascination with artistic failure. Consider his interview with O'Brien, where he contends that the

> driving force behind the books that I write is that I have always liked to risk falling on my face. I am absolutely obsessed by the idea of failing miserably. . . . I like to create problems for myself and see if I can solve them. To me writing is the farthest thing from self-expression. I don't think that I've expressed myself in any of my imaginative writing. My expression of myself, if it exists in my writing, appears in my criticism. If it gets into my other writing, it is disguised in a thousand ways. (26)

This view recalls Vladimir Nabokov's view of art as a deceptive puzzle. Still, while there is little doubt that *Imaginative Qualities* contains moments of self-expression, these do not seem particularly "disguised." As already noted, it would not be difficult to juxtapose Sorrentino's critical commentary, which he admits is a mode of self-expression, with his narrator's critical commentary to "prove" that his narrator is a self-expressive construct. Given that Sorrentino is a hugely intelligent author, one presumes he knows his narrator will come off as autobiographical. What, then, is the "disguise"? How does he intend to transmute the didactic into the aesthetic? Two answers spring to mind. First, though the narrator may seem consistent, closer inspection reveals "him" an involute, polymorphic construct. The second idea is subsumed by the first: "his" narrative is marked by contradictions and self-parodies, lies and "mixed signifiers."

O'Brien and others (e.g., D'Amico) have suggested similar answers. Deriving some of his ideas from the Russian formalists and the aesthetician Etienne Gilson, O'Brien, in "Every Man His Voice," asserts that Sorrentino is centrally concerned with making, not with saying (70-71). He applies this view mainly to *Mulligan Stew,* but he also has important things to say about *Imaginative Qualities.* According to O'Brien, in that novel "there is the controlling presence of a narrative voice whom many take to be Sorrentino himself"; he even quotes a Sorrentino friend, who argues, "Of course that's Gil. I've heard him say those things a million times" ("Every" 75). Because "it would have been easy for Sorrentino to have written himself out of these books, so that the narrator of *Imaginative Qualities* would have borne no resemblance to the author," O'Brien contends "he purposely introduced himself in order to treat this subject formally, finally showing that the 'I' is not *I*" ("Every" 75; O'Brien's italics):

> What Sorrentino figured out was how to use himself in his own fiction, an act whose success depended upon his ability to execute this idea and whose difficulty is demonstrated by the numerous failures of so many writers in the 1960s and '70s to do the same. . . . Sorrentino decided in *Imaginative Qualities* that a narrator need not be "made up" to tell this story of the avant-garde art world of New York. He could use "himself," but himself would be cast in a carefully selected tone and style. In effect, he made himself into a character of fiction, who like any other character, functions according to specific rules. (75-76)

Thus, O'Brien concludes, "in *Imaginative Qualities* the narrator has become, despite the resemblances to the author, another 'I' " ("Every" 76). He does not, for the most part, account for the processes by which personal material becomes impersonal content. What little O'Brien says in this regard (e.g., "cast in a carefully selected tone and style") is, it seems, gleaned from his interview with Sorrentino, where the author argues that "all voices are invented" (15). "Voice is a formal design," he asserts. The narrator is not Sorrentino inasmuch as the former is a flat, unrealistic invention from which all tonally and stylistically contradictory elements have been banished; he lacks the "roundness" and irregularity of the actual man.[17] Still, Sorrentino's procedure for depersonalizing the subject matter of *Imaginative Qualities* is more complex than references to the author's selection of tone and style suggest. While *Imaginative Qualities* may not match the intricacy of *Mulligan Stew*'s devices, it too contains a sophisticated narrator. More important, *Imaginative Qualities* demands a more rigorous act of depersonalization than an autobiographical work like Hemingway's *The Sun Also Rises* (1926) because its subject matter is idea-heavy, because its ideas derive from its author, and, most ironically, because these ideas argue against the expression of ideas in art.

Sorrentino has himself suggested the complexity of his narrator. He tells O'Brien that when he finished, he figured out "how many narrators there are but I can't remember the figure now. There must be at least nine or ten, including those in the footnotes. The first narrator is not the moral guide. He is also being attacked and satirized as much as any other figure in the novel" ("Interview" 14). Of course, as indicated earlier, the initial suggestion that the point of view is a slippery, multifarious construct arrives in the very first scene, where the perspective abruptly shifts from a second-person "you" centered within the consciousness of an anonymous critic to

an irascible, first-person "I" centered within the consciousness of an
anonymous narrator whom Sorrentino refers to as the "first narrator" ("Interview" 14). There are a number of similar shifts in the
novel, with the most noticeable involving the collage elements, i.e.,
the samplings of letters, poems, and essays; the comic lists; and the
footnotes, which are populated by ironic commentators, including
Vance Whitestone and his editorial accomplice, Lee "ZuZu"
Jefferson. By itself, this narrative complexity deserves the comprehensive survey that O'Brien applies to *Mulligan Stew* (a survey I
haven't, unfortunately, space for here). If nothing else, these shifts
clarify one of the ways in which the narrator is "attacked and satirized": witness the disparaging remarks from Whitestone and
Jefferson (129, 195, 208, etc.) anent the irregularities in the
narrator's narrative, remarks that come from "outside" the narrative. Still, it is not at all clear how such remarks would nullify the
primary narrator's status as "moral guide." After all, these footnotes are guilty of the same editorial "sins" that he castigates
throughout (e.g., 75-79). As Sorrentino has admitted, *Mulligan
Stew* contains self-referential material—there are numerous connections between Antony Lamont and his author—yet "no one has
ever said a word about its autobiographical elements" (Andrews
61). The difference is that *Imaginative Qualities* contains a relatively stable narrative; even though it, like *Mulligan Stew,* is a collage of documents and voices, the primary narrator of *Imaginative
Qualities* seems firmly in control. This is what allows one to dis-
criminate between "inside" and "outside." It is also what justifies
the authorial linkage: unlike Lamont, the primary narrator of
Imaginative Qualities fills the same rational, authorial role vis-à-
vis his text as Sorrentino fills vis-à-vis his own. By contrast, in
Mulligan Stew there is no "primary" or "master" exposition to provide a stable context for the other writings. Thus no orienting distinction between inside and outside emerges, and no moral-aesthetic priority is bestowed on any one kind of document. *Mulligan
Stew* seems, then, closer to a "random" collage than *Imaginative
Qualities*.

Sorrentino, I believe, chose to nullify the self-expressive function of his narrative, to render it "useless," in a simple yet subtle
way that has gone largely unrecognized. His narrator lies. Or, more
precisely, the narrator is duplicitous in a literal sense, for he regularly contradicts himself. This art of "mixed signifiers" is an early
attempt by Sorrentino to scramble the referential codes of his
novel, a service performed in more obvious ways by the greater
structural artifice of his later fictions. The most apparent—and
ironic—instances of this wise-guy double-speak are self-reflexive

and involve the ontology and function of fiction. One of the narrator's basic patterns is his tendency to say "this story is invention only," "I'm making this up," or "This is all fiction," only to say "This is all real" in the same (or a proximal) section (9, 49, 46, 30). Likewise, the narrator asserts that "This is not a novel," that this "is a digression: from the novel," and that "there's no plot here to worry you" (11, 197, 57), only to indicate that this "is a novel" and that it has a plot (80, 124). Similarly, characters are framed as real, then as "Totally unreal" (166); first they are based on actual people, then they are pure inventions, unlike anyone who ever lived (see 160). Moreover, there are the narrator's self-canceling assertions, including the rhetorical question, "What is art if not idea?" (133)— which is, of course, posited as an idea within an artwork thick with ideas, many of which explicitly oppose artworks that posit ideas. This asymmetrical way of talking about art's expressive function is related to the narrator's on-again, off-again attitude regarding the social function of art and of his narrative in particular. For example, the narrator notes that Dick, an "invention of the voice," is fiction only, so that he "will teach you utter failure if you try to use his chapter as a handbook for living" (216). This seems clear enough, yet in the same chapter, the narrator himself refers to his narrative as a "handbook," immediately after which he acknowledges his double-speak: "I submit that one may think of it as wiseguy prose" (226-27). In the previous section he refers to his narrative as "an antidote," one that is "to be taken slowly" (191). Yet this function, which is explicitly useful, is also explicitly contrasted with any notion of the artwork as a useful tool: "No tools to be found here with which to build the new society" (191). The narrator then repeats this description at least twice, going so far as to refer to his narrative as "antidote . . . full of ingredients, a specific brew, concocted to ward off the poisons that abound" (198; see also 207). Again, this description would imply an instrumentalist's view of the narrative had the narrator not explicitly rejected such a view earlier.

These features are hardly anomalous. *Imaginative Qualities* contains many other antithetical assertions, most of which are more subtle than those noted above. And beyond the overt contradictions, the novel also contains myriad hypotheticals, phrases that, as they accrete, interrupt the narrative's mimetic and expressive functions by leaving in doubt whether the event in question "really" occurred as described:

He was—let's call him Milt. His name doesn't matter, I don't recall her lover's name, but Milt will do. So [Sheila] said, "Milt, O Milt, fuck me." She whispered then, "Fuck my asshole, Milt, fuck my asshole." . . .

> When she next met her lover, who had, let's assume, a real mous-
> tache and goatee, she wanted him to do what Lou had done. . . . (8-9)

In themselves, phrases like "let's call him" and "let's assume" seem
merely playful—and, integrated with passages like this, their ludic
value is indubitable. But they are not *merely* playful; their perva-
siveness argues against trivialization. As these breezy
hypotheticals accumulate, as the "if you want" is added to the "we'll
call it" and the "Let's say" to the "I'm almost certain" (30, 53, 112,
115), they combine with other moments and types of indeterminacy
and gradually cohere so as to suggest an overall design, one that is
clearly intentional and, it seems, intentionally mute. It might, I
suppose, be argued that the novel is a self-reflexive fiction and that
both its focus on aesthetic ontology and its accelerating indeterminacy are twin conventions of the metafiction that appeared in the
1960s and 1970s. This thesis, however, is tantamount to lumping an
idiosyncratic author with all-those-other-postmodernists, which ignores Sorrentino's modernist emphases on the unity of the artwork
and the autonomy of the aesthetic. Unlike his postmodern contemporaries, he resorts to metafiction in *Imaginative Qualities* and
elsewhere to prioritize design by counteracting the didactic nature
of his medium, his ideas, and his own argumentative tendencies.

Consider a passage that contributes to this design, one that suggests the density of the interpretive obstacles erected by the narrator at the paragraph level. The passage begins with the narrator's
admission that he "once deeply loved Leo":

> There is nothing the matter with Kaufman. He surrendered, that's all.
> There's nothing dishonorable about that, it occurs every day. But in a
> book like this, a slap here, a dash there, a couple of anecdotes mixed
> with gratuitous opinion, a figure can emerge that has little to do with
> the figure as it really exists. Not that Leo exists, but even the invented
> Leo has a set in my mind that is different from the way he will turn out
> here. All these people are follow-the-dots pictures—all harsh angles
> that the mind alone can apprehend because we have already seen their
> natural counterparts. I'm saying that if you know Leo, you'll see him
> plain. If not, you'll see what I let you see. (111)

What does this passage impart to the reader? First, "I once deeply
loved Leo" indicates that a specific Leo existed in the narrator's life
beyond the narrative frame. Next, the first three sentences quoted
above are moral sarcasm; if anything, they mean the opposite of
what they say. The fourth is a non sequitur—though one indicative
of the narrator's misgivings about his representation of Leo, which
he fears might not do justice to the "real" Leo. This indication that a

real Leo exists apart from the narrator's representation of him squares with his statement about past love. This notion is, however, quickly punctured by "Not that Leo exists," the fragmentary clause that opens the next sentence. The pursuant clause suggests that the narrator cannot exactly control his portrayal, cannot exactly transcribe the "imaginative qualities of the actual things" that reside in his mind. The next sentence indicates that Leo, as he is drawn, is a man modeled on multiple people ("their natural counterparts"). This would imply that even vis-à-vis the narrator's "own" reality, Leo is a fiction, a "humor" representing an essential type rather than a specific person. This is supported by the next sentence; the only way the reader could "know Leo" is if he were a generalized character rather than a depiction of a single "real" Leo. Finally, the last sentence, like those that follow it in the narrative, would seem to contradict the notion that the narrator is not perfectly in control.

That is to say, though the passage contains much information, it is not particularly informative. Nor is the passage unique in a chapter that contains logic such as this: "First of all, Leo is really Leo (invented, of course). I mean he is not, was never, and will not be (I'm almost certain) Guy Lewis" (115). Nor in a book that celebrates "photographic" prose while condemning as inartistic "reportage" any "attempt to make a photograph" with words (58, 114). Toward the end, the narrator seems to despair that nothing has been resolved; then, via another non sequitur, he abruptly brightens: "But then, only segments have been given you of these few people. They are in no way representative of anything, necessarily" (215). The reader is again presented with delicately fused contraries. First the people are "in no way" symbolic; then they are not "necessarily" symbolic. "Such the perfections of fiction," the narrator continues, "as well as that honed cruelty it possesses which makes it useless" (215).[18] I submit that the "honed cruelty" the narrator speaks of amounts to deliberate frustration. The narrator presumes that readers approach art hoping to learn, understand, and use. The cruelty of art in his (and, I think, Sorrentino's) view is that "true" artworks are systematically "honed" so as to resist these "improper" goals. Such frustration leaves readers with no choice but to appreciate the artwork in a "proper" way, i.e., by concentrating on its autonomous, autotelic design.

One might, of course, argue that I am approaching these indeterminate passages, statements, and phrases too analytically, too literally—and, perhaps, that I ought to attend long passages like the one quoted above more by "feel" and "tone" than through a line-by-line interpretation. I would counter by pointing out that such a reading would leave us with the traditional one, the one that may be reduced to "Of course that's Gil." But this "feathery" sort of reading is one of the factors that has led to the novel's neglect; it has also led critics, especially those familiar with Sorrentino's oeuvre, to miss the novel's most significant narrative strategies. I do not, incidentally, mean to be guilty myself of contradiction. I recognize that the first half of my argument takes "Of course that's Gil" for granted. This seeming inconsistency is, in fact, part of my point. It is impossible for a reader to ignore these similarities, for they are *there*. However, such a reader must not sift through the text's conflicting ideas, pick out those that he knows match the author's ideas, and dismiss the rest as irrelevant gibberish. A consistent positivist aesthetic informs *Imaginative Qualities* and links it to the rest of Sorrentino's work, but this resemblance between narrator and author is not sufficient to explain the novel in toto. One primary distinction between Sorrentino's criticism and *Imaginative Qualities*—or between his criticism and *Mulligan Stew, Odd Number* (1985), *Under the Shadow* (1991), etc.—is that the criticism generally avoids contradiction and duplicity. Why, if *Imaginative Qualities* were a polemical roman à clef, would that be the case?

Imaginative Qualities is *not* a polemical roman à clef—or at least it was not meant to be. Whereas Sorrentino means his criticism to logically and consistently express his point of view, his aim in writing fiction is an objective, aesthetic consistency that does not express *anything*. Sorrentino can use his own opinions in his fiction and still achieve such a "useless" consistency so long as those opinions are disrupted by divers structural and ideational procedures. Whether or not one judges the author of *Imaginative Qualities* successful in this effort is beside the point. What matters is that he makes the attempt and that, in his later fiction, he carries it to ever-greater extremes. This process begins with *Splendide-Hôtel,* which, though it retains an "I" that may be associated with the author, is a more overtly *fictional* book due to its highly artificial, alphabet-based structure. But a more important and impressive solution to this problem of author-narrator identification is offered by *Mulligan Stew*.[19] There Sorrentino's innovations make it impossible to identify Lamont with his author, so the fact that Lamont (like the narrator of *Imaginative Qualities*) expresses a quirky blend of Sorrentino's opinions, has written books like Sorrentino's, and shares aspects of Sorrentino's background makes no difference.[20] *Mulligan Stew* cannot be interpreted as didactic or autobiographical. This increasing emphasis on artifice persists through *Aberration of Starlight, Crystal Vision* (1981), and *Blue Pastoral* (1983) and reaches its apotheosis in the trilogy of novels aptly entitled

Pack of Lies, which Mackey contends "problematizes the art of fiction, destabilizes the concepts of truth and reality, and in the process brings literature and philosophy to a new consciousness of . . .
the powers and paradoxes of language" (1). Though Mackey interprets the trilogy as a postmodern exploration of a conceptual problem, the philosophical ramifications of the trilogy's techniques are,
I think, a byproduct of Sorrentino's pursuit of modernist uselessness and "negative discourse."

Take, for example, *Odd Number,* the first part of the trilogy and a
novel that includes much the same cast of characters as *Imaginative Qualities.* Like *Mulligan Stew, Odd Number* contains an inventive structure that destabilizes narrative authority. More than
Mulligan Stew, however, *Odd Number* expands on *Imaginative
Qualities*'s tendency to contradict itself at the ideational level. No
fact is factual, and no idea lacks a countervailing idea to render the
former useless. This tendency is in keeping with Sorrentino's self-
description in 1985, the year of *Odd Number*'s release:

> The writers who influenced me . . . agreed with my own artistic neces-
> sities, which are: an obsessive concern with formal structure, a dislike
> of the replication of experience, a love of digression and embroidery, a
> great pleasure in false or ambiguous information, a desire to invent
> problems that only the invention of new forms can solve, and a joy in
> making mountains out of molehills. (*Something* 265)

Indeed, the increasing radicalism of Sorrentino's literary forms
matches that of his criticism—though due to that radicalism, the
forms become, one might say, steadily more difficult to "match."
"Fictional Infinities" (1984) finds Sorrentino mulling the properties
of "Flaubert's famous 'book about nothing,' " which he characterizes
as "an extended and complex list, endless, perfectly useless, and,
ideally, tending toward maximum entropy" (*Something* 330). The
list makes sense in this regard because, according to Sorrentino, it
is "the opposite of that which we think it is, i.e., rather than acting
as a bearer of data . . . the list is actually an *object*" (*Something* 328;
Sorrentino's italics). Similarly, in "Writers and Writing: *Disjecta
Membra*" (1988), he describes the list as "a system of negative narrational energy" that allows words to escape the burden of significa-
tion, which in effect frees characters "from their roles as human sur-
rogates" so that they "become formal elements among other formal
elements" (357, 361). Finally, in "What's New?: The Innovative Act"
(1994), Sorrentino provides another interesting rationale for aesthetic opacity: "Art can be traduced or twisted into yielding almost
any meaning that its audience wishes it to yield. Most pointedly, it is
innovative art which most successfully resists this manhandling,

since it is strange enough, odd enough, to resist such easy consumption and misrepresentation" (*Something* 338).

It is tempting, if simplistic, to think that the critical "misrepresentation" of *Imaginative Qualities* may have spurred Sorrentino to his emphasis on artifice and uselessness. If that were true, not only might one consider *Imaginative Qualities* the crux of his career, one might also consider the various distortions that attended it a boon to American literature. But regardless of the accuracy of this view, it is indisputable that *Imaginative Qualities*—in its structural innovations, its ideational innovations, and its hilarious characters—contains the seeds of Sorrentino's later work. It is likewise indisputable that the book's reception raised questions that have continued to engross the author, as the opening of his recent story "Life and Letters" (2001) makes apparent:

> Some three or four years ago, Edward Krefitz published a story that . . . contained elements of his past life, elements, of course, disguised, twisted, corrupted, embellished, romanticized, and wholly fanciful. A few people recognized themselves as models for characters in the story, and were, predictably, chagrined or flattered, depending on the quality of the fiction's distortion of their being. They all wished, surely, to be *accurately portrayed,* certainly; but there is accuracy and then there is meanspiritedness. So they muttered. (427; Sorrentino's italics)

The story makes short work, so to speak, of the idea that "life" and "letters" have any clear, predictable connection. The protagonist believes his story is accurate in a *figurative* sense; as it turns out, his story is accurate in a *literal* sense that exposes him as a fool and a cuckold. In other words, his "nonfictional" idea of his own life is a hopeless distortion. If nonfiction—which the narrator of *Imaginative Qualities* refers to as a "magic-lantern show" and a "sweet narcotic" (168)—inevitably distorts experience, how can one expect fiction, even "realistic" fiction, to represent life unproblematically?

Perhaps it is time to put such questions aside, fascinating though they are. At this stage, it is appropriate to confess what has likely been manifest all along, that my urge to provide critical correctives is informed by my deep and abiding affection for *Imaginative Qualities*. This novel is, in fact, one of only two that I can honestly say has altered my life—and I know at least two other people who can say the same. Though I have dealt with it here as a work of art and as an intellectual function of its author's aestheticism, make no mistake: *Imaginative Qualities* is the funniest book that I know of. Its satirical images—of, for instance, Anton violating a pizza (167), accompanied in the margin of my copy by an ebullient smiley-face—and muscular wit will be etched in my memory long after my brain has erased the details of almost all the other novels I have ever read. (And that is a beautiful thought.)

The four essays that follow provide fascinating new approaches to *Imaginative Qualities*—approaches intended to stimulate the kind of conversation that will, with luck, reverse the decades of relative silence that have attended the novel. The first is "Fictional Truths: *Imaginative Qualities of Actual Things* between Image and Language," by Tyrus Miller. According to Miller, *Imaginative Qualities* represents Sorrentino's attempt to manipulate art's complex "truth-disclosing capacities" so as to distinguish true art from fake—a mission that places the novel squarely, if at times paradoxically, within "the dimension of social criticism," since its invective focuses on the cultural centers in which fakery proliferates. This mission is made problematic by an obvious question: How can the reader verify that *Imaginative Qualities,* a book that is fabricated from the same "trash" it examines and critiques, is not trash itself, with the narrator just another ingenious faker? Miller explains Sorrentino's answer by placing his attitudes toward truth and mimesis within the context of his various modernist precursors, including Joyce, Eliot, Pound, Lewis, Beckett, and Spicer. In the end, Miller argues, Sorrentino does not in *Imaginative Qualities* fully accept the strategies of any of these exemplary figures but instead adopts an alternative strategy, one that resorts to what Miller dubs "the pornographic simulacrum" so as to forge a new mode of fictional truth-telling that compromises neither aesthetic autonomy nor authorial control. In consequence, Miller's unique presentation of Sorrentino's complex stance toward literary mimesis has the virtue of explaining the radical sexual content of *Imaginative Qualities.*

In "Gilbert Sorrentino's Problematic Middle Child: *Imaginative Qualities of Actual Things,*" Stacey Olster also contextualizes Sorrentino's novel—but whereas Miller focuses on its modernist roots, Olster considers it as an expression of a set of more contemporary, more American imperatives. Thus, after comparing Sorrentino to writers like Robert Coover, John Barth, Donald Barthelme, etc., Olster denies that Sorrentino was "a lone aesthete crying in the wilderness" during the period in which *Imaginative Qualities* was written. She does, however, admit that Sorrentino was rather "extreme" in his formalism, despite the fact that neither his narrator nor his novel quite embodies this formalist ideology—in part because, as the narrator's aesthetic and political manifestos make plain, there is little or no aesthetic distance between narrator and author. Thus the novel is a "problematic middle child" within the author's work, one that does not quite achieve the structural maturity of a later novel like *Mulligan Stew*. In her essay's final section, Olster proposes that various innovations introduced in *Imaginative Qualities* — metafictional devices that, not incidentally, link the novel to its postmodern peers—allow Sorrentino in *Mulligan Stew* to eliminate "the possibility of mistaking [his narrator's] voice for his own," thus allowing him to embody more fully the formalist, aestheticist ideology to which his narrator pays lip-service in *Imaginative Qualities*.

Joseph Tabbi's essay, "Matter into Imagination: The Cognitive Realism of Gilbert Sorrentino's *Imaginative Qualities of Actual Things*," takes an unprecedented approach to the novel, considering it in terms of cognitive science. Tabbi presents Sorrentino not as a metafictionalist or an antirealist but as a more "scrupulous" realist, an identity encoded in his title. According to Tabbi, the narrator and his narrative are true to the interpretative actualities of waking life. The self-consciousness, narrative fragmentation, and flattened (or, in Tabbi's words, "de-realized") characters one discovers in Sorrentino's novel represent his attempt to acknowledge in a dense literary fashion what cognitive science demonstrates, i.e., that exchanges "between the embodied mind and the world produce neither a wholly mental construction nor an objective reality; what they generate is rather a 'dance' that lasts a while, and then fades from memory as new images come to new states of consciousness." In order to illustrate how the novel accomplishes this feat, Tabbi not only submits the novel to rigorous analysis but explains in detail the state of cognitive science, especially its assumptions about art and literature.

The final piece, Kevin Alexander Boon's "Gilbert Sorrentino: Cataloging the *Imaginative Qualities of Actual Things*," explores the author's signature technique, i.e., his use of the catalog (or list), so as to show how *Imaginative Qualities* "confronts the paradoxical qualities of fiction and interrogates the complex (and dynamic) relationship between truth and fiction peculiar to the genre of the novel." In analyzing Sorrentino's diverse manipulation of the catalog in the novel, Boon demonstrates how this device prioritizes design, locates meaning in interpretation, and thereby dispels "the illusion of linguistic referentiality." That said, Boon does not argue that this antirealistic device leads to a meaningless or "entropic" text. Rather, he believes that in disrupting the illusion of unitary literary meaning, Sorrentino's lists reveal the actual richness, the true interactive significance, of the literary artwork. Thus Boon concludes with a point similar to one arrived at by Tabbi: Sorrentino's novel, its lists in particular, "expose that which is absent, the gaps interspersed throughout language upon which meaning necessarily depends, rendering prose opaque, forcing us to confront the truth of the text and the reality of the page, and situating literary art in the author's design."

The essays are followed by a bibliography of *Imaginative Qualities* criticism and a concise checklist of Sorrentino's book-length publications.

Notes

[1] For example, Lou, Anton, and presumably Sheila all write poetry that, in idiosyncratic ways, betrays the influence of William Carlos Williams (whose long, brilliant prose fiction *Kora in Hell* (1920) supplies the novel with its title (see Williams 67)) without exhibiting his characteristic verve, artistry, integrity, and originality. Indeed, the narrator of *Imaginative Qualities* makes the sardonic observation that Williams was "responsible" for Lou's inept poetry "in the way that George Herriman might be held responsible for Roy Lichtenstein. These masters cannot be blamed for the aberrant desires of a minority of the populace. It comes down to: 'Hell, I can do that too' " (35). (This last comment is doubly interesting considering that Sorrentino has noted that his own literary career began in the late 1940s when, after reading Walt Whitman, he thought, "Well, I can do that too" (Robins 279).) The influence of Williams can also be observed at one remove—a remove that debases Williams's influence even further—as in the poetry of so-called nature writers whose "poems have titles like 'Top of Pink Tit Mt.: Cold Beans' " (36). Martin Wright has argued that this title is an allusion to a mediocre poet derivative of Gary Snyder, who, like Lou, is himself (in the narrator's estimation) a mediocre poet derivative of Williams (63).

[2] Guy is a prose writer and a visual artist rather than a poet. I lump him with Leo not because he is a poet but because, like Leo, he is depicted as an artist who for various reasons betrays his own talent.

[3] Sorrentino encodes Sheila's lust for flattery in her section's title, "Lady the Brach." The term "Lady Brach" derives from *King Lear*. "Truth's a dog must to kennel," the Fool tells Lear; "he must be whipp'd out, when the Lady Brach may stand by th' fire and stink" (Shakespeare 1180). According to David Bevington, "Brach" refers to a "hound bitch (here suggesting flattery)" (Shakespeare 1180n).

[4] This "you" is not to be confused with the primary narrator, whose "I" appears abruptly toward the end of the scene. This is the first of many indications that the narrative viewpoint is complex and multiple.

[5] Apparently, this striking jeremiad was influenced by Wyndham Lewis's own energetic satires, especially *The Apes of God* (1930), which Sorrentino calls "Lewis's brilliant assault upon the Bloomsbury of his time" (O'Brien, "Interview" 6): "*Imaginative Qualities of Actual Things*—what I wanted to do with this morass of phony artiness that exists in New York and other places—was directly influenced by *The Apes of God*."

[6] As Sorrentino writes in "Genetic Coding" (1983), an essay in *Something Said,* "My novel *Mulligan Stew* is not truly intelligible unless it is seen as

dependent on the work of Joyce and Flann O'Brien. . . . The novel is, or was meant to be, the end of that process we call modernism" (263).

[7] McPheron's *Gilbert Sorrentino: A Descriptive Bibliography* (1991) remains the Sorrentino scholar's most efficient resource, providing sketches of all the available reviews and critical essays. Unfortunately, the book needs to be updated; it covers Sorrentino's oeuvre through 1989 only.

[8] Oppenheimer and Sorrentino lived in the same West Village apartment building, Westbeth, at the time of *Imaginative Qualities*'s initial publication.

[9] Stephens argues that Sorrentino mocks and critiques the "sad, broken people" of his early, Cedar Bar milieu by skewering them with "*his* voice. He lambasts [*sic*] poetasters, pillories unfaithful wives, vilifies friends who wasted their talents, and he becomes especially nasty to artsy-fartsy types. The fiction writer's voice is judgmental, contemptuous, full of commentary, full of telling instead of showing. Pity the character who gets on Sorrentino's shit list, for this is a writer obsessed with lists" (88, 89; Stephens's italics). The narrator "is" Sorrentino; like other critics personally acquainted with Sorrentino, Stephens has little patience for claims that the voice of *Imaginative Qualities* is an artificial construct.

[10] As O'Brien notes, "Sorrentino insists that he is not the narrator," but "the assumption to the contrary is . . . invited" because "the narrator's opinion's and biases can frequently be traced back to Sorrentino's nonfiction," because "the narrator's books are Sorrentino's," because "the characters in this roman à clef are based on his acquaintances from the New York art scene in the '60s," and because "the narrator's conversational style, so Sorrentino's friends say, is that of Sorrentino hemself [*sic*]" ("Every" 75).

[11] To cite a single example, the narrator of *Under the Shadow* (1991) concludes his narration by noting that the "stars, in their trillions, shone on these people and phenomena, on these credos, tears, and *things,* on this vast desire, shone and shone, meaningless" (137; Sorrentino's italics).

[12] While this idea manifests in Sorrentino's work in ways that appear postmodernist, as an idea that directs us to pay scrupulous attention to the sensuous surface of things, it has a distinctly modernist heritage. Consider, for example, Gertrude Stein's "a rose is a rose," a seemingly simple statement that had profound ramifications for early modernists, including Sorrentino's poetic mentor, Williams (see, e.g., *Embodiment* 22-23), as well as for later modernists such as Susan Sontag (see, e.g., *Styles* 122).

[13] Consider Sorrentino's essay "Jack Spicer: Language as Image" (1966), written a few years before *Imaginative Qualities*. According to Sorrentino, Baudelaire and Spicer "have affinities in that their poetics insist on revelation; there is in both men the belief that the world is there, regardless of what we think it is; it is the poet's task to reveal it" (*Something* 58). Again, the antiessentialist dictum "the world is what it is" is wedded to an essentialist aesthetic, which—though Sorrentino characterizes it here and elsewhere (e.g., *Something* 63-64, 78-79) as antiromantic—is clearly romantic in its insistence that poetry reveals essences, realities, truths, etc. What Sorrentino is saying, it seems, is not generally antiromantic but specifically antisubjective: his view is that reality is fixed, unchangeable, and that the

poet reveals that reality almost unintentionally rather than imposing it or inventing it deliberately. Over the years, as his emphases change, he comes to champion invention and the autonomous, useless artwork that is its own reality rather than the revelation or "handmaiden" of another—a notion, incidentally, that is never fully absent from his work, no matter how contradictory it sometimes seems. But certainly, *Imaginative Qualities* contains an essentialist aesthetic still emphatically insistent on revelation: "In the middle of all the lists and facts," his narrator asserts, "there will sometimes be a perfect revelation. These curious essences" (34).

[14] Though I haven't space to explore this idea comprehensively, the idea of full emotional commitment in both art and love is absolutely crucial to understanding the novel's moral-aesthetic stance. Throughout the book, adultery (and even some nonadulterous sex) is careless, devoid of commitment and true emotional absorption. This is also true of many of the corrupt or just empty aesthetic acts detailed by the book. In *Imaginative Qualities* false artists are typically only marginally involved with the creative process. Thus Anne cannot "understand Leo's involvement with his poem at all. It's throwing a pot, right? You don't get your *life* entangled with it" (136; Sorrentino's italics).

[15] Interestingly, the narrator indicates that he expects this reception. More interestingly, he connects this expectation to Guy, the character with whom he sympathizes more than any other: in a review of a novel the narrator claims to have written under the pseudonym "Guy Lewis," "Craig Garf" writes that the author shows "a curious lack of compassion for his characters" (82; see also 197).

[16] For one distinguished dissenter, see Larry Shiner's *The Invention of Art* (2001), which traces—and roundly criticizes—the historical evolution of this distinction between fine art and low craft. Incidentally, the primary narrator frequently makes this distinction explicit, thus adhering to his author's theory in another important way; he also makes this distinction implicit through his parodies of characters participating in the arts-and-crafts movements of the 1960s, movements that reduce the modernist gulf between artist and artisan and art and craft. (See, e.g., 99-100, 136, 158, 160, 174, 180.)

[17] Compare this idea with a similar one Sorrentino evinces in regard to *The Sky Changes* (1966): "This is not a realistic novel. . . . There would have to be some comic relief, some lightness, some joy. But in my writing of *The Sky Changes,* I deliberately expunged all instances of such things so that the book is a plunge from a dark gray to black" (O'Brien, "Interview" 10).

[18] "Everything it teaches," the narrator continues, "is useless insofar as structuring your life: you can't prop up anything with fiction. . . . Can you see some shattered man trying to heal his life by reading *Tender Is the Night*? . . . There is more profit in an hour's talk with Billy Graham than in a reading of Joyce. Graham might conceivably make you sick, so that you might move, go somewhere to get well" (215). Again, these ideas are directly antithetical to one of the narrator's favorite motifs, i.e., the narrative as antidote. The narrator's antifunctionalist argument is further complicated by the similarities this passage shares with an essay of the same period,

"Empty, Empty Promises, Promises" (1973). (See especially *Something* 253, where Sorrentino wittily points out the impractical value of van Gogh and Rimbaud.)

[19] It is a problem because the author insists on mixing his critical opinions into each of his stews—which, I suppose, is one way of adhering to the clichéd dictum, "write what you know." Like *Imaginative Qualities,* Sorrentino's later work consistently displays such ideas; what he learns to do is to inject such ideas into his work in ways that readers will not automatically brand didactic or autobiographical.

[20] As Sorrentino indicates in his interview with O'Brien, this solution to a recurrent problem struck him as a revelation of sorts: "I suddenly realized that what I thought I wanted to do, I could do, and that was to remove myself from the novel for the first time, to invent a voice and tone that for the first time could in no way at all be identified with me. It was a disembodied voice. It was a tone that permeated the novel and seemed to be cut loose from the man who wrote it. Total fabrication" (19).

Works Cited

Andrews, David. "The Art Is the Act of Smashing the Mirror: A Conversation with Gilbert Sorrentino." *Review of Contemporary Fiction* 21.3 (2001): 60-68.

Armstrong, Peter. "Gilbert Sorrentino's *Imaginative Qualities of Actual Things.*" *Grosseteste Review* 6.1-4 (1973): 65-68.

Creeley, Robert. "Xmas as in Merry." *Review of Contemporary Fiction* 1.1 (1981): 157-58.

D'Amico, Maria Vittoria. "Paradox Beyond Convention: A Note on Gilbert Sorrentino's Fiction." *Rivista di studi anglo-americani* 3.4-5 (1984-1985): 269-80.

Edwards, Paul. Afterword. *The Apes of God.* By Wyndham Lewis. Santa Barbara: Black Sparrow, 1981.

Eilenberg, Max. "A Marvelous Gift: Gilbert Sorrentino's Fiction." *Review of Contemporary Fiction* 1.1 (1981): 88-94.

Elman, Richard. *Namedropping: Mostly Literary Memoirs.* Albany: State U of New York P, 1998.

Emerson, Stephen. "*Imaginative Qualities of Actual Things.*" *Vort* 2.3 (1974): 85-89.

Gilmore, Lyman. *Don't Touch the Poet: The Life and Times of Joel Oppenheimer.* Jersey City: Talisman House, 1998.

Graver, Lawrence. Review of *Imaginative Qualities of Actual Things,* by Gilbert Sorrentino. *New York Times Book Review* 2 July 1972: 6-7.

Kant, Immanuel. *Critique of Judgment.* 1790. Indianapolis: Hackett, 1987.

Klinkowitz, Jerome. *Literary Disruptions: The Making of a Post-Contemporary American Fiction*. 1975. Urbana: U of Illinois P, 1980.

—. Review of *Imaginative Qualities of Actual Things*, by Gilbert Sorrentino. *Village Voice Literary Supplement*. 22 Nov. 1973: 27-28.

Mackey, Louis. *Fact, Fiction, and Representation: Four Novels by Gilbert Sorrentino*. Columbia: Camden House, 1997.

McPheron, William. *Gilbert Sorrentino: A Descriptive Bibliography*. Elmwood Park, IL: Dalkey Archive Press, 1991.

O'Brien, John. "Every Man His Own Voice." *Review of Contemporary Fiction* 1.1 (1981): 62-80.

—. "An Interview with Gilbert Sorrentino." *Review of Contemporary Fiction* 1.1 (1981): 5-27.

Olson, Toby. "Sorrentino's Past." *Review of Contemporary Fiction* 1.1 (1981): 52-55.

Phelps, Donald. "Extra Space." *Vort* 2.3 (1974): 89-96.

Review of *Imaginative Qualities of Actual Things*, by Gilbert Sorrentino. *Booklist* 68.6 (15 Nov. 1971): 274.

Robins, William. "Gilbert Sorrentino." *Dictionary of Literary Biography V5: American Poets since World War II (Part 2)*. Ed. Donald Greiner. Detroit: Gale Research, 1980. 278-84.

Scholes, Robert. Review of *Imaginative Qualities of Actual Things*, by Gilbert Sorrentino. *Saturday Review* 23 Oct. 1971: 88.

Shakespeare, William. *King Lear*. c. 1605. *The Complete Works of Shakespeare*. Ed. David Bevington. 3rd ed. London: Scott and Foresman, 1980. 1173-215.

Shiner, Larry. *The Invention of Art: A Cultural History*. Chicago: U of Chicago P, 2001.

Sontag, Susan. *Styles of Radical Will*. 1969. New York: Anchor, 1991.

Sorrentino, Gilbert. *Aberration of Starlight*. 1980. Normal, IL: Dalkey Archive Press, 1993.

—. *Imaginative Qualities of Actual Things*. 1971. Elmwood Park, IL: Dalkey Archive Press, 1991.

—. "Life and Letters." *Conjunctions* 37 (2001): 427-32.

—. *The Orangery*. 1978. Los Angeles: Sun & Moon Press, 1995.

—. *Something Said*. 1984. 2nd ed. Normal, IL: Dalkey Archive Press, 2001.

—. *Under the Shadow*. Elmwood Park, IL: Dalkey Archive Press, 1993.

Stephens, Michael. *The Dramaturgy of Style: Voice in Short Fiction*. Carbondale: Southern Illinois UP, 1986.

Thielemans, Johan. "The Energy of an Absence: Perfection as Useful Fiction in the Novels of Gaddis and Sorrentino." *Critical Angles: European Views of Contemporary American Literature*. Ed. Marc Chénetier. Carbondale: Southern Illinois UP, 1986. 105-24.

Williams, William Carlos. *The Embodiment of Knowledge*. Ed. Ron
Loewinsohn. New York: New Directions, 1974.
—. *Kora in Hell: Improvisations*. 1920. *Imaginations*. Ed. Webster
Schott. New York: New Directions, 1970. 6-82.
Wright, Martin. "Gilbert Sorrentino's *Imaginative Qualities of Ac-
tual Things*." *Grosseteste Review* 6.1-4 (1973): 61-64.

Fictional Truths:
Imaginative Qualities of Actual Things
between Image and Language

Tyrus Miller

> Not a just image, just an image.
> —Jean-Luc Godard

Already with its puzzling title, Gilbert Sorrentino's *Imaginative Qualities of Actual Things* poses the question of the relations between two categories of being: those qualified as "fictive," "imaginary," or "artistic" on the one side, and those designated as "actual," "nonfictional," or "living" on the other. In addition, the terms *true* or *real* waver unsteadily between these two domains, but come increasingly in the novel's course to stand for the compositional integrity of a written work against any pretense that it refer to something independent of words. Sorrentino prefaces his narrative with a quotation from William Carlos Williams, which lends the book its title and sets up the terms on which it will engage the problems of words and images, the perceiver and the perceived, the imaginary and the actual:

> In the mind there is a continual play of obscure images which coming between the eyes and their prey seem pictures on the screen at the movies. Somewhere there appears to be a mal-adjustment. The wish would be to see not floating visions of unknown purport but the imaginative qualities of the actual things being perceived accompany their gross vision in a slow dance, interpreting as they go. But inasmuch as this will not always be the case one must dance nevertheless as he can. (ix)

Williams here addresses a classic romantic problem, the adequation of the mind's representations to the characteristics of the material object, yet he offers an atypical, unromantic answer. For a late romantic poet such as Yeats, the merging of "dancer" and the "dance" metaphorizes the poetic image's seamless fusion of subject and object, its capacity to intermesh the artistic product with reflections of the productive/receptive processes that shape it. For Williams, in contrast, the metaphor of the dance and of its "images" is an index of a "mal-adjustment" between these phases, symptoms of an irresolvable dissonance in the artistic process. In Williams's poetics, contrary to the celebratory puzzlement of Yeats, one can *always* tell the dancer from the dance: the "image" they create in their dissension signifies first and foremost this very disharmony. For Williams, thus, the dance is not just image, rather just an image.

In comparing the mind's processes to the cinema and insisting that "one must dance . . . as he can," Williams emphasizes that the image is not the product of *mental acts,* but rather emerges through an alien automatism, the intensive passivity of the mind as it is alternately shocked and seduced by what is thrown upon its screen. Still, Williams does not suggest that there might be some orthopsychic posture of mind that could *harmonize* this infelicity of mind and world or correct the epistemological uncertainties born of social and erotic surprise. Rather, he refers to a further fictionalizing *act* of mind that follows the passive moment of imagination, a supplementary act of "interpretation" that implicitly translates to a new dimension the misadjustment of mind and world in which the dance of images is born. (We need not insist on the Nietzschean overtones of the term *interpretation* here; the Jameses, William and Henry, suffice as Williams's intellectual patrimony in this meditation.[1]) In reiterating the disharmony at the heart of things, the fictionalizing, interpreting imagination takes up the chaos of objects as the very inner structure of the artwork, compositionally capturing the temporal shapes in which the phenomena converge and disperse again. But this suggests, then, that interpreted objects somehow occupy a status different from either "real" object or "fictional" images. The dissonant interaction of mind and world spurs the activity of fictionalizing interpretation, which leaves neither pole untransformed.

Although I will explore this complex third status at greater length in what follows, one aspect to mention at the outset is the degree to which Williams's interpretative imagination rematerializes the passionate body dissolved in the romantic imagistic "dance." In a sense, Williams lowers the metaphorical character of the term "dance" insofar as the "act" of interpretation to which he refers is as much an *affective* and *kinesthetic* remotivation of the object as it is a mental activity. Williams's practice of writing is situated among its objects and, literally, moves within them and is "affected" by them. His literary corpus is no more or less than the record of the passion of objects. While Sorrentino's understanding of this embodied aspect of Williams's poetics of fiction is arguably revisionary—he is also attracted, after all, by the negative poetics of Samuel Beckett and Maurice Blanchot—the central role of such passional realities as addiction, sexual misery, and pornographic desire in *Imaginative Qualities* suggests that he too sees the imaginative faculty as an effective mover of the passions.

Literary art, accordingly, reveals its truth insofar as it cleaves to its mission of fictionalizing, *interpreting,* actual things in the light of imagination, thus affecting readers with the passions of love, disgust, shame, sexual desire, and sadness. It is at the level of these basic passions, Sorrentino suggests, more than at the level of represented content, and especially ideological content, that any authentic artistic "communication" with an audience occurs. In the tacit order of the humors that circulate through Sorrentino's book, the volatile vapors of alcohol, the urgent pressure of semen that will have its way, the warm and heavy feminine humors that carry thought toward the lower body, and the black bile of melancholy take pride of place.[2] (Herein, too, lies Sorrentino's debt to such nineteenth-century comic-satirical writers as Sterne and Swift and to the Irish modernists such as Joyce, Beckett, and O'Brien.)

Aside from the satirical and elegiac intentions that emerge and resubmerge throughout the book, then, Sorrentino's narrative also constitutes a consistent statement of poetics and literary ethics in light of an *anthropology* (taking the term with an eighteenth-century flavor) of the arts. This anthropology's underlying view of human nature is an unhappy one, for Sorrentino's human comedy germinates within a dark compost of Machiavelli, Hobbes, Swift, Sade, and (Wyndham) Lewis. As Sorrentino's narrator typically remarks at one point, "If there is one controlling factor that today informs our lives (outside of ignobility, of course), that factor must be greed" (164). But on the basis of this pessimistic anthropology, he goes on to frame the question of the arts and their role in illuminating, if not redeeming, this deep human fallenness. Where, Sorrentino asks, do the arts stand in the order of human nature, shaped as it is by greed, envy, competitiveness, sexual compulsion, and fear? At times via implicit demonstration, at others via explicit argument, his narration suggests that art, especially that of language, is an effort at truth, an endeavor to say the truth about a human nature that has as its most deep-seated instinct its mendacity toward itself and others. Like Williams, with his disenchanted doctor's eye, Sorrentino trains his eye on the physiological mechanisms that so often give the lie to our spiritualizing, idealizing explanations of our desires and actions. For both writers, art is in league with the body's infelicity against the cultural and psychological ruses that sublimate unhappiness into a pursuit of "higher values."

Sorrentino's characters manifest both extremes of this anthropological polarity. At every turn of his narrative, through poetic effusion, intellectual camraderie, or the pursuit of well-being in the business of culture, they seek to evade the desperate energy of their "wild bodies," Wyndham Lewis's apt term for his own anarchically gyrating satirical puppets (see *The Wild Body* (1927)). Anything but stand in the harsh and unflattering light of art, the soul whispers in the inner ears of these characters, anything but face the truth. Sorrentino's art tells the story of their irresistible disavowal of art as such, their terror of the truth that art betrays. The impossible position of art in respect to human nature is, in Sorrentino's novel, the truth art has to communicate, and it shows why the message of its impossibility is the last thing anyone wants to hear. For it is precisely the foreignness of art, its irreconcilability with the compulsions of our averageness, that terrifies: "The artist's particular devotion is the one thing that cannot be reached or tampered with. He is hated and feared—these emotions disguised as admiration. A case in point: a poet can publish a book of beautiful, clear, and powerful poems, which sets off all sorts of terrors in the community of dabblers" (42). Yet terror provokes not only aggression, but mimicry—"admiration," "grudging admiration"—a second-order donning of the artist's smock in a rite that seeks to bring art's estranging power into safe hands. Everyone is an artist, said Joseph Beuys, a consummate showman in an artist's felt hat.

The convergence of fictional invention and the fundamental passions represents the overall artistic perspective of Sorrentino's novel, from which he asserts the value of art against competing claims from the realm of business, sexual life, politics, and so on. Yet it also provides, more obliquely, the dimension of social criticism that the novel also occupies. Thus does Sorrentino's narrator interject in the midst of his attempt to establish the character of Bart Kahane: "Why are people so shabby that even fictitious characters stand revealed as corrupt or damaged? Go ahead, tell me to fulfill my obligations by attacking the society that spawns such corrupt people and dismal art. I am attacking the society. While you make the revolution, I make art" (188-89). To "make art" in the charged context that Sorrentino evokes is not simply a mandarin gesture of withdrawal from the "real" world, but rather a difficult work of clearing space for unwelcome truth-telling, a labor of "determinate negation" in the midst of a totally mendacious culture industry. Genuinely to be making art, in short, means that one is not making cultural journalism, is not making a pile of money, is not making possibly useful contacts, is not making an academic CV, is not making one's friend's or benefactor's spouse, is not making a name for oneself as an enfant terrible at parties and openings, or any of the other forms of making one's way in New York that surrogated for making art. Like Wyndham Lewis's monster satire of 1930, *The Apes of God,* Sorrentino's novel thus attacks that peculiar social complex known as the metropolitan artworld, that compounding and confusion of art, commerce, personal life, journalism, critical cant, and political ideology that characterized the New York artistic-literary community of the late-1950s and 1960s. More generally, he submits to withering satire, at times high invective, a wide range of forms of imitative social behaviors distilled to their essence in this milieu: fake political convictions, fake friendships, marital dishonesty, conformism to commercially or critically successful stereotypes, self-aggrandizement and self-delusion, all under the master sign of fake artistry. As I have already suggested, this imitative behavior—this mimetic demiurgy of fake art—derives, in Sorrentino's view, from terror before the truth-disclosing capacities of the art of fiction.

This is risky ground, however, for an artist to establish a work upon, since fake artists and real artists may very well resemble one another outwardly. At least until the former buy houses in fashionable locations like Vermont, Colorado, and New Mexico (the infernal circles to which Sorrentino consigns the worst sinners against art, places infinitely exiled from the divine light of the intellect that streams from New York), they are not always at first sight distinguishable. Sorrentino's novel is pitched in the very hotbed of fakery and failure, and it depends utterly on its particular forms of pathos and idiocy. Yet as Wyndham Lewis before him had already recognized, opposites tend to contaminate one another, and hence the satirist may end up dangerously resembling the object of his satire. And what, after all, should make us credit Sorrentino's narrator with his vociferous claim to real artistry that might distinguish him from the objects of his invective? Why not see this annoying fabulator as just another species of artworld loser, expressively venting his hard feelings in so-called art while slipping us a few of his favorite pornographic postcards as well?

> People who "recognize" themselves
> in books are never in the books.
> —Gilbert Sorrentino (48)

Implicitly, in the various modes of distantiation, self-deprecation, and reflexive commentary that characterize the narrative voice of *Imaginative Qualities,* Sorrentino gives his answer. He signals his claim to fictive truth through his honest recourse to fabulation, to an art of artifice that dares speak its name. Most immediately, he employs a large repertoire of metafictional narrative devices, including ostentatious intrusions by the narrator, explicit registration of compositional choices like names or settings, footnotes that offer hints to critical interpretation, traces of the editorial process presented as part of the text. Closely related to these devices are his open intertextual importations. Not only is Sorrentino's novel dense with brief quotations and punctual allusions to earlier literary works (indeed, its title is one), but it even includes second-order novelistic characters such as Nabokov's Lolita. In Sorrentino's penultimate chapter, the notorious ex-nymphet of the 1950s appears in the next decade, rather worse for the wear, as the wife of the faux-sculptor Bart Kahane: "Bart is an unreal bore, and Lolita, hopefully, is more unreal than he, being a borrowing of another writer's unreal bore. It is perfectly all right that they should have made it. What is more irritating is to meet real people in the street, at parties, in bars, etc., who have made it the same way. That's not so funny, at all. I mean they are *real*. One can't purify oneself of them through the ruthless selection of art" (205; Sorrentino's italics). Extending to the opposite side the transgressive importation of "outside" figures into his novelistic cosmos, Sorrentino also includes, as walk-on characters, a number of his literary and artistic predecessors and contemporaries: Paul Cézanne, Wyndham Lewis, Norman Mailer, Larry Rivers, Joel Oppenheimer, Robert Kelly, Clayton Eshleman. After comparing the work of his fictive bad poet, philanderer, and snoop "Dick Detective" to that of the living bad poet Tom Clark ("They are poems with less energy than is manifested in the work of Tom Clark"), Sorrentino takes pains to include a footnote to inform us that " 'Tom Clark' is a real name, i.e., the man lives" (222).

Notably, in Sorrentino's employment of these devices, they do not serve—as is often assumed in postmodernist theory—to subvert the authority of the narrator to truthfulness and hence the authenticity of the work, but in fact work to reinforce his claim to veracity. Correlatively, the statements of the narrator emphatically shift the weight of truth toward fictional artifice and suggest that the "non-fictional" is actually only a type of "unreal" fiction, because it is fictional without candor. "Reality" is tangential to nonfiction and fiction alike, which are equally partial and selective. The real is the empire of surprise, mostly unpleasant (but occasionally very pleasurable indeed), that animates representations, but does not form their "content." The real is the "squish" of something stepped on in the street: an imaginative quality of the actual thing. Nonfiction makes the mistake of thinking that once the remaining pulp has been scrutinized, categorized, and properly labeled, the real has been represented. "Nonfiction," Sorrentino remarks, "is a kind of magic-lantern show to captivate the minds of those who think it describes or reveals reality; a sort of sweet narcotic to take you to some other world. While there, you think you're perceptive of everything. But, worse, you think that you can use this when you get back home to the Rock" (168-69). Moreover, when reality itself is corrupted, and mendacity is the primary truth it exhibits, the verisimilitude of fiction and the referentiality of fact diverge: "As a matter of fact, I'm inventing things that may pass as probable or at any rate, possible. If I were to record absolutely the facts about these people, nobody would believe me" (45). Where the facts become incredible—not just surprising or anomalous, but literally impossible to believe—fiction takes up the task of compelling conviction, because it fictionalizes openly.

Yet Sorrentino's narrator is a hard man, and he won't let himself or his readers out of hell in a hurry. As he himself suggests, candor, even this pitilessly dialectical candor of total irony, may be nothing more than the last ditch of the faker. Compare, for example, what the narrator says about the hip cynicism of the nouveau-riche (their *enlightened false consciousness,* as Peter Sloterdijk memorably described the twilight mentality that has internalized the critique, but resigns itself, with unhappy euphoria, to falsity). The artworld success story Bart Kahane was the cynical prophet of the "hip nouveau-riche, a class so modern that *they* call *themselves* parvenus," the narrator observes. "The idea is that one is to forgive them because of their candor" (188; Sorrentino's italics). Yet what of the narrator's candor, laced with more than a hint of guilty conscience, in letting us in on the game of the novel? Is that too to be "forgiven" in the name of his opening his conjurer's hand to the reader's view? Or is the narrator just another puppet in the hand of his author, a more cynically honest sham, perhaps, than figures like Lou and Sheila Henry, who don't know they are shams, but a faker all the same? This last possibility would make Sorrentino's first-person narrator a "broadcasting" structure similar to characters in Wyndham Lewis's fiction, like his eponymous artist character Tarr and the Horace Zagreus/Pierpoint pair in *The Apes of God.* In these satirical novels Lewis channeled his ideas through his characters, even quoting his own ideological treatises, and at the same time rendered them ridiculous, deeply compromised figures in their fictional contexts (see Miller 99ff). My narrator a "busher"?—could well be, the author laughs, and pares the fingernails of his very clean hands.

As Peter Nicholls has suggested in an insightful discussion of Lewis's fiction, this problem of distinguishing the authentic artist from his or her counterfeits was already a central preoccupation of modernist writing in the 1910s and twenties. The so-called men of

1914, Wyndham Lewis, Ezra Pound, James Joyce, and T. S. Eliot—and although outside of the scope of Nicholls's argument, one could add the name of William Carlos Williams here—sought new compositional and stylistic criteria to authenticate art in the face of a "generalized mimetism" that threatened art's integrity. Nicholls notes that in pursuing this goal these writers set themselves apart not only from the major European avant-gardes, such as futurism, expressionism, dadaism, and constructivism, but also from other modernists such as Virginia Woolf, Joseph Conrad, D. H. Lawrence, and E. M. Forster. The cutting edge of this distinction was, according to Nicholls, "their rejection of 'romanticism' in the name of avant-garde modernism," their distrust of "notions of spontaneity and originality which underpinned the ideal of (lyric) expressivity which writers like Woolf and Lawrence seemed to be developing from romanticism" (422). This modernistic romanticism asserted the originality and authenticity of the personal, inner, often unconscious self, hence also sought to exorcise the threat of social imitativeness that reduced personal experience to stereotyped packages. The skepticism of the men of 1914 toward romantic authenticity, however, was rooted precisely in their sense that the intimate self, with its predicates of sympatheticness, spontaneity, receptiveness, fluidity, unreflectiveness, unconsciousness, sincerity, and childlike innocence of code and concept, was a product of imitation par excellence. Centering one's artistic practice on it led in their view to a fuzzy impressionism limited to registering the ever-changing sensory flux originating in the objects and persons of an environment. Such romantic modernism also bore for these writers the stigma of enervated masculinity, the germ of homosexual decadence transmitted from Walter Pater's *Marius the Epicurian* and Wilde's *The Picture of Dorian Gray* to the various products of Bloomsbury, Scott Moncrieff's translations of Proust, and Radcliffe Hall's *The Well of Loneliness*. The reaction of the men of 1914 to this perceived threat was two-fold, with Joyce, Pound, and Eliot representing one response and Lewis a distinctly different one.[3]

In their swerve away from social mimesis and its romantic reflex in the arts, Joyce, Pound, and Eliot recast the mimetic relation between text and reality in terms of intertextuality. As Nicholls writes, the

> function of textual imitation (of pastiche, allusion, citation, translation) in the work of Pound, Joyce and Eliot . . . constantly undermines an aesthetic of spontaneous desire. . . . A literary style thus steeped in self-reflexivity at once reveals the illusion of spontaneous desire *and* presents itself as an alternative model to be copied. That "copying," however, is a process grounded in self-irony, since the fundamental

presupposition of "style" is that desire is always mediated by textuality and thus has to be grasped, as it were, from the outside, from the standpoint of "writing" rather than by an act of imaginative identification. (430)

The displacement of imitation from social and physical objects to a domain specifically of texts allowed these writers to shift the question of artistic value from psychological sensitivity and authenticity to more objective cultural and historical canons of judgment. To put it crudely, these writers found Dante, Homer, Aquinas, and Confucius a more secure bet for their cultural coin than the emotional peaks and troughs of a Virginia Woolf or D. H. Lawrence. Moreover, conceiving of imitation as primarily oriented toward a textual tradition also polemically asserted their conviction that art should be an autonomous, technical, and professional activity, rather than a nearly superfluous extension of psychological, sexual, personal, or political life.

This intertextual mimetic strategy is certainly one explored by Sorrentino and with precisely the literary historical stakes I have just outlined: a modernism centered on Pound and Joyce versus a modernism centered on Lawrence, Woolf, and their lesser peers. One need not stretch the interpretative point, for Sorrentino's narrator carries out polemics of his own and names names:

A friend of mine, years ago, after a first trip to Mexico, was deeply impressed by the Mexican Indians. He had read *The Plumed Serpent* and tripped over it. What most struck him was the image, bright in his mind, of these Indians, squatting by the side of the road, impassive, "their eyes like black stone, onyx, sitting there as if waiting for death." In his speech, "death" came out "Death." Another friend, who *was* a Mexican, said that they were waiting for the bus to come along and didn't feel like standing. So Lawrence and a dozen movies were shaken to their foundations. The first friend was outraged and wouldn't speak to the Mexican friend for two weeks. His Plato was impugned. The world is NOT what I want to make it? He returned to Lawrence in a rage. Those Indians! A bus? A bus!? He was personally attacked, he felt. They were waiting for Death!

The reader will see that what I am driving at is that these words that he is reading—are words. (37; Sorrentino's italics)

You can writhe in the darkest pit and filth of yourself and come up with some dull fragment of *vers libre,* indistinguishable from that of a hundred contemporaries. Thus pain does not guarantee anything. Art, you see, is not interested in your suffering. It is not a muse. Look at Robert Graves—all that palaver about his Goddess, and all those third-rate poems. (35-36)

Lawrence appears here as the "Plato" of the minor poet. Devaluing the particulars of appearance, the facts of everyday life and the realities of the body, he seeks a transcendent, spiritual truth that would transfigure the too sordid reality of a poor, tired man waiting for a bus. Implicitly, Lawrence, like Plato, also clings to his spiritual ideal over any manifestation of it in art, which can only "mimetically" degrade its putative purity and intensity. In the case of both Lawrence and Graves, however, Sorrentino's judgment is clear: he who believes that art refers a "higher" vision will fail to see what is in front of his eyes: the actual appearances of things, the actual order of words. He will betray artistic imagination in favor of a reductive, derivative, egoistic phantasm. Words, not "vision," are the true particulars of literary art.

Yet if Sorrentino takes up the intertextual model of modernism, he does so only with a far weaker sense of mission than his predecessors were able to command. It is with a mixture of admiration and bemusement that he looks back on Joyce's distress that the outbreak of World War II had upstaged the publication of *Finnegans Wake* or Pound's glee that Mussolini really got the Cantos. Sorrentino cannot believe that his (or Pound's, or Joyce's) book will save Western culture, the artist, or anything else—except hopefully the persistence of art itself. Art's claim to reality is precisely its utopian separation from the dimension in which life's problems are experienced, suffered, and, possibly, remedied. If at times the narrator holds out the promise that the book may prove an "antidote" to the poison all around, it is only in a specific and narrow sense. For it is primarily the illusion that art will cure unhappiness that is the poison, and genuine art will only disabuse one of that false hope:

> Can you see some shattered man trying to heal his life by reading *Tender Is the Night*? In the back files of the *Ladies' Home Journal* there may, at least, be found the names of various physicians who will get you to the grave with a minimum of anguish—so they say. There is more profit in an hour's talk with Billy Graham than in a reading of Joyce. . . . Joyce just sends you out into the street, where the world goes on, solid as a bus. If you met Joyce and said, "Help me," he'd hand you a copy of *Finnegans Wake*. You could both cry. (215)

This removal of modernist fiction from the problems of life is not, however, for Sorrentino, disqualifying. On the contrary, it represents for him a paradoxical, doomed, but nevertheless noble gesture of "unworldliness."

Wyndham Lewis, and in his wake Samuel Beckett and Jack Spicer, took a different tack from Joyce, Pound, and Eliot, and developed modes of writing that responded skeptically to the intertextual model. In his critical treatise of the late 1920s, *Time and Western Man,* Lewis thus expressed his distaste for Joyce's and Pound's ventriloquism through previous texts, which, in his view, only shifted the problem of social imitativeness to the temporal realm. As Nicholls explains, for Lewis the preoccupation of Pound, Joyce, and Eliot with the past was "founded on a will to reanimate and humanize that which, properly, is dead (a form of imaginative 'sympathy' re-opens the self to the kind of 'invasion' of which Eliot spoke [in his criticism of romantic poetry]" (431). Pound, as a "man in love with the past," adopted personae and roles in ways that in their structure and function were not fundamentally different from the various figures of Bloomsbury playing at being Duncan Grant (I adopt here, for the moment, the voice of Lewis). Joyce, for Lewis, contaminated his putatively avant-garde prose with the conventionality of the models that he appropriated, parodied, and transformed. For Lewis, the autonomy of the artwork depended on its "deadness"—its exteriority and withdrawal from subjective temporal flux—so that being "dead" and having a distinct, stable identity in time became corollary terms for him, at least in the sphere of art. To seek to reanimate the past, inspiring it with new life, violates both the separateness of the past work and that of present existence.

In *Imaginative Qualities* Sorrentino likewise reveals his doubts whether the brave autonomy that intertextual mimesis seems to offer is really tenable. For example, he has his would-be poets and novelists not only blindly mimic those "bad" writers he clearly dislikes (D. H. Lawrence, John Berryman, Philip Roth, Vladimir Nabokov, etc.) but also mimic badly great writers that he admires— William Carlos Williams above all. Thus as young lovers, Lou and Sheila Henry bond over Williams's *Paterson,* and Lou reads to Sheila from Pound on their honeymoon. "Borrow, borrow," the narrator says of Lou, "you can get into Williams and get the very names of shrubs and wildflowers into your work—anything but the terror that dominates your own life" (35). Anton Harley is similarly presented as a consumer of Williams with neither taste nor digestion, just a sort of selective regurgitation: "No, Anton had swallowed Williams—swallowed is right. He saw in that poet kindness, understanding, wisdom, all the attributes of the patient country doctor. Of course, the absolute darkness and rage of Williams's work escaped him" (158). Insofar as the fictive Lou, Sheila, and Anton seek in Williams's writing a model of how to link poetry (including Williams's own) to life rather than respecting its enigmatic separateness in the dead world of the text, they violate Williams and degrade themselves to epigones and shams.

Even more significant for the narrative voice that Sorrentino adopts, however, may be the examples that Beckett and Spicer represent in reworking the intertextual strategies of modernism. They take Lewis one step further, pushing his views on the deadness of art toward its dialectical exasperation. Let us recall that Lewis's strictures against mixing life and art, his insistence on relating to art and to the past as separate/dead, derived from his desire to purge art of social imitation and to distinguish genuine artistic making from apish fakery. Still, Lewis leaves himself an important hedge: he suggests that his own art, disciplined by his training in the visual arts, resists the imitative blurriness of the changeable "time-world" in favor of the sharp, discrete, "dead" separateness of spatial shapes and forms. For Lewis, in the armored polemical posture of the "Enemy," it is possible as a living author to relate to others without any loss of separateness, that is, as if he were surrounded by dead things. Lewis's artist only has to be tempered in polemical combat to repel the social forces that seek to assimilate him to commerce, fashion, politics, sex, and other extra-artistic domains. His artist need be only a *little* dead to reap the defensive benefits for his art. Beckett and Spicer, however, close this loophole that Lewis left open for himself. They suggest, in contrast, that there is *no* position from which the living can relate to each other or to the other in time (e.g., tradition, the dead) without sacrificing their discreteness from one another. The most minimal state of vitality, which, for example, Beckett's *Unnameable* represents, entails the whole mess of relations to others, to language, to the past. To live, Beckett implies, is to be disseminated among others. Moreover, from the opposite direction, others, other people and the dead, impinge upon us. They chatter in our heads and over our radios, forcing us to utter up their thoughts and write to their dictation. Beckett's and Spicer's texts are thus above all characterized by their continuous demonstration of the impossibility of silencing the alien voice of the other within us.

This recognition at once undermines the intertextual model of Joyce, Pound, and Eliot and calls in question Lewis's response to it as well. Rather than a repertoire of models that can stabilize a new work on the basis of historically guaranteed cultural values, the voice of the other is an uncontrollable irruption of words, words, words. Intertextuality can thus just as easily manifest itself in "sophomoric dribbling" (in the words of Beckett's ex-university man cum derelict, Molloy) as in elegant Eliotic allusion. In Beckett and Spicer, accordingly, most of what appears as allusion is cultural flotsam drifting aimlessly around the space of discourse or even the fragments of a text that breaks apart as it endlessly cites and recites itself. Sorrentino, too, indicates that his own text may be entropically echoing itself. Thus at one point his narrator hints that Guy Lewis and Leo Kaufman, like Beckett's Molloy and Moran, may be two temporal moments of the same character. Or perhaps, if they do not succeed one another narratively, they are at least successive drafts of the same complex of character traits: "It just occured to me that I could make Leo into Guy Lewis before Guy changed his name" (115). Yet he just as quickly withdraws this hypothesis: "First of all, Leo is really Leo (invented, of course). I mean he is not, was never, and will not be (I'm almost certain) Guy Lewis" (115). Similarly, Anton Harley and Lou Henry are cut from the same shoddy material: "Now, what if I were to tell you that Anton is a character in this book, based on a character in this book? That is, Anton is 'really' Lou Henry. It seems complicated, but it isn't, because it wouldn't change the book at all. There is *no* character development whatsoever (I hope) to Lou Henry, so if Anton is Lou, it means nothing. But what is nice about making fiction is that I can do this" (169-70; Sorrentino's italics).

Despite the final remark, however, his narrator's problems in keeping the identity of his characters straight indicate neither the author's sovereign freedom to revise his book in midstream nor his characters' dead passivity in yielding to the author's decisions. Rather, they suggest that in the narrator's world the realms of death (art, fiction, the past) and life are too closely intermingled, lending both spheres an uncontrollable and uncanny life-in-death animation "where the dead walked/and the living were made of cardboard," as the final epigraph from Pound puts it. A reference to Spicer in the "Images of K" chapter may accordingly be taken as a skeptical warning about accepting at face value the narrator's creative bravado: "We were in Max's Kansas City at the time, which bar was invented by Jack Spicer in his book *The Heads of the Town up to the Aether*. The poet creates Max's in the line: 'In hell it is difficult to tell people from other people.' All those Nehru jackets and miniskirts surrounding lobsters and steaks. If you listen closely, you can hear the mandibles working" (149). Yet these "mandibles," as at least the author, if not his narrator, knows quite well, are nothing other than one part of his text gnawing on another—as much as if he had brought in Dante's Count Ugolino for a literary snack at the infernal Max's. Sorrentino, like Beckett, kills off as many of these feebly distinguished larvae and specters of text as he can, dedicating his novel above all to the task of *cancelling* images rather than adding new ones to the world. Viewed in this light, *Imaginative Qualities* appears less a positive narrative than a "graph of specific losses and individual disintegrations" (79).

Beyond the entropic, destructive drive of Beckett's and Spicer's mode of writing, which Sorrentino's text likewise sets in motion, there is another, even more disquieting trajectory that they adumbrate, which would precisely realize Lewis's dream of a wholly dead/separate world of art. If it is impossible for the living author to relate to otherness as if it were dead, a logical possibility remains: that the author is himself, in the very present of writing, unpresent—dead. That is, only if the author is, in the act of writing itself, *already dead* could the separation that Lewis advocated be possible. One cannot, they saw, consistently maintain the artwork in its dead separateness while saving the artist, bristling and armed. So along with the life of the artwork, Beckett, Spicer, and perhaps Sorrentino sacrifice the living artist as well.

Of course, the task of writing as a dead man is an impossibility. But if the very idea of narrative voice presumes that certain structures of enunciation become the linguistic simulacrum of a living storyteller (ultimately referrable to the author), then Beckett and Spicer recast narrative voice as the simulacrum of death—of their own death as authors, their absence from the rustle of words in their texts. Beckett's posthumous voices in the later drama and fiction and Spicer's colloquies of the dead in *For Lorca* and *The Heads of the Town up to the Aether* are precisely maps of this impossible, utopian world in death in which total discreteness might be realized at last. Thus, unfaithfully translating Lorca and writing fictive letters to the dead poet, Spicer speaks as dead man to dead man in a language neither author could claim as "his." In late Beckett dramas like *Footfalls* and *Rockaby,* the playwright arranges structures that exclude him utterly, signifying his muteness and absence of agency in the words. They are closed monologues of isolate dead selves, spatially dispersed between a nonpresent body indicated by an actor's visible body and a silent voice portrayed by an audible tape-recorded voice.

In thus canceling Lewis's half-step back from the brink of suppressing the author as the determining "last instance" of narration, however, Beckett and Spicer also push Lewis's defense against imitation to a paradoxical limit. If Lewis thought to find in the deadness of art a refuge for himself against "aping," a preserve against the uncontrolled effects on art of social imitativeness, Beckett and Spicer cancel the social content of imitation by rendering imitation intransitive and infinite. For in assimilating the author to death, they imitate death itself. The simulacrum of death, however, is an imitation without limits, because it is without an object or model. The image of such an intransitive imitation is that of camouflage and animal mimicry, a paralyzing regression of the figure into its spatial background: Molloy, in his filthy gray-green greatcoat, pressed up against a rock. "Saved by his protective colouring" (137), as Sorrentino writes of the artist in an advanced stage of his disappearance from view.

For the most part, however, in *Imaginative Qualities* Sorrentino's narration does not follow Beckett and Spicer over into this uncanny space of intransitive resemblance—and this, as we shall see, is a significant choice on Sorrentino's part.[4] Instead, he hesitates in the grim forechambers, where death and life mingle in strange shadowy figures. His narrator is tormented, enraged, and paralyzed by the chatter of the walking clichés that populate this realm. More rarely, he is also rent with profound regret and grief for a few of the shades that wander by in the dark. Thus, for example, speaking of Leo Kaufman, a man whom Sorrentino's narrator professes to have loved, fiction becomes a way of mourning the *insufficiently* dead, by conjuring into fictive inexistence a pain that would otherwise be all-too-vivid:

> I look at that book today and the man (whom I loved) who wrote those poems appears in my recollection as some young figure who may as well be buried in one of the bleak cemeteries that break Brooklyn into divers territories of the living and the dead. It was his true, gentle manhood that was killed in those years. Took the garbage out and threw himself away. He himself thought that he himself came back down the alley with the empty pail. But that figure merely looked like Leo. Science fiction. I'd rather not say any of this. But a poet is no common thing. I'd rather he were simply defeated, that his sweet line lost its charge and power. What do *you* know about my life? I hear him say. The poor bastard doesn't know that I invented him, he thinks he's real. (128-29; Sorrentino's italics)

> Puritans and libertines have full-time jobs:
> I mean, that's what they *do*. Read Sade.
> —Gilbert Sorrentino (151)

Up to this point, I have sought to trace out the implicit trajectory of Sorrentino's novel from his adoption of a satirical stance toward social imitativeness to his use of intertextual and metafictional narrative devices, which bring his novel close to the breach between author and text that French criticism of the 1960s characterized as the death of the author. I have also suggested that this trajectory recapitulates key moments in the development of modernism, a legacy to which Sorrentino consciously lays claim and with which he seeks to come to terms. Pound, Joyce, and Eliot performed the crucial displacement of imitation away from social models and refocused it on specifically literary-textual models. Lewis, in turn, offered an acute critical analysis of the limitations of such intertextual mimesis and argued in favor of a "dead" art of distinctions, of separations, of discreteness. Yet as his vivid engagements in the ideological skirmishes of his day and his frequent lapses into conventional narrative and discursive writing suggest, Lewis hardly managed to translate his advocacy of radical "deadness" in art into a consistent literary practice. Beckett's and Spicer's work suggests why Lewis ultimately found this an impossible standard to live up to. Temperamentally unwilling to sacrifice the agency connected to the artist or author, Lewis blocked for himself the only thoroughgoing course into the world of dead, discrete things: to write as a dead man.

Sorrentino retraverses all this terrain in summary in *Imaginative Qualities of Actual Things*. He also signals his awareness of the limits or failures of the modernists' solutions to these problems, at once artistic (insofar as they concern questions of composition and form) and social (insofar as these formal issues relate to the problem of distinguishing art from social imitation). Yet if Sorrentino does not follow Beckett and Spicer in casting the author into the space of death, does this mean in making his narrational choices he has resigned himself to the "enlightened false consciousness" of the postmodern cynic? Does he simply project his own artistic failure onto his narrator, asking his readers to accept failure as a type of artistic form, redeemed by irony? Does he let the narrator's "I" take the rap for the *author's* perplexity before the problems of the modernist literary legacy that he claims for himself?

In this concluding section of my essay, I want to suggest why I believe that the answer to these questions is no. For in at least one aspect of his novel, Sorrentino points positively beyond the modernist narrative impasse, that aporetic form of the novel Lewis forcefully adopted in response to the problem of social imitation and that Beckett and Spicer carried to logical exasperation. Sorrentino's postmodern detour around Beckett and Spicer, however, takes a surprising and problematic form: a mimesis of the pornographic. Or more precisely, it employs what I will call the pornographic simulacrum, which takes the pornographic *image* as a model that words may at once imitate and carry past mimesis into abstract relations.

The pornographic simulacrum functions for Sorrentino as an alternative to Beckett's and Spicer's thanatopic narration because of its specific way of binding language (as the medium of communication, reflection, and universalizing) to death (as the ultimate state of separateness and singularity), in a manner that nevertheless maintains the author as its organizing center. In his critical philosophical study *Sade, My Neighbor,* Pierre Klossowski explicated the paradoxical role of Sade's transformation of perverse sexual acts into a form of literature. Klossowski notes that Sade, because of the extreme nature of the acts that he represents in his novels, forces reflection upon what, if any, might be the difference between the act represented and the act performed independent of the representation. He goes on to consider how attention to this distinction might help illuminate a related question about Sade's work: How does the "pervert," about whom the Sadean characters recount stories, differ from these Sadean libertine narrators? Klossowski suggests that the Sadean narrators/characters raise the inarticulate gesture of the pervert, pursued in isolation and even silence, to an interpretative reformulation in rational language. This interpretative remotivation of the perverse gesture in turn makes it the object of contract, communication, and pedagogical reenactment by the community of libertines. Furthermore, this interpretative activity internal to the novels offers a model for understanding how Sade's narrative discourse affects his readers. By way of his narrator-libertines, Sade employs a language invested with the activity of the pornographic act, yet explictly in the *absence* of the performed act itself. Language and nonlanguage (the silence of the perverted gesture) intertwine in his novels in a mutually disruptive way. The pornographic simulacrum that Sade's writing activates moves the passions of readers—arousing, disgusting, or outraging them. Through these passions, however, it also reacts back on language itself, contaminating the abstract, normative discourses of reason, morality, and politics that it utilizes as its argumentative medium.

Crucial to Klossowski's analysis, however, is what he sees as the *critical* dimension of perversion, which is a negation of a whole order of life in favor of a "dead" repetition of an act focused on a detail of this whole. The pervert, in Klossowski's view, "presents an arbitrary subordination of the habitual life functions to one sole insubordinate function, a craving for an improper object" (23). He thus sacrifices himself to an object that, in its indifference to the utilitarian order of survival, in its being generalized until it constitutes the entirety of the pervert's world and time, represents the death of the human species. "His existence consecrates the death of the species in him as an individual," Klossowski writes; "his being is verified as a suspension of life itself" (23). This negativity of the perversion also has a linguistic dimension, since the communicative use of language is the key means by which human beings create the means to reproduce the human order, through the social norms of labor and sexuality. Yet this implicit insurrection of the pervert against the norms of human life also remains inarticulate, even as it stands against the order of normative communication. As Klossowski notes, "The singular gesture of the pervert *empties all content out of speech at once, since it is by itself the whole of existence for him*" (26; Klossowski's italics). Klossowski identifies Sade's specific literary innovation as that of creating a character-type that will bring the pervert's negative relation to language into a linguistic interpretation: "Sade invents a type of pervert who speaks with his singular gesture *in the name of generality*" (26; Klossowski's italics). When this Sadean character speaks, "the singularity of the gesture that was the motive of his discourse is disavowed in that such singularity is taken to be proper to each one. The content of his gesture is then not singular, for in silence it still had no meaning—and now it acquires meaning in speech" (Klossowski 26-27).

There is no resolution or overcoming of the antinomy entailed by the Sadean character. The key point for Klossowski, rather, is that Sade's characters do not really seek to *convince* others that the content of the singular acts of the pervert are valid for all (a manifest sophism), but rather to create complicity insofar as the interlocutor or reader is led to recognize his or her own *capacity* for such singularity and hence accept the universality of perversion as such. But such complicity implies the disintegration of the normative identity of each participant of such an impossible society. The instrument of such disintegration is the intense affect that pornographic representation of perversion provokes, a unique passion of response that "proves" the *capacity* for singularity that each shares with the pervert, even as that capacity expresses itself differently in each. As Klossowski concludes, "In order for complicity with the pervert to emerge in the normal interlocutor, he, *qua* 'rational' individual, must first be disintegrated. This is possible only by a leap of impulsion or of repulsion provoked in him by the word of the pervert" (28).

It will not escape any reader that Sorrentino's novel has an intimate relation to the pornographic. Within a few pages of the introduction of his first two characters, Lou and Sheila Henry, his narrator offers us the following scene:

> Lou came in to the living room with two Scotches. He was naked, his penis swollen and half-erected. On his face he had painted, with her mascara, a mustache and goatee.
> There is no point in writing pornography here. To be clear, this: instead of mounting Sheila, he masturbated himself and her, while he worked a candle in and out of her anus with great skill, so that Sheila came almost at the moment that she became aware of what he was doing. (8)

This scene segues into a meditation on Sheila's imaginary transformations of the physical act being performed on her at that moment:

> He was her lover. Not even—real, but a man from a dirty book, a blue-movie man, the salesman, the cop, the priest, the man with shoes and black socks on. She thought of him with these things on. No. Rather, she thought of Lou as her lover with these things on. She thought of Lou as Che Guevara with black socks and patent leather shoes, and Che was her lover. He was—let's call him Milt. His name doesn't matter, I don't recall her lover's name, but Milt will do. So she said, "Milt, O Milt, fuck me." She whispered then, "Fuck my asshole, Milt, fuck my asshole." (8-9)

The narrator then makes a leap out of the scene, now extending it into a direct appeal (a staggering Sadean sophism) for the reader's complicity. The perverse, he reasons, is the norm. But this generality of perversion entails the disintegration of identity, since in a system where perversion was general, we would always be misrecognized: we would always be only a partial object, a fetish, a fantasy screen of another's desire. Yet if this disintegration of identity could be carried to its ultimate Sadean conclusion, then we would not be plagued with so many would-be artists using bad art to defend themselves against the crumbling of their selves. Hence—the syllogistic conclusion—in a Sadean utopia of generalized perversion, better art would be assured: "It is clear that Sheila's husband can only satisfy or at the least intrigue her by being someone else. If this is a common experience—which it may well be—among the married, shall we then select the 'perverse' for our observation? We will select then, it would seem, much of our world. . . . Sheila desires what only the man she lives with can give to her. But he cannot give this to her as the man he is. So does he seek his balm in art, thinking that it can establish his ego" (9). In the final twist of this sophism, however, Sorrentino's narrator gives us the full taste of the Sadean "countergenerality" (Klossowski) that the libertine insinuates into the forms of reason. The ultimate marital bliss, the narrator concludes, would be found in reversing the above scene, so that sexual infidelity would evidence the extreme case of fidelity to the spouse. The physically present lover, in this instance, would become nothing more than the contingent and interchangeable screen of flesh on which the beloved image of the spouse is faithfully projected: "Suppose that a lover had moved Sheila to Lou in this way? That the entire situation had swung in the opposite direction? In that case, this couple could have found perhaps, in their marriage—all the pleasure inherent in all the flesh of the world" (9-10).

At this point, attentive reading will reveal that the narrator has carried the reader beyond any shock, revulsion, arousal, or pleasure that the pornographic image might have initially provoked. The pleasure that the narrator invites the reader to share is no longer a mimetic-pornographic one but rather a rhetorical one. The stage of erotic imagination has shifted wholly to the sophistic verbal dialectics of the narrator himself, the pleasure of which the reader is invited to confirm and heighten by complicitous appreciation. As Jean-Paul Sartre observes about Jean Genet's analogous extensions of the images of his erotic reverie into elaborate, highly rhetorical passages: "Words complete our fantasies, fill in their gaps, support their inconsistency, enrich them, enrich them with what cannot be seen or touched. . . . The reason is that there are abstract relationships which can be erotic" (13). Opened to the dizzying possibilities of syntax and syllogism, the pornographic image may be heightened to the point where it metamorphizes into pure paralogism.

If, however, this passage progresses out of the pornographic image toward a kind of seductive paralogism wholly within language, it is nonetheless not accidental that Sorrentino chooses to set the stage for this movement with an initial scene of "sodomy." The term is precise, since what he portrays is not simply a codified sexual practice of anal intercourse, but something presented as and perceived by the actors themselves as aberrant, transgressive, outrageous. Klossowski is careful to underscore this distinction in explicating the special status of sodomy for Sade, who takes it as a kind of summa of all the possible modes of transgressing and aggressing against human life in its character as a finite creation of God. "Homosexuality," Klossowski writes, "which is not an intrinsic perversion, must be distinguished from sodomy, which is":

> sodomy is formulated by a specific gesture of countergenerality, the most significant in Sade's eyes—that which strikes precisely at the law of the propagation of the species and thus *bears witness to the death of the species in the individual*. It evinces an attitude not only of refusal but of aggression; in being the simulacrum of the act of generation, it is a mockery of it. In this sense it is also a simulacrum of the destruction that a subject dreams of ravaging on another of the same sex by a sort of reciprocal transgression of their limits. When perpetrated on a subject of the other sex, it is a *simulacrum of metamorphosis*. . . . The sodomist gesture, transgressing the organic specificity of individuals, introduces into existence the principle of the metamorphosis of beings into one another. (24; Klossowski's italics)

In his second chapter, dedicated to Lou Henry as the first chapter was dedicated to his wife Sheila Henry, Sorrentino's narrator picks up on precisely this metamorphic, identity-dissolving implication of the scene of sodomy in the first chapter. Here, speaking very much in the insurrectionary idiom of the Sadean libertine, he has Lou put on Sheila's lingerie and fantasize a sexual metamorphosis in which she sodomizes him (and again invites the reader's imaginative complicity with the scene):

> He wants Sheila to fuck him. You who read this, imagine your sex changed for a week. I don't speak of homosexuality: that is sexual reformism to rescue one from terror. What I mean is revolution. Or the attempt at it. (Lost from the start.) . . . The impossible desire of the male to be penetrated by his mate. And her imagination, unleashed, as she images herself, heavy with balls and phallus, mounting the familiar body of her husband. To lay these images to rest, the couple may endeavor to explore the sexual possibilities open to them. The realization that they cannot ever become each other strengthens their love or destroys it. (33)

These two scenes of sodomy thus introduce a principle of metamorphosis, a pornographic flux of simulacral forms, into the book. This principle, however, resonates with the apparently sovereign capacity of the narrator to invest his "characters" with new simulacral "identities" through the mere change of a name, through a few new attributes, or through their inclusion within an invented episode. Sodomy and narrative invention, as simulacra of one another, thus exchange their attributes and point toward each other in Sorrentino's novel. Coming almost at the beginning of the book, the two sodomy scenes establish one of the key modes in which the narrator invites his reader to yield willingly to the fictive "tyranny" of his artistic decisions, aesthetic opinions, and critical judgments. Similar scenes accordingly return regularly throughout the book, seeking to reactivate and assure the complicity of the reader: Leo Kaufman's fetishistic dressing up of his partners, Bunny Lewis's encounter with the masochist "Harlan," Anton Harley's fucking of a piece of pizza, April Detective's Catholic-tinged pornographic imaginings as she works her way through the office staff from boss down to mail clerk.

Still, even granted Sorrentino's occasional nods to Sade and the fact that Grove Press (Sorrentino's employer in the 1960s) published key Sade translations in the very period the novel treats, it might seem that *Imaginative Qualities* is far from either Sade's dark moral theology or the aristocratic philosophical reasoning of Klossowski. But if we attend to the underlying problem of Sorrentino's novel, social imitativeness and its implications for art, we can see that his use of pornography, especially its Sadean variety, is more than merely scenic, parodic, or satirical in its intent. For it is in moving the reader toward complicity in perverse singularity that Sorrentino addresses the problem of imitation that lies at the heart of his concerns.

The pornographic in *Imaginative Qualities,* particularly the perverse and fetishistic proclivities of characters raised to the level of generic signs, comes to stand more generally for the author's parti pris for the partial, nonutilitarian insurrection of artistic language against the corrupt prose of everyday life. If William Carlos Williams offered Sorrentino one model of artistic differentiation through a self-reflexive critique of everyday life, Sadean pornography provides an alternative model of per-verting the vocabulary of the everyday into singular terms of art. Perverse generality or generic perversion, for which, as I have suggested, the pornographic image serves only as a point of departure, may initiate participants into art's insurrection by way of aroused passions. In Sorrentino, as in Sade and in Klossowski, the pornographic is thus an intensive pretext before it is a represented content. It is an occasion and instrument for mobilizing intensities of passion that extend beyond the perverse image toward the eroticism of paralogical "abstract relationships"—the stuff of fictional art.

Sorrentino seeks, first and foremost, complicitous readers, prepared to be provoked by the perverse singularity of his narrator, and the pornographic is a cunning means of winning such consent. The successful semblance of communication between perverse narrator and a complicitous reader—a *simulacrum* of communication effected by the pornographic simulacrum in the medium of the passions—in turn "confirms" the narrator's claim to be making real art and not just adding to the legions of imitations that surround him. For his art is the simulacrum of perversion, raised to self-consciousness, made to speak, rendered professional. It counterposes its selective partiality to the norms of labor and communication, which it mocks through its perverse semblance of them. (Art *is* not a "full-time job," but it is *like* one. All its uncanny power lies in the difference.) The whole notion of fictional truth in *Imaginative Qualities,* the narrator's passionate claim for the truth of his fiction, rests on the organized complicity of the reader in the semblance of persuasion that leads from the pornographic image into the generic singularity of art as such. Yet the very first of those readers invited to the orgy is the author himself, who is dis-identified with his narrator but complicitous in all of his perverse ruses. Such complicity is not a mode of *identification,* as in "actual" mimesis, but only *resembles* identification. Complicity is the semblance of mimetic identification between author and narrator and between narrator and reader: the author (or reader) mimics "being like" the perverse narrator and the narrator pretends to believe that the reader (or author) is "like" him in his perversity. This fiction is mutually entertained, only that all might dissolve themselves more violently in the movements of perverse (self-) differentiation.

But complicity, ultimately, can never be organized in terms of truth, which depends on identifiable terms functioning consistently within frameworks of rational norms. Insurrection, sodomy, and art—at their most radical, corrosive of normative identity—always involve a measure of irrational violence, and first of all to the norms of rationality. Any complicity with insurrection, sodomy, or art must sanction the whole grounding "truth" of their fictions, the violence of their simulacral claim on truth itself. For only after this original simulacrum of truth has been granted may the other "perverse singularities" of such fictions be borne toward their improbable generality.

Notes

[1] William James is a key source for modernist considerations of how the interpretative activity of the mind shapes any possible apprehension of the world of objects and of the actions of other people. Especially important are his books *Essays in Radical Empiricism* and *A Pluralistic Universe* (for a more general discussion of the relations between modernist writers and James's thought, see also Schwartz). William James's brother Henry, in his late novels in particular, explores a set of peculiar "interpreted objects" constituted through the often merely tacit relations between his characters. Nothing occurs in novels such as *The Ambassadors* or *The Golden Bowl* without the rich mediation of assumptions about what other characters have assumed was the hidden intention or significance of the event, etc. Thus increasingly, the event itself is bracketed in favor of a complex interaction of multisided acts of interpretation. For a critical discussion of such interpretative structures in Henry James's fiction, see Cameron. (Sorrentino, incidentally, is a passionate reader of Henry James.)

[2] The psychology of humors, which explains character traits according to the predominance and position of certain fluids in the body, dates back to classical medical tracts and had a prominent place in medieval and renaissance medicine as well. In the English literary tradition, Robert Burton's *Anatomy of Melancholy* and Ben Jonson's comedies (e.g., *Every Man in His Humour*) represent key sources of humorial ideas. In his 1927 critical book on Renaissance drama, *The Lion and the Fox,* Wyndham Lewis specifically defends Jonson's "humorously" defined characters against unfavorable comparison with Shakespeare's more psychologically rich characters. Lewis, notably, also entitled one of his *Wild Body* stories "A Soldier of Humour."

[3] William Carlos Williams, arguably, represents a third, sui generis solution aligned neither with the literary montage techniques of the former writers nor with the satirical guerilla warfare of Lewis. Williams's skepticism toward romantic authenticity took the path of a self-reflexive "critique of everyday life" (I allude here to the theoretical work of Henri Lefebvre, who, inspired by the surrealists and later the situationists, took up the task of philosophically examining the structures of everyday life) especially attentive to the ways in which the commitments of the self were inflected by the heritage of common speech and the life of the body. Hence, his life-long insistence on *exactitude* in registering the untidy reality of the American vernacular and the physiological facts of that sociocultural space called New Jersey.

[4] Sorrentino's later writings, especially those that use "generative devices" to displace and confound the immediate intentions of the author, move more emphatically in this "death of the author" direction as adumbrated by Beckett and Spicer. Thematically, also, Sorrentino shifts his emphasis from the "truth telling" function of fiction to its uncanny negativity, in which the mechanisms of language and narration continue to operate in the void from which truth has been evacuated.

Works Cited

Cameron, Sharon. *Thinking in Henry James.* Chicago: U of Chicago P, 1989.

James, William. *Essays in Radical Empiricism and A Pluralistic Universe.* New York: Longmans, Green, 1958.

Klossowski, Pierre. *Sade, My Neighbor.* Trans. Alphonso Lingis. Evanston: Northwestern UP, 1991.

Lefebvre, Henri. *Critique of Everyday Life.* Vol. 1. Trans. John Moore. London: Verso, 1991.

Lewis, Wyndham. *The Lion and the Fox: The Role of the Hero in the Plays of Shakespeare.* London: G. Richards, 1927.

—. *The Wild Body; A Soldier of Humour, and other stories.* London: Chatto and Windus, 1927.

Miller, Tyrus. *Late Modernism: Politics, Fiction, and the Arts between the World Wars.* Berkeley: U of California P, 1999.

Nicholls, Peter. "Apes and Familiars: Modernism, Mimesis and the Work of Wyndham Lewis." *Textual Practice* 6.3 (1992). 421-38.

Sartre, Jean-Paul. Introduction. *Our Lady of the Flowers.* By Jean Genet. Trans. Bernard Frechtman. New York: Grove, 1963. 9-57.

Schwartz, Sanford. *The Matrix of Modernism: Pound, Eliot, and Early Twentieth Century Thought.* Princeton: Princeton UP, 1985.

Sorrentino, Gilbert. *Imaginative Qualities of Actual Things.* 1971. Elmwood Park, IL: Dalkey Archive Press, 1991.

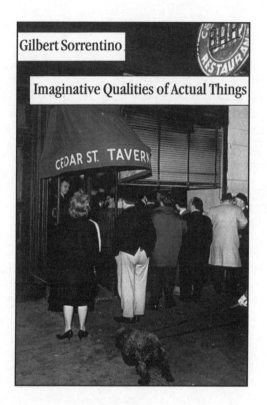

First paperback edition, Dalkey Archive Press 1991

Gilbert Sorrentino's
Problematic Middle Child:
Imaginative Qualities of Actual Things

Stacey Olster

The chocolate was real, the lard was melted, and the vomit that was meant to represent *The Sweet and Pungent Smell of Success* had no smell at all because it was plastic. To prevent the lesson of this last model from being lost on the bewildered viewer, however, artist Sue Williams provided a capsule—and capitalized—summary of the point she wished to make on the floor of New York's Whitney Museum of American Art in 1993:

8,000,000 PEOPLE IN THE
COUNTRY HAVE EATING DISORDERS
90% ARE WOMEN
6% DIE

Strident, certainly, but perhaps necessary in a Biennial Exhibition devoted to "inscribing the personal, political, and social into the practice of art," as the signs by the elevators read. With no *explication de texte* readily available, the striated three-foot-high cubes of chocolate and lard that comprised two parts of Janine Antoni's *Gnaw* clearly failed to make their point about women's pursuit of beauty on the one woman I saw fixing her lipstick in the mirrors that backed the cases of the installation's third section, *Lipslick Display: Phenylethylamine.* The cases contained heart-shaped packages of chocolate taken from the *Chocolate Gnaw* cube and tubes of lipstick made from pigment, beeswax, and chewed lard derived from the swamp into which museum lights were rendering *Lard Gnaw.* For in this world of what Arthur Danto termed "disturbational art" (qtd. in Ross 9), making a point—usually with respect to inequalities experienced because of gender, race, and/or class—was precisely what creative expression had come to be about in the 1990s.

Such a scenario is a far cry from the skewering given the "Revolutionaries of the elegant lofts" and "glittering people who play with vomit" in *Imaginative Qualities of Actual Things* (6), Gilbert Sorrentino's re-creation of the 1950-1960s New York art and literary scene. It is an even more distant cry from the formalism propounded by Sorrentino within that same text as the basis for aesthetic production. Eulogized by Whitney director David A. Ross as "the cynical formalism with which many critics defined the arts of post-war America" (9) and consigned by curator Lisa Phillips to "a backseat to the interpretive function of art and the priorities of content" (53), concern with style would seem to have gone the way of "authorial voice" and "all the emblems of successful art: originality, integrity of materials, coherence of form," according to those who mounted the Biennial (53). Moreover, if form and voice were among the primary traits that, for Sorrentino, characterized modernism in art, so far from modernist concerns did the Whitney exhibitors go, in the view of at least one member of the museum's advisory committee, as to be beyond postmodernism as well: "By giving abstract concepts and formal operations more overt social content, they localize, politicize, and historicize postmodern cultural debates that had been at one time excessively formalist and ethnocentric" (Fusco 81).

And yet, for all Sorrentino's stated emphasis on form, *Imaginative Qualities* seems to be singularly lacking in design. Unlike the chapters arranged in accordance with the letters of the alphabet in *Splendide-Hôtel* (1973) and the eighty-four lyrics linked by the use of the word *orange* that make up *The Orangery* (1978), the eight sections that comprise Sorrentino's third novel adhere to no particular structural principle—each one seems to be just another satirical exposé of a failed artist, and their combination "a collection of 'bits and pieces,' " as the book's narrator admits (11). Conversely, for all Sorrentino's disdain for "ideas" in art, particularly the kind the novel lambastes as "proffer[ring] the most marvelous radical sentiments in utterly degraded and reactionary poetic structures" when expressed in works with titles like "Raincheck for Fidel and Che" (145), the book is replete with diatribes against the United States the equal of any disaffected lefty's—diatribes that cannot simply be dismissed as belonging to the narrator since they duplicate so clearly remarks made by Sorrentino in essays and interviews.

In the case of *Imaginative Qualities,* I do not think it is possible to resolve these apparent contradictions between aesthetic credo and textual artifact. By historicizing Sorrentino's text, however, we can understand how they could have resulted. On the one hand, situating Sorrentino's aesthetic concern with form with respect to similar concerns expressed by American writers during the late 1960s and early 1970s enables Sorrentino's aestheticism to be viewed as typical, however extreme, of the priorities that many accorded form and content during that period. On the other hand, situating Sorrentino's text with respect to his other works corroborates its status as problematic "middle child" in that the novel anticipates the use of narrator in *Mulligan Stew* (1979) without fully completing the move into pure documentation that distinguishes that later work.

Sorrentino, of course, has never shied away from espousing the aesthetic position that underlies all his work. Tracing his deepest aesthetic affinities to his Irish and Italian heritage in an essay entitled "Genetic Coding" (1983), reprinted in *Something Said,* Sorrentino summarizes that heritage as defined by "a relentless investigation into the possibilities of form, a retreat from nature, a dearth of content" (264). Such characteristics—the "coding" that made possible the influence that writers such as James Joyce, Flann O'Brien, and William Carlos Williams later would exert—yielded, in turn, a set of predilections that Sorrentino denotes as his own "artistic necessities": "an obsessive concern with formal structure, a dislike of the replication of experience, a love of digression and embroidery, a great pleasure in false or ambiguous information, a desire to invent problems that only the invention of new forms can solve, and a joy in making mountains out of molehills" (*Something* 265). Anomalous in a collection devoted to previously published reviews of others' works, the autobiographical essay is nonetheless important. Coming late in the collection, it joins into an aesthetic credo many of the points that previously have been scattered throughout the text. Sometimes, those Sorrentino points take the form of outright assertion: "To understand that the world is not ours for the taking, and to understand further that it will not yield up anything that it does not intrinsically possess, seems to me to be the only program that a serious writer can subscribe to"; "writers have only a fistful of ideas, most of which have long been unpopular"; ". . . I do not believe in Originality but consider writers a kind of 'collaborative' band, each adding a stratum to the work done by others, each stratum possible only because of that work" (*Something* 78, 100, 263). At other times, those points take the form of binary opposition, as Sorrentino defines what art is with reference to what it is not: "The novel is an invention, something that is made; it is not the expression of 'self'; it does not mirror reality"; "the poet is not an interpreter, but a revealer"; "things do not *connect,* neither in the poem nor in the life from which it springs: they correspond"; "The artist's job is not to tell you what he *thinks* about it [the world], but is to tell you *it*" (*Something* 26, 55, 56; Sorrentino's italics).[1]

Not surprisingly, Sorrentino's admiration or condemnation of other artists is based on the degree to which they conform to or deviate from these criteria. Paul Blackburn, who learns from the study of the troubadour poets that the "I" of the poem is an artificial creation, writes "a handbook of invented form perfected" (Sorrentino, *Something* 104). John Wieners, who understands that art is "in no way expected to right wrongs or ameliorate anything," composes poems, each of which "holds itself, a closed system" (Sorrentino, *Something* 168, 170). William Gass, who, much like William Carlos Williams, recognizes that people exist "in flashes and glints," writes fiction that "tell[s] the truth in terms of the language and not in terms of the meanderings, psychological or otherwise, of characters" (Sorrentino, *Something* 191). By contrast, Manuel Puig fails as a novelist because he "holds his content to be somehow more than just materials—to be a set of ideas" (Sorrentino, *Something* 210). Worse, John Updike manufactures prose so weighted by a "concatenation of images" as "to conceal the reality they are supposedly revealing" (Sorrentino, *Something* 187). Worst of all, John Gardner relies so much on the "Crippled-Analogue Shuffle," "Garbled-Comparison Hop," and "Down Home Two-Step" for flashy similes and borrows so frequently from the "Warehouse of Hackneyed Phrases" for triumphant clichés as to produce a style so execrable as to be absolutely styleless (Sorrentino, *Something* 216-17).

Significantly, many of these aesthetic criteria are reproduced verbatim by the narrator of *Imaginative Qualities*. He constantly reminds readers that "These people aren't real," but merely "follow-the-dots pictures" that have been "prose[d]" right "into the paper and the shape of the letters" (27, 111, 168). He recalls Williams in denoting the "smallest of flashes" as the "bits of mica" in which "things may be revealed" (34). He acclaims the "perfections of fiction" as so "useless insofar as structuring your life" is concerned that "There is more profit in an hour's talk with Billy Graham than in a reading of Joyce" (215).

Equally significant, many of these same aesthetic criteria also appear in the remarks of other American authors working during the same period. Much like Sorrentino repudiating originality and invoking layering and strata to describe the connection that writers bear to their predecessors, John Barth declared it "too presumptuous, too naïve" for *any* writer "to attempt to add overtly to the sum of 'original' literature by even so much as a conventional short story" in "The Literature of Exhaustion" (33). His portrait of "Echo" in *Lost in the Funhouse* (1968) subsequently typified the position occupied by *every* writer: unable to speak for herself after being punished by Hera for using her stories to distract the goddess from Zeus' infidelities, she "edits, heightens, mutes, turns others' words to her end" (97). Donald Barthelme adopted a similar stance in *Snow White* (1967), turning the words of both the Brothers Grimm and Walt Disney toward the end of producing a fractured fairy tale whose semantic convolutions ("horsewife," "baff," "pelf") satisfy its heroine's desire for "some words in the world that were not the words I always hear" (6), but whose resolution sustains the tradition of its antecedents. The hanging of one of their band having reduced their number to six, the dwarfs incorporate a new member to maintain the status quo and depart in search of another principle, "heigh-ho."

Yet nowhere is Sorrentino's position more representative of his time than in the emphasis it ascribes to form. Perhaps the most well-known exponent of this priority was Susan Sontag, who, in a series of essays written in 1964-65, began relegating content as the "pretext" or "lure which engages consciousness in essentially *formal* processes of transformation" and rejecting "putting art to use—for such purposes as inquiring into the history of ideas, diagnosing contemporary culture, or creating social solidarity" (*Against* 25, 21; Sontag's italics). Celebrating Camp's "love of the unnatural," Sontag went on to advance a postromantic "new sensibility" that "demands less 'content' in art, and is more open to the pleasures of 'form' and style" and in which art exists as an 'object' rather than a vehicle for "individual personal expression" (*Against* 275, 303, 297). Equally early, though, Barth was declaring God a botched realist and reality "a nice place to visit but you wouldn't want to live there" and affirming "the artificial element in art (you can't get rid of it anyhow)" as the point of his work and "technical circus-tricks" as "good clean fun" (qtd. in Enck 8, 11, 6). From that belief emerged the sevenfold-set of Chinese boxes that underlies "Menelaid" in *Lost in the Funhouse,* in which Menelaus tells the reader how he told the sons of Nestor and Odysseus how he told Helen in Egypt how he told Proteus how he told the daughter of Proteus how he asked Helen at Troy why she married him from among her suitors; use of the Fibonacci series of numbers for *Chimera* (1972), in which each of the text's three novellas is 1.6 times the length of its antecedent; and another seven-part structure for *LETTERS* (1979), in which seven correspondents communicate over seven sections in compliance with the seven alphabetical characters that form the novel's title. Based on a corresponding belief that a Platonic paradigm, in which microcosmic City of Man reflected macrocosmic City of God, was being replaced by an Aristotelian paradigm, in which the actual world "was all there was," Robert Coover advanced a similar return to "Design" and the "creation of Beauty" in the *"Dedicatoria y Prólogo a don Miguel de*

Cervantes Saavedra" that introduces the "Seven Exemplary Fictions" of *Pricksongs & Descants* (76; 1969). Commenting, in 1973, on the way that his own "arbitrary commitment to design" manifested itself in *The Universal Baseball Association, Inc., J. Henry Waugh, Prop.* (1968), which employs the seven chapters of Genesis that deal with creation (1.1.-2.3) as the structural key to a story of a man throwing dice for an invented baseball game, Coover recalled his "delight with the rich ironic possibilities that the use of structure affords" (qtd. in Gado 148). Hence, the book's aesthetic joy in baseball's "almost perfect balance between offense and defense" and "beauty of the records system" (Coover, *Universal* 19) is offset by an exposure of the artificiality of its own design, ending neither with a seventh chapter (as the biblical metaphor would dictate) or a ninth (as the baseball pattern would warrant) but with an inconclusive eighth instead.

Such similarities obviously prevent Sorrentino from being viewed as a lone aesthete crying in the wilderness during this period.[2] At the same time, the differences between Sorrentino and these other writers certainly place his position at one extreme.[3] For all the correspondences between Barthelme's recognition that an increasing "trash phenomenon" makes incorporation of all sorts of cultural detritus into art inescapable (*Snow White* 97) and Sorrentino's view that "Nothing in the art of the novel is ever dead" for novelists who compulsively "go rummaging around" (qtd. in O'Brien 5), Barthelme's appreciation of the literary past in particular is far more ambivalent than Sorrentino's.[4] Portrayed as "sometimes dead weight, sometimes live weight" when embodied in the figure of *The Dead Father* (1975) being dragged across a landscape by nineteen followers, that heritage is envisioned as an inhibitory memory "more potent than the living presence of a father" that forces its successors to be "always partly him" (59, 144). Likewise, for all his concern with abstract design and structure, Coover's formalist impulses arise, ultimately, as formulae for psychological succor, based on his conviction that under the "conditions of arbitrariness" in which post-Enlightenment humans live, art can assist in the domestication of terror as novelists "invent constellations that permit an illusion of order" in fiction that "enable us to get from here to there" in life (qtd. in Gado 153, 152).[5] Perhaps most interesting, for all Barth's stated rejection of realism in interviews, his fiction from *Giles Goat-Boy* (1966) onward continually exposes the limits of an aestheticism divorced from the world around it. The title story of *Lost in the Funhouse,* Barth's portrait of the artist as a very young man, depicts Ambrose Mensch's adolescent urge toward creative expression as the product of his suspicion that he is not a "regular person" that, in feeling things that "no normal person feels," he may in fact be a "freak" (93, 88). As a result, his decision at the end of the story to design funhouses for others, each creation "incredibly complex yet utterly controlled from a great central switchboard," is followed by his recognition in the closing line that "he would rather be among the lovers for whom funhouses are designed" (93, 94). And this prioritizing of the real world over the artificial one is corroborated later by the discovery made by the narrator of "Anonymiad," the final piece in Barth's collection. A minstrel who never has "take[n] seriously enough the pretensions of reality" while apprenticing in the court of Agamemnon and Clytemnestra, believing that *To speak for the age . . . was less achievement than to speak for the ageless,*" he ends up stranded on a deserted island, hoist by his proverbial petard after Aegisthus knocks him unconscious with his own lyre; saved from despair by his invention of coded markings he calls *"fiction"* that he writes on goatskins, he finally reaches a critical mass point at which he begins "to run out of world and material" (166, 175, 186, 187; Barth's italics). But with no new experience to provide him subject material about which to write, and the permutations and recombinations of earlier literature already exhausted, he is forced to realize that "The memory of literature, my own included, gave me less and less delight; the 'immortality' of even the noblest works I knew seemed a paltry thing" (188).

Those works of Sorrentino with few pretenses to plot or extratextual relevance—*Odd Number* (1985) and *Mulligan Stew* come to mind immediately—most clearly adhere to Sorrentino's stated preference for artifice over reality. The problem with *Imaginative Qualities,* however, is that it frequently lapses into the kind of disquisitions on the state of the world beyond its covers that its narrator repeatedly renounces. For instance, at one point the narrator invites readers to imagine for themselves the circumstances leading up to and following the twenty activities he lists Leo Kaufman and the female "poem freaks" who surround him as having performed; in this way, readers will obtain "a general picture of the hip New York scene during those years" that the narrator has no interest in writing (121, 122). Yet the very activities listed by the narrator ("Went to parties at the Artists' Club," "Were on hand for Ornette Coleman's opening at the old Five Spot," "Went to innumerable readings in coffeehouses, bars, galleries, churches, and lofts") provide just such a picture (122)—indeed, the narrator's presentation of the Cedar Bar as a post-World War II Deux Margots forms the very background of the entire novel.[6] Or, to give an additional example, at another point the narrator rejects the task of "ruminat[ing] on America," choosing to "leave that to Europeans who have been here about five years or so," who will "tell you all about it, starting with the essential nonseriousness of its art" (101). Yet he consistently punctuates his portrait of the "hip New York scene during those years" that he is (supposedly) not portraying with characters invented "to give the mood of the fading years of the Eisenhower Administration," comments about America in the fifties being "HELL ON WHEELS," and offers conclusions about "the masked pride in surviving at the edge of despair" that joins together the generation that lived through those years in which, quite simply, "America fell apart" (70, 124, 72). More to the point, he traces that very disintegration to the same "nonseriousness of its art" that he has earlier tendered to the Europeans. Having exposed as fraudulent one artist's use of the "Sickness of America" as an excuse for the "disintegration of his artistic powers," he reverses the causal connection in order to diagnose national disease as the product of poetic degradation: "There is no body of work in literature that, conceived of as some kind of diversion from the stringencies of art, will not rot and its putrescence affect the population" (159).

A rather radical conception of literature's impact, to be sure, the narrator's diagnosis recalls remarks made by Sorrentino in a 1963 review of Andrew Hoyem's *The Wake*. Certain that Hoyem's brilliant poetry collection will be ignored by the American literati, much like those of Louis Zukofsky and Charles Olson before him, Sorrentino despairs at the way people remain "dulled to the fact that the language is the only thing that will save us from complete doom as men" (*Something* 150). That those poets most deserving of being called "the keepers of the language" are neglected in favor of those who manufacture "the rubbish that passes for the good, the fine" is, for Sorrentino, the "ticket to our final sellout as a people" (*Something* 151). Hence, the disgust exhibited by the narrator of *Imaginative Qualities* at the relative acclaim accorded William Carlos Williams and Saul Bellow involves more than differences in taste: "I'm rereading *In the American Grain*. You remember that book, right? You *don't* remember that book. Well, you remember *Herzog*? Right! That's a *great* book. All about America—the reality of America" (69; Sorrentino's italics). About which the Bellow book both is and is not. It is not in the same way that Sorrentino finds Marianne Moore's "hysterical, safe" poetry that "*grazes* that which lives" not to be about the maddening America of rot and vigor (*Something* 157, 160; Sorrentino's italics). At the same time, it is in that its reception as "a great book" testifies to the condition of the very nation it studiously avoids depicting between its covers.[7]

What connects that "body of work in literature" in *Imaginative Qualities* to the American body politic it is meant to emblematize is sexuality itself. As the narrator flatly asserts, "America is geared to infidelity" (71). Significantly, it is the complete absence of sexuality that, in Sorrentino's view, dooms Moore's poetry from the beginning of her career to aesthetic anemia: "The poet failed as her language failed, and her language failed because she shut out the real" (*Something* 166). By contrast, the opening lines of *Imaginative Qualities* introduce the correspondence of sexual and artistic betrayal that will pervade the entire book:

> What if this young woman, who writes such bad poems, in competition with her husband, whose poems are equally bad, should stretch her remarkably long and well-made legs out before you, so that her skirt slips up to the tops of her stockings? It is an old story. Then she asks you what you think of the trash you have just read—her latest effort. . . . Is seeing, finally, the hair glossy between her thighs so important that you will lie? About art? (3)

Unfortunately, the narrator's near escape from an aphrodisiac "use of the arts perhaps more common than any other in this time" that makes Sheila Henry "a particular kind of modern-day whore" (3, 8) is one denied to almost every other character. When Sheila's husband Lou responds to his wife's infidelities by sending her out to work ("If she must fuck, he said, in effect, I'll get something out of it"), he only ends up pimping his own poetic talent: "With the composition of the cycle, *Sheila Sleeping,* Lou may be said to have settled into his mediocrity" (41). When, in the case of Leo Kaufman, "America had got him hot" (134), and he alleviates his ardor by buying his wife black underwear and leather boots to model in front of male friends, the dissipation of erotic prowess results in a dissipation of creative prowess. As the narrator explains, "Sex is power. . . . Leo ravaged the products of his powers, so that there was then nothing but for him to ravage their sources. . . . The only thing destroyed in this whole process of liberation was his art" (150-51). And as the book progresses, and characters with at least talents capable of being squandered are succeeded by Stakhanovites like Bart Kahane, who markets art for parvenus in need (187-88), parasites like Anton Harley, who regurgitates William Carlos Williams as rapaciously as he feeds on foods he allegedly fornicates (167), and consumers like Dick Detective, who doesn't fail at art as much as not write it (235), the sexual sellout that opens the book's series of aesthetic sellouts

comes to seem a phenomenon of endemic proportions. Not surprisingly, the anecdote offered as "a curiously American story," involving Bunny Lewis, a "yokel masochist" and a "simply perverse
act carried out in that lavish sterility of the Southwest," occurs in
Taos, New Mexico, a place indiscriminately "destructive of art"
because "everything is art, so that the blanket, the pot, the dinner
on the handmade table, and the poem and painting are all one"
(108, 99).

Taking the lay of the land from the play of the language in this
manner ultimately makes moot all divisions between an art devoted to aesthetics and an art devoted to politics.[8] As Sorrentino
writes in *Splendide-Hôtel,* "there is no politics but the manipulation of power through language. Thus the latter's constant debase-
ment" (17). What the narrator of *Imaginative Qualities* offers as
compensation, however, as "antidote" to "ward off the poisons that
abound" (198), is revelation, specifically, the kind of revelation that
Williams found in the localized "isolate flecks" of "To Elsie," and in
which, as Sorrentino writes, "the whole meaning of a life, or of a
cultural milieu, may be contained" (*Something* 23).[9] The narrator
thus informs the reader near the beginning of the text what his
narrative approach will be throughout it: "In this book, I'll muddle
around, flashes, glints, are what I want. It's when one is not staring
that art works. In the middle of all the lists and facts, all the lies
and borrowings, there will sometimes be a perfect revelation" (34).
As vehicle for such epiphanic condensation, he rejects prose of psychological exploration (45) in favor of prose that approximates photographic illumination, the photo, "if it be not taken by some intelligent and knowledgeable professional," being "absolute
revelation" (58). And if, in the case of Williams, such photographic
revelation yielded "the meaning of the shapelessness of American
life, buried, as it has always been, in the pettiness of our daily routine" (Sorrentino, *Something* 23), so does it provide equally incisive
insights when employed by the narrator, as his description of a ho-
tel-room assignation between Lou Henry and a nameless whore illustrates:

> On the wall of the hotel room there was a framed print of Old Glory, un-
> furled and cracking in the wind. . . . The camera cannot tell this story
> without destroying its root meaning. From love, to sleep, to a shot of the
> flag on the wall. The simplest reader of *Avant-Garde* will understand
> that. The flag. Love. Sordid. America in the sixties, ugghh. While we
> know that's not the point, the point is the sleep, the flag is there. . . .
>   Lou never saw a picture of Old Glory after this that reminded him of
> that room, that girl, that sleep. The picture was *there.* I place it on the
> wall to extract and refine the essence of those two naked bodies, to

make them prose. To make them absolute prose. To prose them. (28-29; Sorrentino's italics)

The division between an art devoted to aesthetics and an art devoted to politics having thus been exposed as spurious by a narrator whose position so conveniently echoes Sorrentino's, one is still left with a troubling conundrum: What differentiates Sorrentino's novelistic presentation from political manipulation? Everything, I would argue, hinges on the voice in which the novel in question is presented. Commenting in 1976 on Dan Rice, one of the two painters to whom *Imaginative Qualities* is dedicated, Sorrentino invokes the word "lyrical" to describe the quality that Rice's work in the plastic arts forced him nonetheless to "read" (*Something* 256). Tracing that quality back to "the creation of a solitary and personal voice that has invented a solitary and personal voice," he concludes: "The man is not revealed in the picture; the man as a painter is" (*Something* 256). Indeed, according to Sorrentino, the man himself could not be so revealed, since the "curious aesthetic 'schizophrenia' " that is an artist's gift produces such an irreconcilable divide between the "man outside" who conducts his daily business and the "man inside" who engages in the creative process that the first is continually surprised by the outpourings of the second (qtd. in O'Brien, "Interview" 24).

In *Imaginative Qualities* Sorrentino attempts a similar division by inventing a narrator who, for all his similarities to Sorrentino, exists as a character unto himself—in fact, more than one character, if one accepts Sorrentino's contention that nine or ten narrators exist (O'Brien, "Interview" 14). Admittedly, the line between the narrator and author often seems so fine as to be nonexistent. This is particularly the case at the beginning of the text when the narrator, dismissing in a footnote the importance of his characters' names, confesses "it would certainly have been preferable to use letters for all of these people, even though I've already done that in a book" (50), so recalling Sorrentino's technique in *The Sky Changes* (1966), his first novel. Shortly afterward, he contemplates rewarding and punishing those same characters by "send[ing] them to Hackettstown in August, to sit in the Warren House in the cool of a 1939 taproom" (53), which, essentially, is what Sorrentino does to the characters in *Aberration of Starlight* (1980) a decade later. That said, the narrator also warns readers against making any such facile equations between characters and actual persons: "People who 'recognize' themselves in books are never in the books. It is the meticulously woven fabric of the ruthless imagination that makes them think they did what the artist says they did" (48). Therefore, as Sorrentino's book continues, the "wise-guy prose" (227) that approximates the author's voice outside the text becomes more and more interwoven with the frustrated angst of the voice that narrates the text. "I see that my problem is identity, i.e., my problem is that I *know* who *I* am," complains the narrator; this "is a big drawback to the writer of today who wants to sell his books" (78; Sorrentino's italics). As well he should know, given his own experience as a writer whose earlier novel, now remaindered in an Anopheles, New Jersey, warehouse, has sold exactly eighteen copies in the Central Valley (82), and whose new work, originally entitled *Isolate Flecks,* already has been rejected by seventeen publishers (125), dismissed by Lee "ZuZu" Jefferson as "merely a *collection* of anecdotes" (129; Sorrentino's italics), and forgotten by fiction editor Vance Whitestone as ever having been submitted to his house at all (125). No wonder the narrator can so easily fashion for his character Guy Lewis a rejection letter written by a bored editor, the stink of which will be recognizable to all who are writers (76). And no wonder the increasing animosity he bears for no-talents like Anton Harley, who approaches the writing of poems as he does the repair of motorcycles, but whose rapacity is evidence of "the spirit that moves the times" (182). Having admitted "What I'd really like to do right now is read *Tristram Shandy*—but with this fifty thousand-dollar advance half spent, it's write, write, write" (79), and fully aware that the prospects for any writing he produces are minimal within "a world of such predators" (182), he starts punctuating his prose with the kind of phrases he thinks will make it more palatable: "This party was in the midtown apartment of a man we shall call, for that is a useful phrase, Horace Rosette"; "The idea of Dick becoming a priest in his late middle age—to employ a needlessly clotted phrase—pleases me"; "I am indebted for this phrase to the 9,000-odd writers who have used it before me" (120, 230, 240). Equally aware that such inclusions turn his tale of aesthetic destruction into a tale of self-destruction, he simultaneously lacerates his prose at the same time that he creates it.

With nonentity and mediocrity both staring him in the face (another useful phrase), the narrator contemplates surrender as the only noble recourse within a hopelessly ignoble environment. "One begins to think that the only escape is to have one's work totally ignored," he states, in a variation of Woody Allen's riposte about not wanting to belong to any club that would have him, only to recognize the fatuous remark as the rationalization that it is: "I myself would embrace this position were it not essentially precious" (205).

But if insufficient fame can be excused on the basis of a corrupt environment, lack of aesthetic quality demands more radical measures. If, as the narrator asserts, self-knowledge is one "big drawback" to "the writer of today who wants to sell his books," not knowing who one's characters are is "The other face of that problem" (78). And so begin a series of remarks that attest to the narrator's increasing loss of creative control as the book progresses. "I'm getting into trouble with these people," he laments, "as soon as I stop watching them, they start moving around on me, and acting in an utterly uncharacteristic way. . . . The prose obeys me, but these people that hide behind the letters are doing God knows what" (102). Guy Lewis shifts from painter to writer without the narrator ever understanding why (84). Anton Harley "sort of walked right in" while the narrator has been busy tacking together Leo Kaufman (158). Dick Detective "seems to be everywhere" (148). Even worse, the characters he is in the process of constructing within the book start appropriating the shapes of people with whom the narrator is familiar outside the book (166). No longer able to distinguish between fabricated and factual figures, suspicious that characters emerging within chapters are not those for whom chapters have been intended (202), surprised by the entrance of Paul Cézanne as a buggering deus ex machina (200), the narrator throws his hands up in defeat (yet another helpful phrase): "Whatever it was it has happened behind my back, that is, these characters rush about among these letters and syllables doing, apparently, as they like. Retreating further and further into the pages, so that my book has become a street guide to some destroyed city" (201).

The narrator's jeremiad is, of course, a familiar refrain to anyone who has read *Mulligan Stew,* Sorrentino's tale of novelist Antony Lamont's attempt to write "an 'absurdist' mystery story" (28). Tired of being an obscure author without even the compensation that coterie status affords, jealous of a brother-in-law whose reissued pornographic books are winning critical esteem and monetary green, and suspecting an ever-widening conspiracy of professors, reviewers, and simple snobs to discredit his name, Lamont is in many ways the direct descendant of Sorrentino's *Imaginative Qualities* narrator. Fearful that his characters "are laughing at me behind my back as they go through their paces to humor me" (126) and astonished to find chapters that seem to have "written themselves" without his knowledge ("I don't even know where the title came from. Let alone anything else!" (246)), he responds with an identical diagnosis: "I don't think I am in *control* here. . . . All right, the story must take a turn on its own, live its own life. But THIS????" (247; Sorrentino's italics).

In contrast to his approach in *Imaginative Qualities,* however, in which correspondences between author and narrator are so close as to make the latter seem like the former "cast in a carefully selected tone and style," as John O'Brien notes ("Every" 76), Sorrentino eliminates the possibility of mistaking Lamont's voice for his own.[10] First, he divests *Mulligan Stew* of any commentary that might approximate his own stance. Thus at the beginning of the novel he establishes Lamont as an author who views art as self expression and treats his main protagonist, Martin Halpin, as an artistic surrogate: "To recast one's chaotic life as purest art—that is the program. . . . In one's self, in the dark shed of the untameable mind, lies the truth, wanting to be released into the line, the sentence, the story or novel" (47). Second, he makes Lamont a function of pure documentation; that is, a figure whose voice exists only in the form of journal, scrapbook, fictional excerpts, and the like. Third, he reinforces that artificiality by populating the text almost entirely with characters whose names derive from earlier works of fiction: Daisy Buchanan and Abe North from Fitzgerald's *The Great Gatsby* (1925) and *Tender Is the Night* (1934) respectively, Ned Beaumont from Dashiell Hammett's *The Glass Key* (1942), Martin Halpin from James Joyce's *Finnegans Wake* (1939), Richard Schiller from Vladimir Nabokov's *Lolita* (1955), not to mention the whole slew of names—Dermot Trellis, Paul Shanahan, Sheila Henry, and Antony Lamont—that originate in Flann O'Brien's *At Swim-Two-Birds* (1939).[11] Therefore, it does not matter that Lamont's three previously published novels, *Three Deuces, Rayon Violet,* and *Fretwork* correspond in theme and style to Sorrentino's three previously published novels, *The Sky Changes, Steelwork* (1970), and *Imaginative Qualities,* or that the eleven pages of rejection letters addressed to "Gilbert Sorrentino" that precede the opening of *Mulligan Stew* portray a publisher's white elephant no different than *Guinea Red* portends to be for Lamont. For when letters from "Gil" follow missives from Flo Dowell, Chad Newsome, and Claude Estee, one concludes that the "Gil" specified is no more meant to denote a real person than those characters from *The Good Soldier* (1915), *The Ambassadors* (1903), and *The Day of the Locust* (1939) are, that, in short, the "Gilbert Sorrentino" who receives the letters of rejection and the "Gil" who writes the letters of inquiry are invented personae who do not so much *reflect* the actual Gilbert Sorrentino as *parody* him.

No longer employing a narrator who, for all his attempts at distancing, still serves as his mouthpiece for the state of aesthetics within the text and the state of the union outside it, Sorrentino is free to cast *Mulligan Stew* as an illustration of the creative process from which art emerges, of that "magic state" he has described in essays and interviews, in which "things that are unknown to the writer in his everyday life are *found,* the clearest example being the discovery of metaphors that will reveal to him what he does not know, that will express to him those things that are there, but there in darkness and obscurity" (*Something* 9; Sorrentino's italics). Earlier in *Imaginative Qualities,* in a vignette involving Guy Lewis and an unfinished painting that is "driving him mad" (83), Sorrentino provides one such example of the process as it applies to the plastic arts. The center of the painting being the source of a problem that Lewis cannot solve, he finally, in drunken frustration and anger, grabs a brush from a can of black enamel and smashes it against the canvas. The result is nothing short of anthropomorphic, a "sign," as the narrator concludes, that "Art is magic" (85): "The painting is forming, it is moving, and Guy steps back, really terrified, looking at the sliding paint in the mellow sun through the dirty windows. The painting is absolutely being opened by something inside it, the black center is the demonic face of some creature that has been inside the painting, inside the canvas, all this time" (84-85). Antony Lamont experiences equal terror in *Mulligan Stew* when "A Bag of the Blues" seems to "write itself" as chapter 9 of *Guinea Red.* Only in his case that terror is the result of his own belief in art as self expression, which makes him think that the "sign" he receives from the chapter's unexplained appearance is a sign of his own incipient madness (293). But because Sorrentino has replaced the *Imaginative Qualities* narrator who declaims with the *Mulligan Stew* character who is pure documentation, he can *show* in the later book the point he has had to have *told* in the earlier one. Therefore, Lamont's learning that he must surrender himself to the madness that he feels is engulfing him rather than resist it is illustrated in the surrendering experienced by his own artistic surrogate, Martin Halpin, to the wiles of Corrie Corriendo and Berthe Delamonde, "two evil spirits incarnate" (296), who perform "tricks and marvels of magic that had never been known before" at the nefarious Club Zap (362).

As it turns out, they don't. For after having "flogged" their patrons into "a state of ecstasy" by "flashy sleight of hands," Corrie and Berthe conclude their act with name-the-card tricks of the most common variety, "simple parlor frou-frous that any amateur, with but a pinch of practice, can bring off" (375). What makes for the uniqueness of their act, then, is not the unusual nature of the tricks themselves, but the fact that Corrie and Berthe perform them without dissembling. As Halpin is forced to realize, "It mattered not that I caught the banal signal words whereby the sluts pulled off their raggedy trick, i.e., 'yes,' 'right,' 'that's right,' 'fine,' as well as silences used discreetly. Each was tried and true-blue and yet the saps abounding thought all was 'mystery' " (380). The artifice is freely admitted.

And having admitted much the same when Lamont has Halpin— and by extension himself—fall prey to the kind of magic the two women practice, Lamont can reap the benefit of their conflated surrenders. "She Is the Queenly Pearl," the first chapter to emerge from this acquiescence to magic, ends on an image of pregnancy, an image of fertility that becomes especially appropriate when the work in which it issues exchanges the hackneyed mystery of *Guinea Red* for the exuberant comedy of *Crocodile Tears,* Lamont's rewrite. Because this second kind of novel does not emerge until the second half of *Mulligan Stew,* we as readers are allowed to see both the process by which it emerges and the aesthetic principles that give it shape. "I like the 'Pearl,' " writes its father with new energy. "And I confide to you, O notebook, that I'm even a little *proud* of it!" (248; Sorrentino's italics). Well he should be, given the consequences that a freely admitted work of art can have on those very rare occasions when, according to Sorrentino, the "absolute falsehood of artifice" can be turned "by magic into truth" (137).

Notes

[1] The more astute commentators on Sorrentino's work correctly recognize that his emphasis on "revelation" and "correspondence" does not presuppose an art completely removed from the world from which it takes its elements. Thus Johann Thielemans's observation that "This is not the time for an 'innocent' realism," which is followed by his listing of the myriad ways in which a language of representation has become suspect, still concludes with the statement: "My point is that such an awareness changes the relation of the text to reality, but has not completely severed it from it. Fiction is never that pure, and we always read narrative statements as testimonies of the way in which we perceive the world, of which both language and literature are part and parcel" (116-17). Or, as David Andrews succinctly notes, "words are artifactual, that is, simultaneously artificial and factual" ("Gilbert Sorrentino" 41). As Andrews also realizes, this means that there is no "final difference" between the "artificial" works of Sorrentino, like *Splendide-Hôtel* (1973), *The Orangery* (1978), and *Under the Shadow* (1993), and the "realistic" works, like *The Sky Changes* (1966),

Steelwork (1970), and *Aberration of Starlight* (1980); all are consistent in "find[ing] subtle and inventive ways to manifest their artificiality *and* to register their fascination with the objective reality that is refracted in, and remade by, their surfaces" ("Gilbert Sorrentino" 50).

[2] In making this statement, I do not mean to imply that aesthetic design was the only quality advanced by American authors during this period, as the following juxtaposed examples clearly indicate: Barth's "Literature of Exhaustion" was published the same year as William Styron's *The Confessions of Nat Turner* (1967); Coover's *Universal Baseball Association* was published the same year as Norman Mailer's *The Armies of the Night* (1968); and Sorrentino's *Imaginative Qualities* was published the same year as E. L. Doctorow's *The Book of Daniel* (1971).

[3] See, in addition, the essays included in Raymond Federman's *Surfiction: Fiction Now . . . and Tomorrow* (1975) for position statements similar to those of Sorrentino. Indeed, in supplementing the views that "fiction will no longer be regarded as a mirror of life" or "be judged on the basis of its social, moral, psychological, metaphysical, commercial value" (8, 9) and that characters exist only as grammatical "word-beings" with the view that fiction "exposes the fictionality of [a] reality" that "does not exist, or rather exists only in its fictionalized version" (13, 7, 8), Federman exceeds even Sorrentino's renunciation of representational art. See, as well, Ronald Sukenick's description of Bossa Nova style (43-45), the leading examples of which he finds in Steve Katz's work.

[4] As anyone familiar with Sorrentino's work knows, that "rummaging around" also includes pilfering from his own works. As he admits to Barry Alpert in the *Vort* interview, "I've always used almost everything that I can put my hands on. I hardly ever throw anything away" (13). Sorrentino then explains the rationale behind this practice of aesthetic recycling: "Because I always know somewhere I'll be able to use it. I'll write something that I know is really rotten, see. And I'll keep it and know that somewhere, some place in the future I'll be able to use it as an instance of something that's rotten. I keep things like that, I mean I keep all sorts of things: old poems of mine that are terribly embarrassing. But they're very valuable because they show an absolutely embarrassing poem. One can also take lines and phrases out, things that are ludicrously bad, *sincerely* bad" (13; Sorrentino's italics).

[5] As Coover also admits, his subversion of the very structures he establishes within his works derives from an awareness of how frequently imaginative ways of grasping the universe can harden into dogmas when forced upon people outside of his works (Ziegler and Bigsby 84).

[6] For additional discussion of the role played by the Cedar Bar in the 1950s-60s New York art scene, see Sorrentino's interview with Barone (242-44) and his remarks on *"Neon, Kulchur,* Etc." (304-05).

[7] For more straightforward comments about the way the United States "died in the '50s" (10), only to be reborn as a country that alternately evokes "strained and unreasoning laughter" or "morbid, bleak sobbing" (14), see Sorrentino's interview with John O'Brien (9-14).

[8] It also, as Andrews has forcefully argued in his concluding chapter on "Aestheticism in American Literature," differentiates American aestheticism

from European aestheticism ("American" 385-418). See, as well, the head-note that opens Sontag's essay on Jean-Luc Godard (1968): " *'It may be true that one has to choose between ethics and aesthetics, but it is no less true that whichever one chooses, one will always find the other at the end of the road'* " (147; Sontag's italics).

[9] As Thomas H. Schaub argues, Williams's distinction between "copying" and "imitating" is comparable to Sorrentino's distinction between "signaling" and "inventing" (442). For an extended discussion of the way the latter terms facilitate apprehension of the actual, see Schaub 435-49. For the clearest portrayal in Sorrentino's fiction of that process of apprehension, see the section introduced by the letter "W" in *Splendide-Hôtel* (55-56).

[10] Sorrentino's remarks to O'Brien on this subject are worth quoting in full: "I suddenly realized that what I thought I wanted to do, I could do, and that was to remove myself from the novel for the first time, to invent a voice and tone that for the first time could in no way at all be identified with me. It was a disembodied voice. It was a tone that permeated the novel and seemed to be cut loose from the man who wrote it. Total fabrication" (19).

[11] In taking to an extreme many of the techniques introduced in *Imaginative Qualities*—such as the use of lists and the appropriation of characters from other works of fiction—*Mulligan Stew* does satisfy the desire "of doing anything I damn well pleased" that became a possibility to Sorrentino while working on the earlier text (qtd. in Alpert15).

Works Cited

Alpert, Barry. "Gilbert Sorrentino: An Interview." *Vort 6* (1974): 3-30.

Andrews, David. "American An/Aesthete: A Study of Aesthetes in American Literature, From Edgar Allan Poe to Gilbert Sorrentino." Diss. State U of New York at Stony Brook, 1997.

—. "Gilbert Sorrentino." *Review of Contemporary Fiction* 21.3 (2001): 7-59.

Antoni, Janine. *Gnaw*. 1992. Saatchi Collection, London.

Barone, Dennis. "An Interview with Gilbert Sorrentino." *Partisan Review* 48 (1981): 236-46.

Barth, John. *Chimera*. New York: Fawcett, 1972.

—. *Giles Goat-Boy or, The Revised New Syllabus*. New York: Fawcett, 1966.

—. *LETTERS: A Novel*. New York: Putnam's, 1979.

—. "The Literature of Exhaustion." *Atlantic Monthly* Aug. 1967: 29-34.

—. *Lost in the Funhouse: Fiction for Print, Tape, Live Voice*. 1968. New York: Bantam, 1969.

Barthelme, Donald. *The Dead Father*. 1975. New York: Penguin, 1986.

—. *Snow White*. 1967. New York: Atheneum, 1980.

Coover, Robert. *Pricksongs & Descants*. 1969. New York: Plume NAL, 1970.

—. *The Universal Baseball Association, Inc., J. Henry Waugh, Prop.* 1968. New York: Plume NAL, 1971.

Enck, John J. "John Barth: An Interview." *Wisconsin Studies in Contemporary Literature* 6 (1965): 3-14.

Federman, Raymond, ed. *Surfiction: Fiction Now . . . and Tomorrow*. Chicago: Swallow, 1975.

—. "Surfiction—Four Propositions in Form of an Introduction." *Surfiction: Fiction Now . . . and Tomorrow*. Chicago: Swallow, 1975. 5-15.

Fusco, Coco. "Passionate Irreverence: The Cultural Politics of Identity." *1993 Biennial Exhibition*. Curator: Elizabeth Sussman. New York: Whitney Museum of American Art/Harry N. Abrams, 1993. 74-85.

Gado, Frank, ed. *First Person: Conversations on Writers and Writing*. Ed. Frank Gado. Schenectady: Union College P, 1973. 142-59.

O'Brien, John. "Every Man His Voice." *Review of Contemporary Fiction* 1.1 (1981): 62-80.

—. "An Interview with Gilbert Sorrentino." *Review of Contemporary Fiction* 1.1 (1981): 5-27.

Phillips, Lisa. "No Man's Land: At the Threshold of a Millennium." *1993 Biennial Exhibition*. Curator: Elizabeth Sussman. New York: Whitney Museum of American Art/Harry N. Abrams, 1993. 52-61.

Ross, David A. "Preface: Know Thy Self (Know Your Place)." *1993 Biennial Exhibition*. Curator: Elizabeth Sussman. New York: Whitney Museum of American Art/Harry N. Abrams, 1993. 8-11.

Schaub, Thomas. H. "Williams, Sorrentino, and the Art of the Actual." *William Carlos Williams: Man and Poet*. Ed. Carroll F. Terrell. Orono: National Poetry Foundation/U of Maine at Orono, 1983. 435-49.

Sontag, Susan. *Against Interpretation*. 1966. New York: Anchor-Doubleday, 1990.

—. *Styles of Radical Will*. 1969. New York: Anchor-Doubleday, 1991.

Sorrentino, Gilbert. *Aberration of Starlight*. 1980. Normal, IL: Dalkey Archive Press, 1993.

—. *Imaginative Qualities of Actual Things*. 1971. Elmwood Park, IL: Dalkey Archive Press, 1991.

—. *Mulligan Stew*. 1979. Normal, IL: Dalkey Archive Press, 1996.

—. "Neon, Kulchur, Etc." *TriQuarterly* 43 (1978): 298-316.

—. *Odd Number*. San Francisco: North Point, 1985.

—. *The Orangery*. Austin: U of Texas P, 1978.

—. *The Sky Changes.* 1966. Normal, IL: Dalkey Archive Press, 1998.

—. *Something Said.* 1984. 2nd ed. Normal, IL: Dalkey Archive Press, 2001.

—. *Splendide-Hôtel.* 1973. Elmwood Park, IL: Dalkey Archive Press, 1984.

Sukenick, Ronald. "The New Tradition in Fiction." *Surfiction: Fiction Now . . . and Tomorrow.* Ed. Raymond Federman. Chicago: Swallow, 1975. 35-45.

Thielemans, Johan "The Voice of the Irresponsible: Irresponsible Voices? On Gilbert Sorrentino's *Mulligan Stew.*" *Representation and Performance in Postmodern Fiction.* Ed. Maurice Couturier. Montpellier: Delta, 1983. 113-29.

Williams, Sue. *The Sweet and Pungent Smell of Success.* 1993. 303 Gallery, New York.

Ziegler, Heidi, and Christopher Bigsby. *The Radical Imagination and the Liberal Tradition: Interviews with English and American Novelists.* London: Junction, 1982.

Matter into Imagination: The Cognitive Realism of Gilbert Sorrentino's Imaginative Qualities of Actual Things

Joseph Tabbi

The Cognitive Dance

The book for a time enjoyed some notoriety as a roman à clef. It made enemies, it caused a stir, and it was then largely forgotten as the living models for the characters, like the author himself, left the scene. It was read by some for its scathing portrayal of local poets and downtown painters, for its faces and names—the ones dismissed by John Cale and Lou Reed as posers, self-abusers, or "just alcoholics." Not since William Gaddis's *The Recognitions* (1955) had the New York scene been so well described from the inside (which is to say, from the perspective of a young writer who had gotten to know the "insiders" before he, or they, had yet made it into the mainstream). But the author himself—if we can isolate and identify Gilbert Sorrentino among the many voices and narrators in the book—never intended for readers to dwell on the book's characters, or its plot, or its Greenwich Village ambience (hinted at in the photograph of a crowd gathered in front of the old Cedar Bar, reproduced on the cover of the Dalkey Archive edition of 1991). These staples of novelistic fiction are decidedly among the actual things the author wants subordinated to their own, and his, imaginative qualities.

In the book itself, typically, "No attempt [is] made to describe this famous bar, thank God" (63n). The tavern and the photograph are ephemera, and so, it would seem, are the men and women shown there, backsides to the camera. The outlines of one man's cheeks show through his pulled-up pants as he waits by the door to the bar. Behind him is a dog pulling at a leash and sniffing at his feet. Everyone seems to be looking at something through the window to the bar, while the doorman eyes the waiting patrons warily. Once alive, and part of a "scene," these figures are now literally "cardboard" figures. In the words of the book's closing quotation from Ezra Pound, they belong "where the dead walked/and the living were made of cardboard." Or perhaps they are like "pictures" in a movie, as in the epigraph from William Carlos Williams: "In the mind there is a continual play of obscure images which coming between the eyes and their prey seem pictures on the screen at the movies. Somewhere there appears to be a mal-adjustment. The wish would be to see not floating visions of unknown purport but the imaginative qualities of the actual things being perceived accompany their gross vision in a slow dance, interpreting as they go" (ix).

Framing the book, this epigraph from Williams and the closing quotation from Pound should not be taken metaphorically. What the quotations describe, and what is enacted in Sorrentino's text, is essentially a consciousness at work. As images pass between the perceiving subject and the world of "things perceived," they come to life not in the mind's eye nor in themselves, but in some middle zone, the cognitive space of "interpretation." Exchanges between the embodied mind and the world produce neither a wholly mental construction nor an objective reality; what they generate is, rather, a "dance" that lasts a while, and then fades from memory as new images come to new states of consciousness. This is how the mind works, adjusting (or mal-adjusting) its expectations to things as they are encountered and giving dimension and palpability to what is in reality—perceptually, in the eye's "gross vision"—not even a blur: every conscious perception, as cognitive researchers now realize, involves the "activation or deactivation of widely distributed areas of the brain" (Edelman and Tononi 55). These independent subsystems or mental modules nonetheless remain in communication with each other, "interpreting as they go" (in Williams's words), and generating patterns of recognition, repetition, and variation largely from within themselves. What the eye alone objectively "sees" is only one small part of a patchwork quilt largely lost to symbolic representation, in need of something further, something interpretative, before its perceptual "prey" can be brought to consciousness. The qualities Sorrentino derives from Williams are not imaginary, they're *imaginative*; fictive rather than fictional; made over in the mind's active imagining, not made up; and registered on the page so that the reader can extend the interpretation and take part in the cognitive dance.

Usually when an author forswears representation and fills his narrative with metacommentary and self-consciously "literary" effects, he is thought to be working against the mainstream and his work is filed—and then dismissed—as metafiction: fiction about fiction, not about life, and so unlikely to win over a reader's willing suspension of disbelief in the encounter with the made-up but plausible world of realist fiction. The metafictionist, it is often said, is more interested in literature than in life, composition to the exclusion of creation. But Sorrentino is not an antirealist writer; in fact, he is striving toward a more scrupulous realism. By attending "to the way the sentences fall" and by presenting events "in only the clearest contours—what is salient," his narrator wants to achieve what he calls "a perfect fiction: reality" (114). Realism remains the goal, and so does the pursuit of character—despite the narrator's determination to excise any section that threatens to flesh out his characters or make them "walk off the page" (27). Their reality, the narrator insists, comes not from the likelihood that they are based on real people known to him, but precisely because the people he "knows" are derealized, broken up, made to disappear: "They should, rather, walk into the page" (27).

Numerous critical discourses have emerged that attempt to account for our time's shifting actualities. Those who contribute to these discourses have largely ignored Sorrentino's novel, and we have, in turn, been ignored by Sorrentino. His narrative persona doesn't leave much room, for example, for critiques based on class ("I hate the rich") or gender ("while she was, in effect, a particular kind of modern-day whore, there was none of the whore's finesse about her; she had little sexual style")—or, for that matter, for critical approaches based on race, status, psychology, or craft.[1] Critique itself is dismissed outright: when confronted with perspicuous social criticism by right-thinking people, the "polite thing is to listen as if you didn't know about any of this, then agree and add some indictments of your own" (101). What the author objects to in these critical approaches—and literary avoidances—is what I would call their colonizing tendency, the way they lose sight of particulars in pursuit of an abstract pattern. Where critical discourse desires topicality and devotes itself largely to the changing actualities, literature is unique in its attention to wholly imaginative qualities. If I propose in this essay to bring in the apparatus of cognitive science, a powerful new discourse with its own corporate branches and colonizing ambitions, that is because those who work in the field are at least interested in what interests Sorrentino: "fitting mind to material circumstances" and asking how it is that matter, in its turn, gives rise to mind in the first place.

The Unity of Knowledge within the Universe of Consciousness

The cognitive model I will be using, derived from Gerald Edelman and Giulo Tononi, is valuable for literary studies because it shows how one can sustain a commitment to materialist explanations without denying the uniqueness of the specific products of a specific mind. Unlike the various materialist discourses cited above, their approach is not *reductive*. Indeed, so far from wanting to colonize literature as merely one among many cultural productions, Edelman and Tononi remain skeptical as to whether consciousness studies can be extended to literature at all. Unlike E. O. Wilson, for example, who in his influential book *Consilience: The Unity of Knowledge* wishes to expand scientific description to the study of all evolutionary and cultural products (including literary texts), these two neurobiologists feel compelled to *limit* the province of scientific description. They open their book, *A Universe of Consciousness,* with the observation that "consciousness and mind," long marginalized as "legitimate concepts" for scientific study, are now central in many disciplines. However, after seventeen dense chapters opening the field of cognitive studies to a vast "material order as it gives rise to mind," Edelman and Tononi close by identifying at least one set of objects that is *not* "fit . . . for scientific study"— namely, "meaningful sentences in ordinary language or, even better, poetic exchanges as they are enacted by sentient humans" (222).

Whereas a self-proclaimed reductionist such as Wilson would not hesitate to subject meaningful sentences and poetic exchanges to the same "testable laws and principles" that science has gathered in the study of nature (53), Edelman and Tononi would regard such an explanation as at best a trivialization. The explanation and meaning of human utterances, they argue, "rest on too many unique historical patterns; on multiple ambiguous references; and, in the case of a unique poetic utterance . . . , on an incomparable sample" (Edelman and Tononi 222). Not *all* meaningful relations are fit objects for scientific study, even if we believe (as Edelman and Tononi do believe, no less than Wilson) in the evolutionary basis of consciousness and its products. Knowing that our emotions and responses to an art are engendered by our biology, Wilson wants to abstract from this knowledge a set of "biologically evolved epigenetic rules" that will lift our cultural explanations outside of history and outside of the contingencies of any one mind or body. Edelman and Tononi, by contrast, make evolution's throughgoing historicity central to a model in which consciousness emerges, like everything else in nature, out of elements that were already in place. Like everything else in nature, consciousness is also governed by rules— but they are rules of a special kind that emerge dynamically out of the conscious system's own operations. We might describe such rules as algorithms—the way that Wilson and, more elaborately, Daniel Dennett and the community of artificial intelligence researchers have described conscious systems. But even so, the algorithms at work in the brain should not be confused with those at work in a computer. Unlike a computer, consciousness cannot be programmed by a system or authority outside itself. A mind can be informed; it cannot be *instructed*.

Edelman has often cautioned against false analogies between the mind and a computer, and these cautions are rightly extended to those who would equate literary patterns and (more recently) hypertext networks with the associational processes in a reader's mind. No literary description should be based on a scientific reduction, but there is no reason not to use cognitive theory to identify what is distinctively literary about works of literature as they emerge out of specific cultural environments. Given the economic and cultural materialisms that now dominate literary studies, consciousness continues to be marginalized (even as it becomes ever more central in the sciences). Yet a cognitive approach promises to revive the object of literary analysis as it asserts itself within and against the media environment. A literary theory based on cognitive selection rather than computation may be, like Edelman and Tononi's conception of consciousness, appropriate to the exploration of the unity of literary form in the current environment of distributed and differential information.

Assuming that natural selection is no less a force in the evolution of consciousness than it is in nature, Edelman and Tononi posit that a defining feature of higher-order consciousness is its ability to select, "at any moment, one out of billions of possible conscious states" (22). Consciousness, then, is posed as a formal problem of creating unity out of complexity, a problem that is consistent with what any writer must face when creating a literary work in an environment of information, cultural diversity, and multiple media of communication. The work is formally unified; its environment is complex, differential, and informative — and so it is comparable to the vast material order that, in the brain and in nature, gives rise to consciousness. Like consciousness, a literary work in progress can at any moment make a selection (via the author) from a vast range of preformatted, shared, and widely recognizable expressions made familiar by the mass media — namely journalism, television, film, and other electronic media. Out of all the uncountable phrases that can be taken for example from popular songs of a given era — merely one resource within the overall media environment — how many selections are needed before a characterization counts as "literary"? Consider this highly literary sampling taken from the Bunny Lewis section of *Imaginative Qualities*:

> It was clear that her heart was broken. She was carrying a torch, she took a lot of time out for tears, she won't die, she'll live on, she gets that old feeling, there'll never be another Guy, she won't forget the night she met him, the songs of love are not for her, she dances with tears in her eyes, her love for him meant only heartaches, she'd like just one more

chance, willows weep for her, every street's a boulevard of broken dreams, she covers the waterfront, she can't show her face, she smokes, she drinks, she never thinks about tomorrow, sometimes she can't even think of his name, sonnets she writes of him, she's aware her heart is a sad affair, their love went out just like a dying ember, she'll never smile again, half a love never appealed to her, she rushed in where angels fear to tread, she has those blues in the night, she's got it bad, she doesn't want to walk without him, she'll remember April, he'll never know just how much she loves him, she falls in love too easily, she should care, it was like a trip to the stars, he came, he saw, he conquered her, oh, how they waltzed. . . . (95)

This elaboration—which is of a piece with a number of more explicit listings in the book drawn from various cultural contexts—is not entirely ironical (I imagine) in its intent or effect. Sorrentino does not seem to me to be writing from a superior position; his point is not simply that Bunny has allowed the clichés of popular culture to affect her own most private affections. Whether or not one or all of these phrases would have actually passed through her consciousness at this moment, they are all *available* to her, no less than they are obviously available to the author. Maybe he can't get the damn songs (and at least one quotation from antiquity) out of his head, and so he puts them here, on the page. They produce an odd reality effect: Sorrentino's character, like any woman of the time, *could have* drawn on any one of these phrases or song titles in thinking about her love relationships. The mass media have succeeded— more extensively and across more social strata than earlier, orally transmitted or printed circulations—in creating an environment of information that one cannot *not* know. Neither should it matter that Sorrentino's particular selections in this passage are now—more than thirty years later—unlikely to be recalled by a new generation of readers. But these media are not about remembering. Like most of the mind's operations, they are in the main about forgetting, about freeing capacities and enabling consciousness to attend to the here and now.

For a writer working in the modern media environment, ignoring its images and its various verbal messages is not an option: the images and messages are present as a publicly accessible, distributed cognitive background against which any focused, personal, and conscious understanding has to set itself. And this, too, helps explain the strength of the media, what creates their overall all-over reality-effect. Neither the media nor distributed cognition can burden itself with too much memory; the task of each is not to store up past events indiscriminately for eventual recall and meditation but rather to delete traces of the past so as to free up capacities. What is held in mind or kept on file from the past signifies only by comparison with present developments, and past events will be recalled only if they can show up differences, constructing the present as *news*. Such cognition could hardly be less congenial to the ordinary process of literary self-creation, which has traditionally been about remembering, not forgetting: Recollection in tranquility. News that stays news. A madeleine. Literature after Wordsworth, Pound, and Proust has evolved ways of its own to bridge the gap and to make the past present; but meditation in literature is out of synch with the flows of mediated time.

What distinguishes Sorrentino's own expression from the song titles and lyrics that he folds into his text is not so much a difference between high and low art, the formally realized and the formulaic. Rather, by elaborating one woman's media environment at such length, Sorrentino is purposely pushing these mediated expressions into the past, helping along the media's own process of forgetfulness, and so freeing up space for other, more conscious, hence more "literary" purposes and responses. Whereas the mass media are committed largely to entertainment and the reporting of current events, literature is broader, committed to remembering the past and projecting a future in terms selected out of, but not seriously attuned to, the lingua franca, and retaining in its formal outlines a range of older forms and knowledges that may be inappropriate to the mass media, where they appear outdated and cumbersome, but which widen the range of formal inventions and cognitive possibilities. As Sorrentino's narrator remarks at various points, the literary work is "To be taken slowly, as an antidote" (198; see also 191).

The cognitive-evolutionary model, then, provides a hypothesis about how the literary text is indeed distinguishable from contemporaneous verbal but nonliterary texts. Rather than help us explain the meaning of a particular work, it gives us a set of constraints within which specifically literary form and meaning can emerge. So a sentence or a poetic exchange is not something to be judged from outside—indeed, it is not in need of scientific "explanation" at all. These modes of expression are to be understood, instead, as emergent features of a higher-order consciousness, a product of the unique capacity of consciousness to use its own operations as a way of reflecting back on itself. As Edelman and Tononi write,

> Our position has been that higher-order consciousness, which includes the ability to be conscious of being conscious, is dependent on the emergence of semantic capabilities and, ultimately, of language. Concomitant with these traits is the emergence of a true self, born of social interactions, along with concepts of the past and future. Driven by

primary consciousness and the remembered present, we can, through symbolic exchange and higher-order consciousness, create narratives, fictions, and histories. We ask questions about how we can know and thereby deliver our selves to the doorstep of philosophy. (208)

If literature is regarded, thus, as Edelman and Tononi regard consciousness, as "not an object but a process" (9), then the cognitive model offers much more than another externally generated set of rules for talking about literature. What it describes is not the meaning of particular sentences or poetic exchanges, but the material grounding that makes a work of literature unique and historically specific. By attending to this material base—in print or electronic media—critics can recognize works of literary imagination as resulting from a particular, individual embodiment and the mutual exchanges, past and present, among authors, readers, and the various media that constrain expression.

Among practicing cognitive scientists who acknowledge a fully material basis for both consciousness and cognition, Edelman and Tononi are the most insistent on "the fact that consciousness is embodied uniquely and privately in each individual; that no description, scientific or otherwise, is equivalent to the experience of individual embodiment" (208). Likewise, among contemporary American authors, Sorrentino has been the one who insists most strongly on the uniqueness and autonomy of the literary work. That insistence, while it can be attributed to his own oft-stated commitment to a modernist aesthetic, does not necessarily imply a turning away from the wider cultural environment or the communicative sphere of the social. So far from separating literary study and the sciences, self-enclosure and self-referentiality in the arts are actually preconditions for communication between the different cognitive realms.

Observing Sorrentino's Observations

"In this book," says Sorrentino's narrator, "I'll muddle around, flashes, glints, are what I want. It's when one is not staring that art works" (34). That these "flashes" are the stuff of consciousness— "the flashing perversity of the human brain" (39)—is made explicit a few pages later, in a separate context having to do not with the author's intentions but with the impression made by one character, the poet manqué Lou, on his wife Sheila. Only the word "flashes" connects the two passages—that and a complex of related ideas important to a book that, if it is about anything, is about literary failure. Lou is a man who "willed himself into poetry" (35), a hopeless ambition within the book's terms, which construe literary integrity as the only morality: it is said at one point, for example, that the "careless and perennial" adulterer is immoral because he "lacks imagination" (17). Lou's perversity, which so shocks and disgusts Sheila, is not to be destroyed emotionally by her confession of infidelity; instead of making him jealous, her "brief, 'searing' (her word, I'm sorry) affair" with a "hip girl" only gets him worked up so that he "rapes her, with all her clothes on, on the couch, after dinner" (38). Their mutual willfulness, a frustrated desire to affect others in a certain way, is part of the pattern that links Lou and Sheila. Lou can try writing a poem by the force of will; Sheila can betray a husband with a lesbian lover: it is no more possible, however, to coerce a response from a poem's reader than to will a husband into outrage.

So while the husband's "perversity" describes, on one level, his excitement rather than jealousy at his wife's unfaithfulness, it is also, in a flash, "the perversity of the human brain" itself. Like poetry, and like sexual response, human cognition works by indirection. It is always notoriously in the place where it's not, meaning things we don't know that it means, doing things (like walking, or talking, or raising a glass to our lips) that we could not do if we stopped even for a moment, while doing them, to think about them. Cognition is marked by what critics have termed "a CONSTITU-TIVE lack of context" (Wilden 134), a built-in inability to recognize itself and its environment that gets expressed, in Humberto Maturana's well-known formulation, as a literal blindness: "every world brought forth necessarily hides its origins. By existing, we generate cognitive 'blind spots' that can be cleared only through generating new blind spots in another domain. We do not see what we do not see, and what we do not see does not exist" (242). The most heightened consciousness will not always let us see all we might want to see—least of all how others perceive *us*. In literature as in the operation of consciousness, reality is what one sees when one is not looking. And Sorrentino, uniquely to my knowledge among contemporary authors, recirculates the private interpretations and social observations that inform a life and give it substance, "pushing reality so hard that it [falls] over on its back and [becomes] a kind of fantasy" (76), as the narrator, repeating the observation of a friend, says elsewhere.

It is this recirculating consciousness, and not the fact that he writes about writing, that creates the distinctly literary reality of Sorrentino's work—its worldly distance; its characters at once modeled on the living and purposely drained of all life and sympathy; its disdain of both the literary and nonliterary languages that it uses with such extraordinary facility. Like Don DeLillo, another Italian-American novelist from the boroughs, Sorrentino keeps a slight distance from what he has managed to possess. Imaginative qualities do not transcend the sordid actualities that the work is "about"; the qualities emerge from the actualities, forming a realm that is more mindlike, more lasting, and, finally, more real than the characters and scenes which, in life, may have served as the author's starting point. Sorrentino's particular aesthetic—call it a cognitive realism—arises from what the narrator has observed in his characters, from how they observe each other and how we readers, in turn, observe their observations and those of the narrator as well: "I would like to have a long talk with Lou," the narrator says, "and tell him what I've made up about him, except that he would laugh at me, and tell me about my novels . . ." (45). An inability to get outside oneself, to imagine what it is like to be *seen,* is a serious moral failing of many of the book's characters. And so is the related narcissism that assumes one knows oneself well enough to identify with a fictive character: "People who 'recognize' themselves in books are never in the books," claims Sorrentino's narrator (48). One is what others see when one isn't looking.

This is how Sorrentino creates the "characters" that populate *Imaginative Qualities*—by putting himself into their situations and imagining what they might think of him even as he, the author, makes them up: "What do *you* know about my life? I hear [Leo] say. The poor bastard doesn't know that I invented him, he thinks he's real" (129; Sorrentino's italics). What Sorrentino is after in these seemingly self-contradictory passages is a representation not of character as a set of positive features, mannerisms, ways of speaking, or other identifiable "qualities." Every Sorrentino character is a "man [or woman] without qualities," like the hero of Robert Musil's novel, who is referenced in *Imaginative Qualities* (126). What is being sought, rather, is the mental life of an ordinary person, a "poor bastard" such as Lou, as he "strives daily to make sense of his life, that is, he tries not to die all at once" (45). Marking an advance on "repression" in psychoanalysis (with which it might appear cognate), the "blind spot" in cognitive studies is materially real and capable of being formulated in the terms of information theory and neurobiology. The study of cognition is less subjective than conceptual; less interested in the unconcealment of childhood trauma or the exposure of universal drives than in revealing (in Sorrentino's words) "the pattern" each life, uniquely, forms (118). Rooted though cognition is in the actualities and, especially, materials of consciousness and communication, a cognitive realism does not seek materialist *explanations* for the mind's creative life. Sorrentino's narrator, unlike his psychoanalytically minded contemporaries, doesn't want "to dissect or remove the artist's brain to see what makes him compose. What they [his contemporaries] find, of course, is another troubled man, in the case of the artist, a man who is perhaps more deeply troubled. There is no place for an artist here any more. He has been officially dismissed in favor of the entertainer" (46).

That literary art has to be more deeply troubling than psychoanalysis and more demanding than entertainment does not mean that it should be "difficult" necessarily or more complex in its handling of personalities. Literature's demands on the reader are of a particular sort: an author seeks from his readers not understanding so much as the capacity for imaginative projection: "this story is invention only," we are told early on: "Put yourself into it" (9). What a literary author should be aiming to bring into existence is not only a communication but rather the coordination of independent minds. The reader is one part of the book's environment, and this reader in turn is environed by many of the same trappings, the same social furnishings, public phrasings, romantic and literary aspirations that preoccupy the author and the characters he has momentarily and sequentially put himself into. Such proliferating mental environments are not the author's subject; they are not what's communicated. It is rather via these actualities that the reader finds a field of possible selections, a multiplicity out of which the author has created a unity—not in the old, organic sense (a correspondent breeze uniting mind and world, their life the eddying of nature's "living soul")—no: what is being produced is more akin to the self-generating unity of conscious experience itself, the way at any given moment we are thinking *this* thought, speaking *this* word, or remembering *this* event rather than some other thought, word, or event. The unity we take for granted actually embeds great complexity, since what we hold in mind is informed by everything we are not aware of—although we could become aware of these alternatives at any moment, just as our minds are free (within certain constraints) to move from one thought to the next.

An ability to make a selection, to say what comes next, could well be what lies at the origin of an author's creative or self-generative power. In a book such as *Imaginative Qualities* narrative sequence has less to do with the gradual accumulation of events and character traits or life decisions than with Sorrentino's marking of a continuing passage from one unity to another. Such a book is not modeled on the movement from fictional beginnings through multiple middles eventuating in a single significant conclusion: "stories that are replete with sadness and despair never end at all: they stop" (114). Rather than impose an ending on his material, Sorrentino offers up sequences, collections of "bits and pieces" (11n) analogous in their continuity to the continuity we experience in moving from one thought to the next, without our consciously experiencing a break in the sequence. How this is so, nobody has yet explained.

This Is Not a Novel

Sorrentino calls the book a collection of "bits" in the first asterisked footnote:

*This is not a novel. More a collection of "bits and pieces." (11n)

Thirty years later, under the title *This Is Not a Novel*, David Markson would publish a work of fiction whose narrator, like Sorrentino's, aspires to do away with the staples of novelistic fiction:

A novel with no intimation of story whatsoever, Writer would like to contrive.

And with no characters. None. (2)

Plotless. Characterless.

Yet seducing the reader into turning pages nonetheless. (3)

In the absence of such actualities as plot, character, setting, etc., what is it that seduces the reader into turning pages? Wouldn't it have to be a power on the same order as that which moves the mind from one thought to the next?

Given what's known to date about the relation of consciousness to its material substrates, the origins of that power are no less mysterious—no less a fiction—than the driving force behind a cognitive fiction by Markson or Sorrentino. Our limited knowledge need not limit understanding, however. Although we may not be able to specify precisely "how matter becomes imagination," to cite the subtitle of Edelman and Tononi's book, at least we have an idea of what needs to be explained—namely, the selection of conscious states out of largely automatic and unconscious cognitive environments (a process whose formulation by Edelman and Tononi coheres nicely with the selective processes out of natural environments that unconsciously direct evolution). What interests me further about these theories is how the uniqueness and self-generating autonomy inherent in conscious experience can also be used to describe what is unique about literature as an art. What Edelman and Tononi identify as the defining feature of consciousness—a unity capable of embedding great complexity that changes constantly from moment to moment, from one conscious state to another, without our sensing any break—could just as well define all that is literary about Sorrentino's work.

Call it hypertextual, this literary network of distributed "flashes": the work is certainly collaborative and seemingly endless, as everyone likes to claim about electronic hypertext. And hypertext, like Sorrentino's fiction, is also mindlike—if by this we mean not the false analogy between a mind and a computer. A mind is not, like a computer, programmable from somewhere else: it can only generate its thoughts from within itself—like the poem in New Criticism whose meanings are self-entailed, or (better still) like a Möbius strip whose internal topography is indistinguishable from external reference. What is mindlike in the work of literature is the author's selective activity, which takes place, like the operations of consciousness, within cognitive environments whose "enormous variety of discriminable states" remain "many orders of magnitude larger than those available to anything we have built," including our current distributed network of computers (Edelman and Tononi 32).

"Prose is endless," Sorrentino admits: "Tell it to the Marines. It is the texture I love" (47). The particular prose embodiment—the salient contour, the shape and weight of a sentence, a verbal patterning—all this allows one writing mind to effect a corresponding sensibility or set of interests in another mind reading. There is, of course, no way, in literature or in science, that the sequence of thoughts produced in one person's head can be identically reproduced in the head of another person: these are self-generating, autopoietic processes. What we can do, however, is to coordinate thoughts through a common attention to words that have been fixed in place on a page, *this* word, in *this* sentence, "in relation to all the others in this book" by Sorrentino (169). The communication is not between an author and a reader—but rather between the two together (at a distance) via the page that unites them. This is why so much attention is paid, in Sorrentino and affiliated writers, to the materiality of the book itself—and to all our systems of registering experience (in passing thoughts, notebooks, manuscripts, and books). Sorrentino's "lists and facts, all the lies and borrowings" leading by indirection to a "perfect revelation" (34); David Markson's private archive of world art, music, literature, deaths and lives, together with numerous "inconsequential perplexities" noted down for no special reason (*Wittgenstein's Mistress* 79); Harry Mathews's cookbooks and his private journals of "everything" recordable in everyday life; Lynne Tillman's literal-minded efforts "to find words" and put them on the page in a certain order (7-37): instead of taking a writer away from life and into himself or herself, the coordination of reading minds facilitated by such technologies of inscription is what makes the social possible and presentable in a work of literature.

There is no entering the mind of an author: the reader is and must remain "an outsider who thinks he knows best" (27), but the author knows no better. Sorrentino has no greater access to the mind of a character in his fiction than you or I. What Sorrentino does have, however, is the capacity to register observations of characters in prose, to "prose them," to "Prose them right into the paper and the shape of the letters" (29, 168). His narrator disapproves of the practice, popular at the time, of allowing misspellings into narrative as if reality itself could be changed and customized to the author's individuality. Such a practice assumes that words represent things "off the paper," whereas what is changed by orthographic tampering is something far more important to art, "the reality of the true prose": "In the mawning is not In the morning. People who write 'mawning' think the language has a true 'reality' off the paper" (169).

Sorrentino's argument is subtle, even if the discourse is easy to dismiss (with a Bronx cheer, over martinis in midtown, or in the margins of the manuscript as it languishes in-house). We could easily imagine Sorrentino in the notes having one of his characters express impatience at the author's impatience: "V. W.," the editor, "ZuZu," the editor's assistant and sometime traveling companion, or the narrator himself in a self-critical mood. The dismissal itself could then be dismissed in a parenthesis, as in this one (197): "(Don't tell me that this is a digression, this whole book is a digression: from the novel. . . .)" By now a number of critics have pointed out how none of the author's voices and personae—not even the ubiquitous "Dick Detective"—commands a final authority, and this is true (and truly frustrating). But rather than chalk up this authorial elusiveness to a perverse desire for metafictional amusement or some anti-authoritarian streak in the culture of the time in which it was written, I want to keep the focus on the specifically imaginative qualities of mind in the book, which forbid *any* program or authority from being imposed from outside the mind (or the book) itself. "The beauty of fiction," says Sorrentino's narrator, "is that it goes two ways, at least. Out, into the world of the reader's experience and in, into the stringencies of the writer's tyranny" (111).

A tyranny that has "stringencies," that works collaboratively with the reader and submits willingly to the constraints of a literary art—down to the linguistic and phonetic materials out of which it is made: this is all formally consistent with the mind's autopoietic closure, a reflexive internal organization that does not preclude communication but in fact makes communication possible. For communication depends not on a mind's openness to the environment, but on the ability of any two self-possessed and self-enclosed minds to *shut* out noise (consider Michel Serres's excluded third party or "parasite" and Niklas Luhmann's disorganized "environment") in order to focus on what is written on a page or projected on a screen, in terms whose meaning is subject to interpretation but whose formal conventions are agreed on in advance. Sorrentino's insistence on observing the driest of dry conventions is in fact crucial to any understanding of literature as an art—to knowing where its real freedoms are won, and how damaging are its spurious freedoms, such as the freedom to mess with the spelling of words. Unlike the particularities of expression or symbolization, which can be created and revised at will by every author, the materiality of the page, once fixed, *has* to be kept whole and intact. The page is a set of conventions, a cultural construction, to be sure—except that, unlike other constructions, this one is foundational. As historian of science Adrian Johns has shown at length, it took ages for this particular construction to achieve its modern form, and only in the past hundred years or so have the book and the page achieved the stability that allow us to consider them "natural." The success of the construction, Johns argues, can be appreciated by just how well the book hides its nature *as* a construction. And when we tamper with the book (as we are doing collectively in the current transformation from print to electronic textuality), when we try bringing its reality as a medium into consciousness, we risk interfering with one of the material supports for consciousness and its cultural expression. Certainly it is possible that hypertext will replace the book, but for this to happen, we will need to have in place an entire structure—including settled conventions about spelling and so forth—so that we can again forget the medium and therefore begin to communicate through it.

The material organization of the mind is doubtless also a construction and hence just as arbitrary, although time frames in the case of the mind are much longer: its constraints were given by evolution, not by culture or economics. But in neither case—within the mind or on the material page—are we to treat such conventions as if they were like other, personal or wholly cultural, constructions. For those characters who think they can get away with a full-blown social constructivism, Sorrentino reserves his deepest scorn and, at times, much sadness. These are people whose lives are spent in classrooms, chat rooms, bedrooms, and offices — and who, because they recognize the arbitrary nature of the signs of life, think that they can change life merely by changing the signs, by manipulating symbols to suit a personal vision or a new utopian plan for the organization of an ideal society. In the same way that these people express their individuality by experimenting with spelling, they try to change themselves by changing sex partners, by undergoing psychoanalysis, by serving meals off unmatched tableware, or by "meticulously destroying" a prose style (57).

Do not suppose that this last, literary, failing is of a lesser order than the rest. If the identity I am drawing between the settled materiality of everyday life and the necessary transparency of prose on a printed page seems far-fetched, consider in closing the case of Guy Lewis, whose prose style (before he was influenced by Hemingway) once possessed "the sort of sweet clarity that presages a distinguished career" (57). And consider, then, how Sorrentino applies the same adjective to another set of male writers and artists, who betray their own "true, gentle manhood," lose their "sweet line" of prose and poetic lineage, and forfeit their creative power because they think their sexuality (and the secrets they make public about their lovers) can survive the process of being brought fully into consciousness (128-29). Leo Kaufman, for example, a writer of real talent who has become a character in the book, "ravaged the products of his powers, so there was then nothing but for him to ravage their sources. And all the time, he thought that he was freeing himself from inhibitions. And he was" (151).

But repression is not the main trouble. All told, Leo "was happy" to be rid of his inhibitions: "The only thing destroyed in this whole process of liberation was his art" (151). The labor needed to make an art depends, at its source, on a settled structure that one can agree is beyond art, beyond our abilities to put it into discourse. Self-consciousness is surely needed in the making of an art. But consciousness cannot extend to its own sources any more than a written word can do what it says: a mind is not a computer, and prose is not a code. The work's freedom and autonomy depend in no small part on our *not knowing,* on what we cannot and must not know of our own lives and the lives of others. This not knowing is neither anti-intellectual nor defensive in trying to preserve for its characters a separate and autonomous literary space. Not knowing is what frees the characters into reality, so that they can "rush about among these letters and syllables doing, apparently, as they like. Retreating further and further into the pages, so that my book has become a street guide to some destroyed city" (201). Neither a city of words nor the city that was home to the characters in life, this particular "destroyed city" exists only as a lost materiality, a structure of actualities that continuously undoes itself through its own invention.

From the perspective of cognitive studies, the destroyed city that is nonetheless foundational is like the vast material basis of cognition whose existence must be forgotten so that a higher-order consciousness can emerge. Only by *forgetting* its supporting structures can conscious activity take place at all—even as, for example, the self that emerges after we have learned a language forgets the specific sequence of social interactions that were needed to acquire language in the first place. The "conscious and, above all, self-conscious" individual never ceases to be present (Edelman and Tononi 198). And so it is the writer's obligation not to settle into a fixed view of the formative interactions or the characters with whom, in life, one has interacted. The creation of "narratives, fictions, and histories" depends on "the ability to be conscious of being conscious" (Edelman and Tononi 208), but this condition must, of necessity, change from moment to moment. So to maintain a viable self-narrative, the author needs to *de-realize* the characters and the environment with which one's own, "true self" interacts, and out of which an enabling self-consciousness emerges (Edelman and Tononi 208).

According to Sorrentino, failure in art can be more interesting than success under terms that are set elsewhere—in popular journalism, for example, or in any of the communications and informational media that environ the literary but are not in themselves capable of literary expression: "Norman Mailer knows what I mean," says Sorrentino's narrator. "What is the difference between twenty shiny armies of the night and one failed deer park? Fail in the terms you are helpless within. Terror of art" (128). This insistence on enclosure within the literary is not a way of shutting out the social; it is instead a precondition for the forming of new relationships, the generation of potentials for further interaction, keeping the conversation going among sympathetic minds. The authors Sorrentino honors in the book—Mailer in his early, almost-forgotten novels (*Barbary Shore, The Deer Park*), along with "Hart Crane, Weldon Kees, Scott Fitzgerald, Hemingway"—are those who "fell apart in their own work" (128). They are also men who, like Sorrentino's character Leo, tried to will themselves into "relevance" and an outspoken manliness whose generative potential, like the "sweet line" of their prose, "lost its charge and power" (129). A true self can indeed be heard through the several personae in *Imaginative Qualities,* but its truth lies in the author's willingness to court fragmentation in an ongoing literary development. The self, like the art it produces, is what it is and not anyone or anything else—even if we can only know "what it is" in relation to everything that is not the self and not the work. The book, like the mind itself, is differential and distributed, which would account for the scathing, seemingly absolute negativity Sorrentino's narrator brings to every topic he discusses in *Imaginative Qualities*. The more positive, imaginative qualities are harder to identify, but they are no less a presence in the book than the consciousness that made it.

Notes

[1] The quotations in this passage are taken from 100 and 8, respectively. For examples of how Sorrentino's narrator dismisses the other styles of critique named here, see 92, 6, 91, and 47, respectively.

Works Cited

Edelman, Gerald M., and Giulio Tononi. *A Universe of Consciousness: How Matter Becomes Imagination*. New York: Basic Books, 2000.

Johns, Adrian. *The Nature of the Book: Print and Knowledge in the Making*. Chicago: U of Chicago P, 1998.

Markson, David. *This Is Not a Novel*. Washington: Counterpoint, 2001.

—.*Wittgenstein's Mistress*. 1988. Normal, IL: Dalkey Archive Press, 1997.

Maturana, Humberto, and Francisco Varela. *The Tree of Knowledge: The Biological Roots of Human Understanding*. Boston: New Science Library, 1987.

Sorrentino, Gilbert. *Imaginative Qualities of Actual Things*. 1971. Elmwood Park, IL: Dalkey Archive Press, 1991.

Tillman, Lynne. *The Madame Realism Complex*. New York: Semiotext(e), 1992.

Wilden, Anthony. *System and Structure: Essays in Communication and Exchange*. 2nd ed. London, Tavistock, 1980.

Wilson, E. O. *Consilience: The Unity of Knowledge*. New York: Knopf, 1998.

Gilbert Sorrentino: Cataloging the Imaginative Qualities of Actual Things

Kevin Alexander Boon

Sorrentino's playful novel *Imaginative Qualities of Actual Things* confronts the paradoxical qualities of fiction and interrogates the complex (and dynamic) relationship between truth and fiction peculiar to the genre of the novel. As with all writing that threatens the sanctified conventions of reading by exposing itself as an artifact, *Imaginative Qualities* thwarts the delusions upon which fiction so thoroughly depends: that fiction is somehow representationally "true," that something beyond the mundane text can be apprehended. This blatant literary honesty is accomplished largely through the author's extensive use of the catalog, or list, as a rhetorical device analogous to brushstrokes on canvas—an apt analogy considering the narrator's admission that he wants us to "remember this book the way you remember a drawing" (27). The brilliance of *Imaginative Qualities* rests in part on how the novel's many catalogs reveal how meaning is formed by writers and readers alike.[1] More specifically, *Imaginative Qualities* exposes the site where meaning is constructed by employing catalogs to foreground design as the primary aesthetic element of prose, hence dispelling the illusion of linguistic referentiality—for, as David Andrews puts it, a Sorrentino catalog is meant to elude "the inartistic, information-bearing function of language, making it . . . an object rather than a series of ciphers in simulation of other objects" ("Reading" 3).

Some discussion has been made of Sorrentino's "idiosyncratic use of the list" by the author and his critics (see, e.g., Andrews "Reading" 3). Of the list, Sorrentino himself claims that "If the elements are disparate enough, the list yields little information, and if the elements have, or seem to have absolutely nothing in common, the list becomes transitively useless: it is a world of language that yields no meaning, or that yields meaning only in terms of itself" ("Fictional Infinities" 329). Commentaries such as this have understandably led several critics to claim that Sorrentino's lists are entropic. Sorrentino's other novels also contribute to this view. In *Odd Number,* for example, Sorrentino's narrator states that

If the catalogue, or any catalogue or list, is understood to be a system, its entropy is the measure of the unavailability of its energy for conversion into useful work.

The ideal catalogue tends toward maximum entropy. (144)

It is important to keep in mind that Sorrentino claims that the list becomes "transitively" useless, which is not to say that it is universally useless. When he refers to the list as potentially entropic—as he also does, incidentally, in "Fictional Infinities" (see 330)—he is narrowly defining energy as the energy necessary to carry meaning to and from an object, not the energy used to produce meaning when confronted by an object nor the energy needed to create an object.

It is also important to note that Sorrentino makes little distinction between a catalog and a list (I use the terms interchangeably). Some critics do, however, distinguish between them. For example, Louis Mackey, in his monograph study of four of Sorrentino's novels, articulates such a distinction: "A list may be defined as an unprincipled catalogue, as conversely a catalogue is a principled list . . . As opposed to the catalogue, the list, by refusing to pretend that it is anything but a random enumeration and an arbitrary ordering, renounced the rhetoric of totalization. The only principle that governs the list is the principle: in principle this could go on forever" (36). Although, in general, I agree with much of what Mackey says about Sorrentino's lists, I disagree with his classifications. Randomness is a perception rather than a objective quality, a presumption of unpredictability. How something is perceived, Paul Watzlawick notes, may "have nothing to do with probability, but rather with our idea of order" (55). The randomness or arbitrariness of a list says more about how readers assign "exclusive meaning, importance, and prominence" than it says about the essential character of the list (Watzlawick 55). In the absence of any objective criteria, it is not possible to determine accurately which lists "pretend" randomness and which lists "pretend" order (Mackey says, for example, that Whitman's catalogs in *Leaves of Grass* "produce the effect of encyclopedic totality" (36)), rendering Mackey's distinction between lists and catalogs untenable. To claim that one list is "principled" while another is not, is merely to say that a particular reader can attach (or *predict*) the list's relevance to an existing notion of order.

What an audience does or does not make of Sorrentino's lists matters little in Sorrentino's aesthetic. Sorrentino claims that "The artist . . . hasn't got an audience" and notes that "I never think of an audience, really. I think of my own pleasure" (qtd. in O'Brien 7). Thus Sorrentino's experience when writing his novels is not an analogue for the reader's experience when reading them. Nor does Sorrentino suggest in his critical comments that he expects readers to identify the authorial intentions "behind" his fictional works. Instead, Sorrentino admits that when he reads back over something he has written and sees "something that strikes . . . [him] as being marvelously subtle or beautifully structured, [he] think[s] of friends . . . who might read it and see it" (qtd. in O'Brien 7), further implying that the structure that he intends is not presumed by him to be necessarily apprehendable by readers. What a reader makes of a list involves interpretation, an imaginative act that, as the title suggests, is of central importance in *Imaginative Qualities*.

Sorrentino's lists are entropic only if we define the work they are not doing in terms of conventional representation. If we consider their potential for meaning, their pull toward meaning, they are, it seems, even more energetic than conventional narratives. Sorrentino dismisses prose that is referentially "useful," and *Imaginative Qualities* openly dismisses its own external references, but this only increases the novel's potential for meaning. The less referential a text is, the more it *may* mean. In eschewing referentiality, Sorrentino produces an aesthetic object, a static artifact, that resists any singular or totalizing reading—and that invites interpretation by stimulating the imagination upon which interpretation depends.

For example, *Imaginative Qualities* offers the following list of proper names:

John Ashbery
Vladimir Nabokov
Norman Mailer
Kenneth Koch
Bruce Jay Friedman
Kenneth Noland
Mark Van Doren
Richard Lippold   (207)

Sorrentino's narrator invites us to "Study . . . [these names] and try to determine the author's intent in setting them down" (207). The possibilities are quite literally endless, as there is no way of knowing with any certainty why these eight names are placed here, what the relevance of their sequence is, or why Sorrentino positions them within this particular list. The potential for meaning is greater in this list than in more familiar rhetorical structures, such as when April frames the salutation of a letter to a lover as "My dear Dick" (235), or even more so when the narrator of *Imaginative Qualities* claims that "America is geared to infidelity" (71).

Meaning or significance is produced by the quest for totalizing interpretations that do not, in any absolute sense, exist. Interpretation ends at the point when something is presumed to have been fully understood. Through his use of innovative devices, the catalog in particular, Sorrentino moves away from writing that promotes fixed or unitary meaning toward writing that engenders possibility, invites interpretation, and incites the imagination—writing, that is, that produces aesthetic objects rather than utilitarian conduits for unitary literary meaning.

Sorrentino's use of catalogs cannot be restricted to the obvious. There are numerous lists in *Imaginative Qualities,* many with self-identifying titles, such as *"Some Things Sheila Henry Disliked about Lou Henry, 1963-1967"* and *"A Clutch of Things Lou Henry Liked Before He Became a 'Serious' Writer"* (20, 49; Sorrentino's italics); there are also untitled but enumerated lists, such as the list of Bart Kahane's paintings from the Gom Gallery brochure that Dick Detective wrote for Kahane's one-man show, as well as the list of questions for would-be editors (186, 77-78); and there are, moreover, untitled, unnumbered lists, such as the list of wishes for Guy Lewis (80). It should also be noted that not all of the novel's lists are graphically presented as lists. The narrator's suggestions for Guy are laid out vertically, in listlike fashion:

> Allow him to be loved.
> Give him a stiff penis.
> Make him realize the value of his early collages.
> Let the deaf-mute Lena hear his voice, a miracle.
> Let him fail with some grace.
> Let him not see himself in this prose.
> Allow him to strike out the acknowledged slugger of the barroom team.
> Let him see that those particles of language, the bones of the very letters themselves, . . . can be marshaled, crafted . . . into the absolute image of the old photograph. (80)

But the narrator's catalog of Sheila's superficial desires is not so explicitly presented as a list, for it is laid out horizontally and embedded in a paragraph: "Take me to the zoo. Fly me to the moon. A new blender to make a pineapple-spinach frappé. No cavities. An orgy at the home of John Lennon" (22). Sorrentino could have had his narrator organize this list vertically, as,

> Take me to the zoo.
> Fly me to the moon.
> A new blender to make a pineapple-spinach frappé.
> No cavities.
> An orgy at the home of John Lennon.

But verticality alone does not make a list a list (or a catalog a catalog). This point is made clear by the horizontal "list of the things Anton Harley ate at the party" (172): "18 small cucumber sandwiches; 21 small watercress sandwiches; 11 miniature egg rolls; 2 large roast beef sandwiches; 1 large Virginia ham sandwich; 1 large turkey sandwich; 2 platefuls of potato salad; 1 plateful of coleslaw; 2 dill pickles; 7 deviled eggs; 1 pussy" (172).

In other words, not only does *Imaginative Qualities* discourage distinctions between lists and catalogs, it raises questions about distinctions between catalogs and other rhetorical forms, such as the "outline" (123)[2] and the *"collection"* (129)[3]—and in the end, it questions the distinction between a list and literary prose in general. After all, any sequence of items is a list. Thus Lou's removal of "a pair of stockings, panties, and a garter belt" (33) from Sheila's drawer qualifies, for example, as list, as does the narrator's presentation of Sheila's imagined future: "A future of college towns, trees, frost on the lawns, alert faces of Lou's adoring female students. . . . Literary parties, weekends and holidays in New York . . ." (21). Once any prejudicial or restrictive definition of what a list comprises is dismissed, lists spring up on virtually every page of Sorrentino's novel. Some in the form of options. Some as characteristics. Some as full paragraphs. Sheila's masturbation scene in front of Nathan's Famous in Coney Island, for example, is presented twice—two full paragraphs of narrative that constitute a brace of possible narratives (21). Leo's trip to the zoo is also presented as a set of options (116). These multiple perspectives on the same (albeit fictional) event are akin to cubism in literary form.

Furthermore, if a catalog can consist of paragraph-length items, then the difference between paragraph lists and the eight chapters of the book is only a matter of degree. The novel as a whole can be characterized as a list of narrative vignettes describing eight people, eight failed artists—some bad, some unrealized, and some who "surrendered" or succumbed to the mediocrity that can accompany popularity and financial success (111):

1 *Lady the Brach*
Sheila Henry, "who writes such bad poems" (3) and is "a terrible poet" (177)
2 *Brooklyn-Paterson Local*
Lou Henry, c.f., *"Things Lou Henry Would Have Been Better off Being* . . . A good poet" (32; Sorrentino's italics)
3 *The Butcher Cut Him Down*
Guy Lewis, who at his best as a prose writer is "better than average" (76), but who "battered and chipped at his prose until it changed . . . to a shambles of abstract egoism" (61)

4 *And Other Popular Songs*
    Bunny Lewis, who "drew . . . painted . . . could play the clari-
    net and piano" (90), but whose life was "Desperately normal,
    and filled with the most incredibly uninteresting phenom-
    ena" (93)
5 *Images of K*
    Leo Kaufman, "a poet of brilliant gifts" (113) who "surren-
    dered" (111), and whose poems as "he came to be more of a
    poetic figure . . . shed their strength" (126-27)
6 *Radix Malorum*
    Anton Harley, who "made the most hopeless poems" (155)
    that "were, at the center, dead" (158)
7 *Many Years a Painter*
    Bart Kahane, who could have been "a mediocre painter, and
    a slightly better sculptor," but who became "a remarkably
    successful and wealthy decorator" (204-05)
8 *Amethyst Neon*
    Dick Detective, who wrote "inept conglomerates of words . . .
    rotten [poems]. . . concrete turds" (217)

This structure is implied when the narrator confesses, "I don't understand the motivations of these characters I've invented. I could
make up a good list of them" (34), and then repeatedly denies that
Imaginative Qualities is a novel. The text forms a catalog of catalogs, containing lists embedded in lists embedded in lists. But these
are not lists that make for boring reading (despite the narrator's
implications to the contrary). They prompt interpretation. Language is not, for Sorrentino, transparent. It cannot " 'represent'
things," cannot "take their place" (169), as he makes clear in his
condemnation of Anton's writing and "poets" who write words such
as "mawning" instead of "morning": "People who write 'mawning'
think the language has a true 'reality' off the paper. The difference
between a good writer and a bad one—or, the difference beween a
writer (take your choice out of the millions around) and an artist—
is that the former thinks the words are pictures, and so on. He
thinks they 'represent' things, and take their place" (169). A distinction is made here between a writer and an artist, with the claim
that an artist "is a slave to the fact . . . that they [words] represent
nothing" (169). An artist does something that writers do not; that
something is directly related to ideation. Leo Kaufman, the only
decent poet in the novel, is described as a man with "ideas" (134),
but ideas are not enough to create art, as the novel also offers examples of "dullard[s]" and bad painters who have ideas but who do
not produce art (133).

The epigraph from William Carlos Williams and, to a lesser degree, the postscript from Ezra Pound provide insight into what the novel exposes about the way meaning (or literary *art*) is produced. The key passage in the epigraph is as follows: "The wish would be to see not floating visions of unknown purport but the imaginative qualities of the actual things being perceived accompany their gross vision in a slow dance, interpreting as they go" (ix). What we are invited to desire—indeed told we *should* desire—are not merely "gross vision[s]," such as objects, items in a list, words on a page, sentences in a paragraph, chapters in a book, and so forth. What we should desire is to *perceive,* along with objects, their "imaginative qualities." Thus the empirical is wed to the imaginative and the interaction of these two—the "slow dance" of Williams's quotation— involves interpretation. The cognitive process of apprehending art, in Sorrentino's discourse, privileges and depends on imagination and interpretation.[4]

Consider what Sorrentino's narrator writes after providing a list of "twenty things that Leo and some of these enraptured girls [Leo's lovers] did during those two years [spent without Anne]" (121): "If the reader will take all these things, and imagine for himself the events leading up to them, the places through which Leo and his various loves passed to get to do these things, and the events that followed these things, he will have a general picture of the hip New York scene during those years. In other words, the reader is asked to write the book that I have no interest in writing" (122). This passage outlines the relationship between imagination and interpretation. In the paradigm informing Sorrentino's use of lists, imagination is not merely Williams's apprehension of "floating visions of unknown purport" (ix), not merely the processing of mental images,[5] but the production of meaning based on what is imagined in an intentional way about the real. To be real in an intentional way is to be the product of a design. This is what Sorrentino's narrator asserts when he says "Art is selection" (47). *Imaginative Qualities* is a design, a literary pattern consisting of listed items. It dispels the illusion that narrative carries unitary meaning in favor of a multiply meaningful "texture," which the narrator confesses to "love" (47). To put it most succinctly, Sorrentino designs the catalog, and readers make it meaningful. It is the interaction between the reader and the gaps among the listed items that engenders meaning. As readers move back and forth between the text and what is imagined about the text (the "slow dance"), they interpret.

Plainly, Sorrentino's catalogs are designed to have a particular texture. They are not random, but in terms of meaning, they are arbitrary. That is the artist's contribution to the work: he designs the catalog, he is the one who "subtly link[s]" the items together (157). Quite simply, he writes the list. But the list, once written, is not referential, as Sorrentino repeatedly reminds us throughout the novel. His characters are "the flattest of people," for they are "made out of words"—and those "words . . . are words" (169, 157, 37). Words, then, are not pictures; "they represent nothing . . . [and we] pay homage to them on their terms" (169).

This idiosyncratic, nonreferential use of the list links *Imaginative Qualities* to the rest of Sorrentino's oeuvre. Discussing *Mulligan Stew* in an interview with John O'Brien, Sorrentino confesses, "I would like to bust the goddamn novel apart and put it together again for once and for all and prove to myself that fiction is real unto itself, that it is total invention, that it is total prose, that it is the absolute reality of fiction that matters in terms of writing fiction" (18). The nonreferentiality of prose renders it incapable of transmitting reality. Only the prose is real. What the artist *means* is not important (except, of course, to the artist) for it is not (cannot be) transferred via language from the mind of the artist to the mind of a reader. What does get transferred, what does accompany the text is the artist's design, the product of the artist's selection process. And it is the imaginative qualities of the various and diverse words/phrases/sentences (linguistic items cataloged) that the artist has chosen that, in the reader's experience, contribute to the production of meaning. The site where this occurs is located between items, between lines, between *things,* in the imaginative realms between words. This is not a transcendent experience, as some, perhaps even Sorrentino, might claim, but a product of human consciousness.

Indeed, what Sorrentino's fiction implies is similar to the phi phenomenon, where movement is perceived when one spot in one location is turned off and a similar spot in another location is turned on. Just as Nelson Goodman and others questioned the human mechanism that allows viewers to "fill in the spot at the intervening place-times along a path running from the first to the second flash *before the second flash occurs*" (qtd. in Dennett 114; Dennett's italics), Sorrentino's catalogs raise the question of how readers are able to compose a narrative (or perceive a narrative that is wholly absent) in the narrative gaps between narrative utterances—in the space between catalog items. This addresses a linguistic process seldom examined, but nevertheless central to literature. A catalog, broadly defined, is merely items in sequence; thus there is nothing to prevent us from viewing a poem or fiction as a form of catalog—a type of list. "Poetry is fiction" (169), the narrator tells us, and even when fiction is composed of phrases and sentences in a traditionally formed narrative, there are content gaps between the phrases and sentences. If readers could not imagine what fills those gaps, fiction would not be possible any more than film is possible without persistence of vision and the phi phenomenon.

What I am positing here is that the process that makes it possible for us to see a series of still images of the second hand on a clock jumping several seconds with each consecutive image at a rate of twenty-four frames per second as the fluid motion of the second hand through every point on the clock's face (even those points for which no image actually exists) is similar to the process that makes it possible for us to construct a fluid narrative from a series of stagnant phrases placed in sequence. The latter is a type of psi phenomenon, a process that fuses what is imagined with what is actual, thus making interpretation possible. The imaginative interpretation of actual prose (i.e., "isolate flecks," in Sorrentino's Williams-inspired terminology (124)) is the function of the reader. The selection of those "isolate flecks" that the reader interprets is the function of the writer. And the writer achieves art when his design greatly stimulates a reader's imagination, or a reader's impulse toward interpretation. Any connection readers make between prose and their lives is a result of the "meticulously woven fabric of the ruthless imagination" (48). The writer selects a design ("woven fabric") or creates a design via selection, which the reader interprets by exercising his or her imagination to narrate connections between items in a list.

Sorrentino is clear about the distinctions between the experience he is having writing *Imaginative Qualities* and the experience of others reading it. He engages his imagination in the writing of the book, using, as he says, his "experience (plus inventions and lies)" (43). He admits that he is more interested in "manipulat[ing] these inventions" (169) than in pleasing readers. When he says, "This list is a bore to read but was interesting enough to compile, based as it is on hazy memory and on the imagination" (68), he shows that two processes are at play: his and the reader's. His advice to readers is: "Take the list or leave it. This book is for me" (69). Clearly he does not expect his aesthetic experience writing the book to transfer to readers, but he does expect his design to be apprehended by readers. The text is planned (124); it has form; it contains Sorrentino's design. Its design is what distinguishes it as art. Sorrentino's narrator says, "Prose is endless" (47), but art is selective design. He invites readers (those, that is, who decide not to leave the book) to "think of the words . . . in relation to all the others in this book" (169). He invites them to interpret his design, rather than align his prose to external referents.

Sorrentino offers an analogy to illuminate reading as a process of engaging one's imagination to fill in the gaps between linguistic objects. In his chapter on Leo Kaufman, his narrator claims that "All these people [characters] are follow-the-dots pictures—all harsh angles that the mind alone can apprehend because we have already seen their natural counterparts" (111). This analogy is apt, as "follow-the-dots pictures" contain design but no referent. They are, like lists, a collection of points with no essential relationship between each other, only an imagined relationship.[6] Of Leo Kaufman, Sorrentino writes that "in a book like this, a slap here, a dash there, a couple of anecdotes mixed with gratuitous opinion, a figure can emerge that has little to do with the figure as it really exists. Not that Leo exists, but even the invented Leo has a set in my mind that is different from the way he will turn out here" (111). The Leo that is read is not the Leo as Sorrentino writes him, and neither Leo references a real Leo—or, as Sorrentino's narrator goes on to say, "The beauty of fiction is that it goes two ways, at least. Out, into the world of the reader's experience and in, into the stringencies of the writer's tyranny" (111).

In *Imaginative Qualities* Sorrentino fully realizes[7] the potential of the list as a prose device and informs our understanding of the function of fiction at its most paradigmatic. In drawing attention to the text as merely text, he makes us aware of the larger operations of literature: the communication of art through textual design and interpretation, by way of the interplay of our own imaginations with the objet d'art. The postscript by Pound that follows the text proper might leave one to wonder if it is Sorrentino's characters who comprise the walking dead and the living who are "made out of cardboard," or if Sorrentino is attributing these qualities to the actual people who inspired his fiction. But in close reading of the work, Sorrentino leaves little doubt that fixed referential parallels among the imagined characters his words inspire and the actual people who may or may not have inspired those words are untenable. Fiction, in the end, is inescapably fiction.

Mackey points this out in his discussion of *Odd Number* when he claims that "the only truth in fiction is its exposure of the indeterminacy of all discourse. Truth and reality are never more than the imagined terms of the nostalgia for a truth and reality never possessed. The greater art is the art that embraces this paradox" (37). His point is well made, but truth's and reality's roles in fiction should not be too quickly dismissed. It is not that Sorrentino is necessarily *not* referring to actual experiences when he writes; it is simply that language is incapable of transporting those experiences to readers. And it is not that readers do not construct references between Sorrentino's text and their actual experiences; it is simply that any connections readers make between fiction and reality are arbitrary and controlled by expectations. Art does not record or preserve truth or reality; it destroys it for its own sake. This is what is implied when Sorrentino writes that "Prose will kill you if you give it an inch, i.e., if you try and substitute it for the world. What I am trying to do, through all this murk, is to define certain areas of destruction" (112). As Sorrentino's narrator repeatedly claims, the "book is about destruction" (167). The "hour of blissful sleep that [Lou] had enjoyed . . . with a whore in a hotel room" (27) is ineffable, because any attempt to capture it in prose, even Sorrentino's, reduces it to nonreferential language. *Imaginative Qualities* illustrates this impossibility. Its catalogs expose that which is absent, the gaps interspersed throughout language upon which meaning depends, rendering prose opaque, forcing us to confront the truth of the text and the reality of the page, and situating literary art in the author's design.

Notes

[1] Sorrentino's engagement of the list should not be divorced from the word's etymology and the ability of the word *list* to summon ear and mind: to list is to hear and to desire. From its Old English (*list*) and Old French (*lest*) roots, the term also connotes art, as it is associated with craft, wisdom, and cunning.

[2] Sorrentino claims, at one point, that what he is trying to do is "give you an outline of Leo's basic activities" (123).

[3] ZuZu Jefferson criticizes the book as "merely a *collection* of anecdotes" (129; Sorrentino's italics).

[4] Some would argue that this is a misreading of the quotation by Williams. In the absences of punctuation, we may, at our discretion, punctuate the passage as we wish, which presents us with a variety of possible readings. Andrews, for example, reads the phrase as "The wish would be to see not floating visions of unknown purport[,] but the imaginative qualities of the actual things being perceived accompany their gross vision in a slow dance . . . ," and thus claims that Williams is saying we "would like to access reality directly, . . . but we cannot," thus we "long for objectivity" but are "stuck with subjectivity" ("Re"). I agree that the passage can be read that way, but in the absence of linguistic certainty, there is no way to privilege this reading over another. The fact that Andrews and I interpret the passage differently supports the central axis of my argument: that prose is a static, nonrepresentational artifact, which, like other aesthetic art forms, stimulates the imagination in the presentation of its design, in an inverse relationship between determinacy (read: familiarity) and its potential for variant interpretations in the imaginations of its readers. There are several

reasons why I imagine the passage to mean that "imaginative qualities" are desirable. Two of the most significant are that I find no nostalgia in Sorrentino's dismissal of referentiality, thus no desire for a more accessible "reality" and that in entitling his work *Imaginative Qualities of Actual Things,* Sorrentino posits "imaginative qualities" as things to be desired. To read it otherwise would be to imagine an imaginative writer writing an imaginative novel about the undesirability of imaginative qualities.

[5] Sorrentino frequently criticizes film (and photography), claiming, as Williams does in the epigraph, that merely processing images is a "maladjustment." Several times in the novel Sorrentino implies that a "movie shot" is inferior to art (33).

[6] My interpretation of Sorrentino's analogy assumes, of course, that the dots are not labeled.

[7] Inasmuch as anything can be fully realized.

Works Cited

Andrews, David. "Gilbert Sorrentino." *Review of Contemporary Fiction* 21.3 (2001): 7-57.

—. "Reading Gilbert Sorrentino." Unpublished essay, 2001.

—. "Re: ALA Conference." E-mail to Kevin Alexander Boon. 5 Jan. 2002.

Dennett, D. *Consciousness Explained.* Boston: Little, Brown, 1991.

Mackey, Louis. *Fact, Fiction, and Representation: Four Novels of Gilbert Sorrentino.* Columbia: Camden House, 1997.

O'Brien, John. "An Interview with Gilbert Sorrentino." *Review of Contemporary Fiction* 1.1 (1981): 5-27.

Sorrentino, Gilbert. "Fictional Infinities." *Something Said: Essays by Gilbert Sorrentino.* 1984. 2nd ed. Normal, IL: Dalkey Archive Press, 2001. 323-30.

—. *Imaginative Qualities of Actual Things.* 1971. Elmwood Park, IL: Dalkey Archive Press, 1991.

—. *Odd Number.* 1985. *Pack of Lies: Odd Number, Rose Theatre, Misterioso.* Normal, IL: Dalkey Archive Press, 1997. 7-146.

Watzlawick, Paul. *How Real Is Real: Confusion, Disinformation, Communication.* New York: Vintage, 1976.

Selected Critical Bibliography: Interviews, Reviews, and Articles on Imaginative Qualities of Actual Things

Andrews, David. "The Art Is the Act of Smashing the Mirror: A Conversation with Gilbert Sorrentino." *Review of Contemporary Fiction* 21.3 (2001): 60-68.

—. "Conclusion: Aestheticism in American Literature, Part III: From Williams to Sorrentino." "American An/Aesthete: A Study of Aesthetes in American Literature, From Edgar Allan Poe to Gilbert Sorrentino." Diss. State U of New York at Stony Brook, 1997. 385-418.

—. "Gilbert Sorrentino." *Review of Contemporary Fiction* 21.3 (2001): 7-59.

—. " 'Something Has Sure As Hell Happened': Gilbert Sorrentino, *The Review of Contemporary Fiction,* and Provocative Fiction." *Bridge* 1.4 (2002): 138-43.

—. "Under the Shadow: David Andrews on Gilbert Sorrentino." *Hunger Magazine* 4.2 (also designated 9): 95-102.

—. " 'A Vulgar, Cruel, and Mad Tongue': Gilbert Sorrentino's Regenerative Fiction." "American An/Aesthete: A Study of Aesthetes in American Literature, From Edgar Allan Poe to Gilbert Sorrentino." Diss. State U of New York at Stony Brook, 1997. 334-84.

Armstrong, Peter. "Gilbert Sorrentino's *Imaginative Qualities of Actual Things.*" *Grosseteste Review* 6.1-4 (1973): 65-68.

Barone, Dennis. "An Interview with Gilbert Sorrentino." *Partisan Review* 48 (1981): 236-46.

Bronk, William. "The Person of Fiction, the Fiction of Person." *Sulfur* 4 (1983): 168-72.

Caserio, Robert. "Gilbert Sorrentino's Prose Fiction." *Vort* 2.3 (1974): 63-69.

Charles, May. "A Postmodern Challenge to Reference-World Construction: Gilbert Sorrentino's *Mulligan Stew.*" *Style* 29.2 (1995): 235-61.

Creeley, Robert. "Xmas as in Merry." *Review of Contemporary Fiction* 1.1 (1981): 157-58.

D'Amico, Maria Vittoria. "Paradox Beyond Convention: A Note on Gilbert Sorrentino's Fiction." *Rivista di studi anglo-americani* 3.4-5 (1984-1985): 269-80.

Eilenberg, Max. "A Marvelous Gift: Gilbert Sorrentino's Fiction." *Review of Contemporary Fiction* 1.1 (1981): 88-94.

Elman, Richard. *Namedropping: Mostly Literary Memoirs.* Albany: State U of New York P, 1998.

—. "Reading Gilbert Sorrentino." *Review of Contemporary Fiction* 1.1 (1981): 155-56.

Emerson, Stephen. *"Imaginative Qualities of Actual Things."* Vort 2.3 (1974): 85-89.

Emmett, Paul. *"The Sky Changes*: A Journey into the Unconsciousness and a Road into the Novels of Gilbert Sorrentino." *Review of Contemporary Fiction* 1.1 (1981): 113-29.

Gilmore, Lyman. *Don't Touch the Poet: The Life and Times of Joel Oppenheimer*. Jersey City: Talisman House, 1998.

Gontarksi, S. E. "Working at Grove: An Interview with Gilbert Sorrentino." *Review of Contemporary Fiction* 10.3 (1990): 97-110.

Graver, Lawrence. Rev. of *Imaginative Qualities of Actual Things,* by Gilbert Sorrentino. *New York Times Book Review* 2 July 1972: 6-7.

Hutcheon, Linda. *Narcissistic Narrative: The Metafictional Paradox*. Waterloo, Ontario: Wilfrid Laurier UP, 1980.

Jacobs, Barbara. "The Art of Gilbert Sorrentino." Diss. New York U, 1984.

Klinkowitz, Jerome. "The Extra-Literary in Contemporary American Fiction." *Contemporary American Fiction*. Ed. Malcolm Bradbury and Sigmund Ro. London: Edward Arnold, 1987. 19-37.

—. "Gilbert Sorrentino's Super-Fiction." *Chicago Review* 25.4 (1974): 77-89.

—. *Literary Disruptions: The Making of a Post-Contemporary American Fiction*. 1975. Urbana: U of Illinois P, 1980.

—. *Literary Subversions: New American Fiction and the Practice of Criticism*. Carbondale: Southern Illinois UP, 1985.

—. "Poetry in the Novel: American Fiction of the Last Eight Years." *Poetry Australia* 59 (1976): 61-69.

—. Rev. of *Imaginative Qualities of Actual Things,* by Gilbert Sorrentino. *Village Voice Literary Supplement* 22 Nov. 1973: 27-28.

Laurence, Alexander. "Gilbert Sorrentino Interview." *The Write Stuff:* Interviews (1994). 7 pp. 7 Dec. 2000. <http://www.altx.com/int2/gilber.sorrentino.html>.

Mackey, Louis. *Fact, Fiction, and Representation: Four Novels by Gilbert Sorrentino*. Columbia: Camden House, 1997.

McHale, Brian. *Postmodernist Fiction*. New York: Methuen, 1987.

McMullen, Kim. "Necessary Fictions: Fictional Reflexivity in Works by Vladimir Nabokov, Flann O'Brien, Gilbert Sorrentino, and John Barth." Diss. Duke U, 1986.

McPheron, William. *Gilbert Sorrentino: A Descriptive Bibliography*. Elmwood Park, IL: Dalkey Archive Press, 1991.

Miller, Anthony. "Sorrentino's Synthetic Ink-quisitions." *ebr* 7 (1998). 7 Jun. 2001. <http://www.altx.com/ebr/reviews/rev7/r7mil.htm>.

Mosley, Nicholas. "Gilbert Sorrentino and *Mulligan Stew.*" *Review of Contemporary Fiction* 1.1 (1981): 153-54.

—. "*The Review of Contemporary Fiction.*" *Bridge* 1.4 (2002): 149-51.

Mottram, Eric. "The Black Polar Night: The Poetry of Gilbert Sorrentino." *Vort* 2.3 (1974): 43-59.

Nufer, Doug. "No End to Trying: Gilbert Sorrentino's Novel Novels." *Stranger* 10.5 (19 Oct. 2000). 13 Aug. 2001. <http://www.thestranger.com/2000-10 19/bookguide3.html>.

O'Brien, John. "Every Man His Own Voice." *Review of Contemporary Fiction* 1.1 (1981): 62-80.

—. "An Interview with Gilbert Sorrentino." *Review of Contemporary Fiction* 1.1 (1981): 5-27.

—. "Gilbert Sorrentino." *Dictionary of Literary Biography Yearbook: 1980.* Ed. Karen Rood, Jean Ross, and Richard Ziegfeld. Detroit: Gale Research, 1981. 310-14.

Olson, Toby. "Sorrentino's Past." *Review of Contemporary Fiction* 1.1 (1981): 52-55.

—. "Sorrentino's Opus." *Bridge* 1.4 (2002): 157-58.

Phelps, Donald. "Extra Space." *Vort* 2.3 (1974): 89-96.

Rev. of *Imaginative Qualities of Actual Things,* by Gilbert Sorrentino. *Booklist* 15 Nov. 1971: 274.

Robins, William. "Gilbert Sorrentino." *Dictionary of Literary Biography V5: American Poets since World War II (Part 2).* Ed. Donald Greiner. Detroit: Gale Research, 1980. 278-84.

Schaub, Thomas. "Williams, Sorrentino, and the Art of the Actual." *William Carlos Williams: Man and Poet.* Ed. Carroll F. Terrell. Orono: National Poetry Foundation, U of Maine at Orono, 1983. 435-59.

Scholes, Robert. Rev. of *Imaginative Qualities of Actual Things,* by Gilbert Sorrentino. *Saturday Review* 23 Oct. 1971: 88.

Selby, Hubert. "Gilbert Sorrentino." *Review of Contemporary Fiction* 1.1 (1981): 48-51.

Sorrentino, Gilbert. "*Neon, Kulchur,* Etc." *TriQuarterly* 43 (1978): 298-316.

Share, Bernard. "On Giving Up Fictioneering." *Review of Contemporary Fiction* 1.1 (1981): 168-70.

Stephens, Michael. *The Dramaturgy of Style: Voice in Short Fiction.* Carbondale: Southern Illinois UP, 1986.

Thielemans, Johan. "The Energy of an Absence: Perfection as Useful Fiction in the Novels of Gaddis and Sorrentino." *Critical Angles: European Views of Contemporary American Literature.* Ed. Marc Chénetier. Carbondale: Southern Illinois UP, 1986. 105-24.

—. "The Voice of the Irresponsible: Irresponsible Voices? On Gilbert Sorrentino's *Mulligan Stew.*" *Representation and Performance in Postmodern Fiction.* Ed. Maurice Couturier. Montpellier: Delta, 1983. 113-29.

Waugh, Patricia. *Metafiction: The Theory and Practice of Self-Conscious Fiction.* London: Methuen, 1984.

Wright, Martin. "Gilbert Sorrentino's *Imaginative Qualities of Actual Things.*" *Grosseteste Review* 6.1-4 (1973): 61-64.

A Gilbert Sorrentino Checklist

Fiction

The Sky Changes. New York: Hill and Wang, 1966. San Francisco: North Point Press, 1986; Normal, IL: Dalkey Archive Press, 1998.

Steelwork. New York: Pantheon Books, 1970; Elmwood Park, IL: Dalkey Archive Press, 1992.

Imaginative Qualities of Actual Things. New York: Pantheon Books, 1971; Elmwood Park, IL: Dalkey Archive Press, 1991.

Splendide-Hôtel. New York: New Directions, 1973; Elmwood Park, IL: Dalkey Archive Press, 1984.

Flawless Play Restored: The Masque of Fungo. Los Angeles: Black Sparrow Press, 1974.

Mulligan Stew. New York: Grove, 1979; Normal, IL: Dalkey Archive Press, 1996.

Aberration of Starlight. New York: Random House, 1980; Normal, IL: Dalkey Archive Press, 1993.

Crystal Vision. San Francisco: North Point Press, 1981; Harmondsworth: Penguin, 1982.

Blue Pastoral. San Francisco: North Point Press, 1983.

Odd Number. San Francisco: North Point Press, 1985.

A Beehive Arranged on Humane Principles. New York: Grenfell Press, 1986.

Rose Theatre. Elmwood Park, IL: Dalkey Archive Press, 1987.

Misterioso. Elmwood Park, IL: Dalkey Archive Press, 1989.

Under the Shadow. Elmwood Park, IL: Dalkey Archive Press, 1993.

Red the Fiend. New York: Fromm, 1995.

Pack of Lies. Normal, IL: Dalkey Archive Press, 1997.

Gold Fools. Los Angeles: Green Integer, 2001.

Little Casino. Minneapolis: Coffee House, 2002.

Poetry

The Darkness Surrounds Us. Highlands: Jonathan Williams, 1960.

Black and White. New York: Totem Press, 1964.

The Perfect Fiction. New York: Norton, 1968.

Corrosive Sublimate. Los Angeles: Black Sparrow, 1971.

A Dozen Oranges. Los Angeles: Black Sparrow, 1976.

Sulpiciæ Elegidia: Elegiacs of Sulpicia. Mt. Horeb: Perishable Press, 1977.

White Sail. Santa Barbara: Black Sparrow, 1977.

The Orangery. Austin: U of Texas P, 1978; Los Angeles: Sun & Moon, 1995.
Selected Poems: 1958-1980. Santa Barbara: Black Sparrow, 1981.

Criticism

Something Said: Essays by Gilbert Sorrentino. San Francisco: North Point Press, 1984; 2nd ed. Normal, IL: Dalkey Archive Press, 2001.

Gilbert Sorrentino
Photograph by Vivian Ortiz

From the home of Marguerite Young
Photograph by Miriam Fuchs

Interview with Marguerite Young

Miriam Fuchs

The following dialogue took place when Marguerite Young was hospital-
ized in June 1993. The exchange moves rapidly between topics of discussion and is sometimes disjointed. Young was ill at the time, but readers
will recognize the marvelous and illogical statements as characteristic of
Young's own form of logic and, in addition, that her statements often allude to anecdotes and events in *Miss MacIntosh, My Darling.* I have omit-
ted a small amount of material that Young requested not be quoted, the
two pages published in my edited *Marguerite Young, Our Darling* (Dalkey
Archive Press, 1994), and some paragraphs that were not recorded clearly
enough to be transcribed and edited. I have, however, included names as I
heard them, which means that the spelling may not always be accurate,
and the anecdotes as Young elliptically told them. Readers will also notice that I often changed the line of questioning while trying to get specific information from Young, with varying degrees of success. Rather
than researching every detail that Young offered in our last talk, I prefer
to leave her responses as a tribute to her astounding talent, imagination,
and insistence on "truthfulness."

After preliminary greetings, Young began to describe the preparation of
her Debs manuscript at Knopf. Published as one volume and edited by
Charles Ruas, it was entitled *Harp Song for a Radical: The Life and Times
of Eugene Victor Debs* (1999).

MARGUERITE YOUNG: She [the editor] has tremendous understanding. We have to cut it in such a way that the three volumes will
be the Bible of modern prose, the Bible on your table. This is because I will have done the most massive epic achievement ever done
by a woman in the Western . . .
    MIRIAM FUCHS: Women have not generally written epics.
    MY: No, they haven't. . . . See, I have to cut it to fit it all in one vol-
ume, the Bible, on every coffee table in America . . . the Bible of the
American psyche. She [the editor] said, "What you're really writing
about is not Debs, it is America." Well, I knew that.
    MF: Does that mean you have the second volume done?
    MY: Well, for the second volume we have to put in just the first
two or three chapters. It's the best.
    MF: What is the title of your second volume?

MY: Well, the first is *Prelude in the Golden Key: The Life and Times of Eugene Debs.* The second is, oh, let's see, I forget—the last is *Harp Song for a Radical,* from the Pullman Strike. I forget now. It has Mrs. Lincoln and it has all the many wonderful things about Lincoln that you never knew.

[The discussion moves to Marguerite's friend, the poet Amy Clampitt, from whom I had received a letter about her contribution to *Marguerite Young, Our Darling.*]

MY: I love Amy. You know what happened? Well, I met her the first day I ever came to New York. She was in love with a man, a stone deaf man, who wouldn't marry her because . . . I don't know whether she . . . he said her high heels made too much noise, and her earrings . . . which is true if you're listening to the vibrations. But she adored him. She cooked spaghetti and meatballs for me the first day I arrived in New York. I've known her since the first day I ever arrived.

MF: Dalkey Archive Press recently sent me the manuscript of *Inviting the Muses,* a collection of some of your early writings. You recall, yes, that your stories, essays, and book reviews are going to be published soon?

MY: Is there one in it called "My Grandmother's Foot"? Oh, I love that, and that was about Lillian Blumberg. The story is about Lillian and her grandmother's foot, which was accidentally buried in the wrong grave. So when they dug up the parts to attach on Resurrection Day, it was her grandmother's hand.

MF: So that story is true.

MY: Yes, it's true, and I told the story in her voice. You would know it was Lillian if you ever heard Lillian talk. And Lillian made a pact that she would allow me to write whatever I pleased . . . there are many more things I didn't get around to telling about Lillian. But Lillian gave birth to an angel's foot and an angel's wing and I don't know what else while she was in the hospital with hallucinations. I understand that now. This boy, a young writer, was in love with her and very, very devoted to her. And his mother came, and she said, "Well, son, since your baby is only imaginary, a stone baby, you don't have to marry her, you just come back home with me." He said, "Mother, if she loves me enough to have an imaginary stone baby by me, I'm marrying her and I'm going to make it real." And he did. And Lillian went out to Berkeley and she educated that guy, and he became a brilliant sociologist. And then she had a daughter by him, a red-headed daughter, and she educated that daughter to be one of the foremost news commentators. I forget the daughter's name. And she died sitting on a park bench, in Berkeley, with her hand holding on to her little dog. The story is only about twenty pages, and it really is hilarious.

MF: I've begun reading the articles in *Inviting the Muses* that you originally wrote for magazines such as *Mademoiselle* and *Vogue*. There's an article about Marianne Moore in which you describe visiting her in Brooklyn. You wrote, "She has a box of wild bird feathers. And bluebird's feet. She offered me a bluebird's foot. She offered me some eagle down, which she says is getting scarcer." Did you visit her, and did Moore give you a bluebird's foot?

MY: Yes, although I think she said that it wasn't a bluebird, it was something else much more interesting. I forget now, but whatever I said was true.

MF: There is an editor's note somewhere saying that in addition to taking a Ph. D., you've written two books of poems, taught school, worked in the stock market and in an electric chair factory." I didn't bring the note with me, and now can't remember if it really did say an "electric chair factory" or whether I'm veering off into my own imagined memories. Can you help me out here?

MY: It was a chair factory. But I never did take a Ph. D. I did all the work and walked out on it. I wish I hadn't, but I did. I did all those things.

MF: You worked in an electric chair factory?

MY: Oh yes, when I was first out of high school. And that was the most interesting, strange, horrifying experience, and Carson McCullers thought it would be smart to tell everybody that I used to work in an electric chair factory.

MF: Did you also work in the stock market?

MY: Yes. David L. Payne. He was writing his memoirs, and he . . . I wrote his biography. He said to put in a lot of stuff about early Indiana and how beautiful it was. He was very funny. Oh God, I worked for him for four years without a vacation.

MF: In those magazine articles surely you were laughing to yourself at how the editors and readers would receive the fantastic anecdotes in them.

MY: It was all true. . . . If I said it I saw it. I don't remember now. I ought to read those pieces sometime. The bus driver, too.

[I briefly read aloud a few passages from *Miss MacIntosh, My Darling*.]

MY: Well, it was said to be true, it was a legend, you know. What I liked was the girl who was going to take the football team to heaven. Cedar Rapids. *O-see-the-rabbits*. The little boy thought he was going to see the rabbits. I heard that. Don't you know where the girl was dancing? You know the man who measures the wind tonnage of music over the Brooklyn Bridge? It's true. And you know Harpo [got] inside a bicycle wheel with his harp? It's true. Everything I've written is true. I don't make up anything.

MF: Why did you open *Miss MacIntosh, My Darling* with the young couple, Madge and Homer?

MY: I was looking for the model Middle West, remember? But I never found it because there isn't any.

MF: Yes, I do remember, and I suspect that most readers have been struck by the degree of violence. There's Gertrude, who murders one husband, then marries his brother, then kills him too.

MY: Yes, well, it's true, by the way.

MF: Why did you write so many book reviews?

MY: I was a book reviewer for the *New York Times* and the *New York Herald Tribune*. I got a lot of money, but the reviews meant a great deal to me. Also, the work gave me a chance to write (like "The Death of Virgil") beautiful reviews for people who needed them. Like Kurt Wolf. I very much enjoyed writing them. And Marianne Hauser was a person I wrote about. She is a wonderful writer.

MF: What about the story "Old James"?

MY: Yes, that is a personal favorite. That was in the anthology of the best . . . I could have edited that piece, if the editors had known I wanted to. I like to write about books. And I made money that way and it was years before I got any money from anybody [else]. No, it wasn't a drain on my energies. What drained my energy was teaching in three or four universities, going way out to the Fordham campus and then Seton Hall and Great Neck. It was awful.

MF: Is *Angel in the Forest* a defense of utopia or a defense of socialism?

MY: Neither one. It's just the way I saw things. By putting in everything I could.

MF: Is the story of the seven suitcases in Rome true? This is told on the jacket copy of the first edition of *Miss MacIntosh, My Darling*. It says that seven suitcases of the manuscript were lost in a train station in Rome, but located by seven men from Cook's who had to use seven wheelbarrows to retrieve them.

MY: True, but it was Gare Lazarre in Paris. I think in the palace. Peter Prescott said in his review, "Good God that they had remained lost. . . ."

MF: How does your prose in the Debs book differ from *Miss MacIntosh, My Darling*?

MY: It's just as beautiful. In some ways . . . well, it's equal . . . it is not. . . none of the books, by the way, not one of them is . . . they remain at a high level and that's what, she [the editor at Knopf] says, makes it so beautiful. Utopia is not in the realization, it's in the words, only in words do they exist because when you get there, it isn't what you thought it would be. That's what Walt Whitman said too.

MF: So, in the Debs manuscript is your emphasis really on utopia? Are you using Debs and socialism as particular manifestations of utopianism?

MY: It's the tragic-comic history of American socialism. *Prelude in the Golden Key*. I forget the second volume, but it's lovely. And the third, *Harp Song for a Radical*.

MF: You once said to me that Miss MacIntosh was the one character you most nearly invented. You knew the others, but she was your invented character. Why was she, in particular, the invented character?

MY: That's right. I don't know. I had to invent somebody who was sensible, or who seemed sensible. She hailed from What Cheer, Iowa, and there were headlines, "What Cheer Makes National Press." It seems that there was a What Cheer, Iowa, and that there was a Macintosh in it, but I didn't know that then.

MF: You also once said to me how you would advise people to read *Miss MacIntosh, My Darling,* and you said that they shouldn't take it so seriously. They should read it for the humor.

MY: They can always read it again, if they like it. At different periods in your life you see a different book.

MF: Do you consider yourself to be a writer of humor?

MY: Absolutely. I don't think there is such a thing as tragedy, it's tragic-comic. Everything is like the two Mr. Spitzers. You know, is he alive or is he dead? However, the black coachman, he's one of my favorite characters. Or the twin house. Or the old suffragette chock full of wedding dresses.

MF: Does your Debs manuscript include independent sections as *Miss MacIntosh, My Darling* does?

MY: Absolutely. Did I tell you that I've returned to writing poems? It's very funny. I found out that I can write beautiful poems, very different from what I wrote a long time ago. [She begins to recite them.] "This is I, Louisa May Alcott, who should be called . . . This is I, Louisa May Alcott, who should be called Louisa May Not Alcott in view of the prohibitions placed upon the child of three to confess her sins and make her feel that it was progress. And repent." The poetry is very wonderful, and all these ladies, all these people, rather, are people who recur in the Debs manuscript and are his immediate background.

MF: Are all of your recent poetic voices those of women?

MY: There are two men. I can't remember who they are now, but I wrote one . . . it really is beautiful. One of them is four and a half pages. Another is "I, Susan B. Anthony. I, Susan Be(e) in her bottom

Anthony," and "I, Harriet Beecher Stowe." That's the one I love the most. And on and on: "I, Margaret Fuller." "I, Josie Baker."

MF: Have you written an "I, Marguerite Young"?

MY: No.

MF: What made you return to poetry after all these years?

MY: Because I know how to do it. I found that I can write poetry. It's as easy for me—and good poetry, this is a beautiful poem—as rolling off a log. And all these men and women are in the background of the Indiana and America from which Debs came. They are the background of the times. They are really beautiful.

MF: Are any of these speakers, or characters in your work, extensions of yourself?

MY: I don't write about myself. I never did. You've been doing that. For Marguerite.

[The conversation continues briefly about Young's age, then comes to an end. Marguerite Young died two years later in 1995.]

Marguerite Young
Photograph by Miriam Fuchs

Book Reviews

Richard Powers. *The Time of Our Singing*. Farrar, Straus & Giroux, 2003. 631 pp. $27.00.

For Richard Powers, in fictions that are among the most invigorating and humane of the last fifteen years, art is a place, a sheltering space apart where characters, socially angular to the point of nerdy eccentricity or emotionally terrorized by the malevolence of the real world, gratefully seek protective retreat. Powers enriches this exploration of the imagination through a familiarity with contemporary sciences, finding within such unpromising theorizing rich metaphors that give depth to this dynamic of retreat and return. *The Time of Our Singing* is Powers's most compelling treatment of this theme, a generational narrative of a biracial family that is as well a deeply affective meditation on time, racial identity, and the complex engine of memory, big ideas that are here offered within a narrative of heartbreaking poignancy in which (without that forced sort of *Forrest Gump* hokiness) characters confront, even participate in the landmark moments of midcentury history, from Hiroshima to the L.A. riots.

At the historic 1939 Marian Anderson Easter Sunday concert at the Lincoln Memorial, an African American woman, a promising Philadelphia gospel singer, chances to fall in love with a European immigrant—a lapsed Jew, a mathematician, and theoretician—whose family had disappeared into Hitler's concentration-camp archipelago and whose work will come to figure in the Manhattan Project. Perhaps naively, they determine that they will raise their three children beyond race. The narrative tracks their difficult struggles to achieve racial identity amid the harrowing crosscurrents of an America compelled to examine just such questions. What forges the family is a love of music, all kinds, that provides a gentle refuge from the hard press of street racism. In such a climate of harsh division (haunted by the shadows of Hitler's ethnic cleansing and of Hiroshima), Powers offers breathtaking descriptions of the harmonies of music, the difficult intimacies of love, and the abiding matrix of family. And he ruminates on time itself: the father spends his university career theorizing on time as a continuum, which Powers himself tests formally with a narrative that shuttles throughout more than fifty years and in a closing chapter that audaciously borders on speculative fiction. Lingering within the enthralling narrative space that Powers here constructs, a reader feels indeed in the presence of a generation's voice who, only in his midforties, may just now be coming into his full. [Joseph Dewey]

William Gaddis. *Agapē Agape*. Afterword Joseph Tabbi. Viking, 2002. 113 pp. $23.95.

Although anything by William Gaddis is a major literary event, this final work marks his exit with a whimper. Not so much a novel, *Agapē Agape* is an inconsistently dramatized monologue delivered by a dying man who bears many resemblances to Gaddis himself. As he weathers the effects of illness and prescription drugs, he rants about the loss of artistic authenticity and the impoverishment of an individual life in this age of technologized production and consumption. Many of his remarks about the mechanical reproduction of art echo ideas famously developed by critics like Walter Benjamin, Hugh Kenner, and John Berger (though according to Joseph Tabbi's superb afterword, these ideas first occurred to Gaddis independently). In certain intellectual circles, it has become second nature to worry over the ambivalent trade-off between the democratization of culture and the resultant loss of artistic standards and achievement. Gaddis himself has dramatized this trade-off much more successfully in his long novels *The Recognitions, JR,* and *A Frolic of His Own.* Even though, as Tabbi has noted, Thomas Bernhard looms behind this work as a significant new influence, Gaddis enthusiasts looking for anything particularly original in *Agapē Agape* will be disappointed. But for anyone who wants to see the familiar Gaddis references and themes played out one last time, it's an extremely interesting final testament of a great artist facing that most ruthless of all democratizers, death: "problem is you have to be wiped out. Have to be reduced to this herd anonymity, humiliated and eliminated as an artist like Melville." In its occasional autobiographical sincerity, the sadness of this testament can be painfully direct. But in its final few pages, some of the mortal gloom lifts in a way reminiscent of a motto from Schiller that sustained Melville during his own depressing last years: "Keep true to the dream of thy youth." For Gaddis this has always meant sustaining hope in "that self who could do more." And for those of us who know *The Recognitions,* these final pages can leave us with the comforting reminder that Gaddis was indeed "that Youth who could do anything." [Thomas Hove]

William Gaddis. *The Rush for Second Place: Essays and Occasional Writings.* Ed. Joseph Tabbi. Penguin, 2002. 182 pp. Paper: $14.00.

William Gaddis, probably the greatest American author of the past half-century, authored mountains of innovative, satirical fiction that spanned five critically acclaimed novels. He was less prolific in his production of nonfiction, publishing barely a handful of substantial essays. With this brief collection, scholar Joseph Tabbi nicely ballasts those pieces with Gaddis's unpublished work and corporate writing. The result is more of a scrapbook than an anthology, but thanks to Tabbi's expert editing and telling commentary, *Rush* manages to extend the ideas found in Gaddis's novels and provide insight into the preoccupations of this deeply private author. Readers familiar with Gaddis will recognize the themes in this collection. The title essay and "Old Foes with New Faces" are rigorous criticisms of capitalism and religion, respectively, deliberations on American culture that will no doubt recall *JR* and *Carpenter's Gothic*. Additionally, there are various notes and project outlines that provide a certain voyeuristic penetration into Gaddis's career-long obsession with the player piano. He was able to pull this disparate material together to create his final work of fiction, *Agapē Agape*. The more substantial pieces, such as the aforementioned title essay, bear a style similar to that of his fiction, and it is his style that ultimately defines his work as art. Gaddis layers his exposition with voices—Alexander Solzhenitsyn, John Maynard Keynes, Mary Baker Eddy, to name a few—and unattributed references to flesh out his highly charged observations. Still, as Tabbi points out in his introduction, Gaddis's style is not multifarious for the sake of being difficult. Moreover, it is emblematic of "his determination to grapple with" the "thoroughly transforming conditions" of the world he inhabited. Tabbi does a great job of contextualizing the disparate fodder that makes up *Rush,* which is a fine compliment to the work of a vastly underappreciated artist. [Christopher Paddock]

Hubert Selby, Jr. *Waiting Period*. Marion Boyars, 2002. 197 pp. $22.95.

This novel is the extended monologue of a man obsessed with death. He is planning his own suicide, but when a delay occurs in obtaining a gun, he changes purpose and decides to kill those he thinks deserve to die. The question raised in the title—whether the novel will only describe waiting—is answered once he moves into action. His first target is an official in the Veterans Administration whom the narrator thinks has cheated him out of his rightful benefits, and he devises a plan to plant *E. coli* culture where it will contaminate the bureaucrat's food. During this planning, the narrator justifies his actions by reflecting on the presence in America of a right-wing gun culture without suspecting that he may be just as much a prisoner of his own obsessions. Short inset passages in italics give external images of the narrator and balance the subjectivity of his monologue. Selby skillfully builds a picture of an isolated individual whose interaction with waitresses and shopkeepers remains minimal throughout, scarcely more than banal greetings or orders. The irony of the novel lies in the new purpose the narrator feels when he embarks on a killing spree. His *E. coli* plan succeeds better than he had hoped, killing more than the bureaucrat. His account takes on a new upbeat tone. He jokes to himself, speculates about how the law would deal with him, and even starts creating news reports about himself by feeding spurious information about the "Russians" responsible for his bomb and wearing a Groucho Marx moustache when detonating it. The disguise reflects his adopted role of joking commentator on American society, one that he combines with a Bonnie-and-Clyde tradition. The conclusion to the novel underlines the irony that a bomber should give the strongest final affirmation: "life is worth living afterall." [David Seed]

Steven Millhauser. *The King in the Tree*. Knopf, 2003. 224 pp. $23.00.

Steven Millhauser's work has always had a romantic quality about it. His characters are dreamers who revel in the wonderment of imagination or are victimized by their own obsessions. But readers expecting surreal, subterranean landscapes and a longing for nostalgia may be heartbroken, for the three brilliant novellas that comprise *The King in the Tree* are all tearjerkers of sorts, each a variation on the theme of heartache: these are tales of love lost, betrayed, or unrequited. *Revenge* is a powerful tale of shattered identity and betrayal. As the narrator leads a potential buyer through her charming old house, she reminisces about the times she shared with her recently deceased husband. As she moves from the kitchen to the back porch, from the study to the guest bedroom, she gradually reveals enough to make her guest, and the reader, increasingly uncomfortable, creating a dynamic tension that carries through to the end of the story. *An Adventure of Don Juan* finds the hero of the title in search of new conquests. After becoming restless with his promiscuous lifestyle in Venice, he travels north to England in search of more meaningful relations. The pace and intimacy of his surroundings force him to delve inward and lead him to question his self-worth. The title novella is also set in the world of medieval fantasy. It is a retelling of the story of Tristan and Ysolt, a tragedy of deception and deprival. Millhauser's version is a strained love triangle in which the king, his queen (Ysolt), and his nephew (Tristan) are all perpetually denied the object of their affection. Much that is here is what you might anticipate from Millhauser—his writing is perceptive and startlingly efficient, and there are yet elaborate underground structures to wander through. Such detail, however, works to support more intimate, if not tragic, discoveries. [Christopher Paddock]

Norah Labiner. *Miniatures*. Coffee House, 2002. 402 pp. $23.00.

Following up *Our Sometime Sister* (2000), Norah Labiner successfully funnels her energies into this marvelously layered novel, which sprints in abecedarian fashion across chapter headings from "Appomattox" to "Zion," lingering over a sense of disaster and loss. In the process, *Miniatures* raises self-reflexive questions about fiction and reality, these tied to the frame of biography, both in the narration itself and the stories narrated. *Miniatures* presents the experience of Fern Alice Jacobi, sometime traveler and housecleaner, age twenty at the time of the story and her entry into the writerly Lieb household; she becomes the wife Brigid's confidante. This couple, resonating with Plath-Hughes and Jane Eyre-Rochester connections, occupies a house "haunted" by Owen Lieb's first wife, Frances, also a writer, an earlier suicide. Fern's own biography, as it turns out, parallels that thought to be Brigid's, who suspects her kinship to a major author, one obsessed with the same themes of writing, love, loss, and disaster as *Miniatures*. Parallels, perhaps one should say "mirrorings," abound, and Labiner's writing, con brio, combines the most literary of allusions to the most worldly—from those early travel books, Genesis and the *Odyssey,* to the more contemporary *Through the Looking-Glass* as well as to the horrifically real Nazi extermination camps. Frances Lieb wrote, "I long for the tiny world, when we were miniatures of ourselves"; that simple line contains the undercurrent of determinism that drives the doubling, recurring interplay among characters, texts, fiction, and life, leading to a final uncertainty about Fern's version of all she "tells" us. This flat, tightly edited response does not convey the excitement and amazement I enjoyed in the reading of *Miniatures*; I recommend it highly to anyone interested in the games of literature and life. [Richard J. Murphy]

Camilo José Cela. *Boxwood.* Trans. Patricia Haugaard. New Directions, 2002. 211 pp. $25.95.

Like the densely branched and intricately sculpted shrub that Camilo José Cela takes for the title of his final novel, *Boxwood* is a complex adventure that weaves and branches through varying narratives, including traditional wisdom, folklore, history, superstition, seafarers' stories, and autobiography. Cela himself has called it "a book of adventures passing through the confused sieve of the memory." The Nobel Prize-winning novelist and father of *tremendismo* has continued toward a path of greater experimentalism with content, structure, and language. *Boxwood* represents Cela's fullest realization of *tremendismo,* which combines aspects of existential philosophy and "brutal realism" with a surreal atmosphere. This is produced via a flowing narrative whereby tales of ships lost at sea collide and merge with other tales, such as one that describes the cure for cancer as "ashes from the head of a rabid dog steeped for nine days in vinegar." His method of intertwining stories dismantles conceptions of linear time through artifice and narrative expansion. One of the many recurring scenes of dialogue that interrupt the storytelling sequences calls attention to this murkiness of time and perception: " 'Isn't this a little garbled?' . . . 'Like life itself?' " The recurring tales and tumbling motifs begin to coalesce, and patterns emerge that are both illuminating and dynamic. The inertia of shipwrecks, superstitions, and anecdotes becomes less blurry, and what arises is a commentary that reveals humanity in its often horrid but hopeful incarnations. He writes: "Don't you know that vultures hatch their eggs within my heart? Time passes gently and uncertainly, like the trees which grow without anyone realizing, this growth business has more to do with the throb of intuition than with the sense of sight." Cela's creative process and methodology are foregrounded, and the text becomes a treasure trove of possibilities and potential discoveries. [Mark Tursi]

Andreï Makine. *Music of a Life.* Trans. Geoffrey Strachan. Arcade, 2002. 109 pp. $19.95.

Andreï Makine's powerful new novel opens in a provincial train station in the middle of a snowstorm. There, an unnamed narrator finds himself stranded amid a sea of fellow travelers, whose collective patience in the face of a long and unpleasant delay seems a microcosm of the Soviet condition. The principal story that Makine unfolds in the pages that follow is the tale, told to the narrator, of one of these travelers—one of these constituent elements of *homo sovieticus,* in Alexander Zinoviev's phrase—but it might stand for many a life derailed by Stalin's purges. Alexis Berg, promising young pianist, his parents arrested and soon to be exiled, finds himself forced to flee his home two days before his first public recital. World War II and the borrowed identity of a dead soldier provide a temporary but transformative cover for the young exile: he feels his way through the fog of love and betrayal that awaits him at war's end with well-calloused hands. Berg's story is tragic, but it is not unremittingly grim. As in all Makine's writing (which once again has been beautifully translated by Geoffrey Strachan), even the darkest textures are shot through, at least fleetingly, with light, or as in this typically evocative moment, light and music: "[Berg] left the room, took a few steps along the corridor, had no desire to go farther. What he saw was enough for him. A deep blue velvet dress, the glow of fair hair, a right hand he could see when it slipped along towards the high notes. . . ." Makine is no stranger to the art of compression; his earlier novel, *Confessions of a Fallen Standard Bearer,* was a model of resonant concision. Still, if *Confessions* carried within its own slender frame the heart of a novel, *Music of a Life,* 109 pages of love, war, loss, and music, constitutes an epic. [Laird Hunt]

Touré. *The Portable Promised Land.* Little, Brown, 2002. 256 pp. $23.95.

It takes a certain panache, and certainly some talent, to pull off a single name. Not to worry: Touré, the *Rolling Stone* writer and self-proclaimed tennis champ of the current literary elite, exhibits both in this new collection of short stories. His prose is aggressive and hip, his characters outrageous, and his stories, for lack of a better word, outlandish. How else to describe Huggy Bear Jackson's tripped-out Cutlass Supreme, creeping down the street at fifteen m.p.h. and suffering from brownouts, in "Steviewondermobile"; the wicked restaurant Jamais in "The Playground of the Ecstatically Blasé," which serves, among other delicacies, the finest rhinoceros testes you've ever tried; or the demise of the philandering Right Reveren [sic] Daddy Love, who serves his congregation in an abandoned three-story KFC? But the eccentricities of character and situation mask a deeper tragedy below the surface of Soul City, Touré's fictional stand-in for New York City. Indeed, many of these stories seem preoccupied with a group of black artists and thinkers, mostly musicians, whose voices speak only in absentia. Their names are repeated over and over: Marvin Gaye, Curtis Mayfield,

Biggie Smalls (Christopher Wallace), Tupac Shakur. And others too: King, Basquiat, Clemente, Malcolm, Charlie Parker. Their absence, it seems, is the foundation on which the city and these stories are constructed. Touré's Soul City, ultimately, is a metropolis of loss, whose citizens lack leaders and whose true founders have long since passed. *The Portable Promised Land* marks the entrance of a talented new voice in American letters, and if Touré already sees himself in the company of writers like Wallace, Franzen, Moody, and Eggers—he's by no means on their level yet—we might forgive him his hubris. He does go by only one name, after all. [Rob Mawyer]

José Saramago. *The Cave.* Trans. Margaret Jull Costa. Harcourt, 2002. 307 pp. $25.00.

With *The Cave* Saramago returns again to the novel (his last book was a non-fiction work on Portugal), using the form to provide a critique of capitalism and mall culture, with his habitual attention to language and his long multivoiced sentences. At the book's heart is Cipriano Algor, an aging potter who lives with his daughter Marta and her husband Marçal in a small village. Cipriano has been selling his pots to The Center, a quickly growing assemblage of apartments and "a succession of arcades, shops, fancy staircases, escalators, meeting points . . . endless numbers of ornaments, electronic games, balloons, fountains and other water features, platforms, hanging gardens, posters, pennants, advertising billboards, mannequins, changing rooms, the façade of a church . . . " This discontinuous and nonparallel list goes on, both suggesting that The Center contains everything within its walls and that the quality of anything consists only of its illusive commodity value. When The Center cancels their order for his pots, replacing them with plastic vessels, Cipriano begins to try to make ceramic dolls, hoping to sell these to The Center. In the meantime, Marçal, who works as a guard at The Center, is given residency privileges, and he and his pregnant wife and Cipriano make preparations to move into The Center. As Cipriano thinks, "from now on everything would be little more than appearance, illusion, absence of meaning, questions with no answers." Indeed, once in The Center, the trio begin to make disturbing discoveries that in the end drive them back out into the world again, unsure of what they want to do but certain they do not want to remain in The Center. Though *The Cave* is the least impressive of Saramago's three most recent novels (the others being *Blindness* and *All the Names*), it becomes undeniably compelling in the last seventy pages. Saramago, though eighty, remains an original writer. [Brian Evenson]

Maurice Blanchot. *Aminadab.* Trans. and intro. Jeff Fort. Univ. of Nebraska Press, 2002. 199 pp. Paper: $22.00.

It is only within the last ten to fifteen years that Maurice Blanchot's work has found its way into English translation, and he still remains relatively unknown. One of the most important authors of fiction and theory, Blanchot's work continually challenges the limits of form and language, continually forces us to question what we know and how we put that knowledge (if it in fact exists) into a language that always resists us. *Aminadab,* the last of Blanchot's narrative works to be translated into English, now allows us to view his work in its entirety. Written in 1942, *Aminadab* is Blanchot's second novel, and in it he leads us on a journey with his protagonist, Thomas, as he makes his way through a bizarre boardinghouse. Believing a woman has gestured for him to enter, Thomas quickly becomes lost in the house's multitudinous interior spaces, and he encounters a range of grotesque characters along the way. Clearly Blanchot means for us to see the novel as an allegory, but this novel—perhaps more than his other fictional work—holds together as a "novel." In Blanchot's other work, the line between the fictional and the theoretical is far less distinguishable (*The Step Not Beyond* comes most readily to mind). As with other translations of Blanchot, this edition from the University of Nebraska Press includes an excellent introduction by Jeff Fort. Nebraska has been at the forefront of bringing Blanchot's work into English translation (along with Stanford UP, among others), and this volume, with Fort's introduction, joins earlier translations by Ann Smock of *The Space of Literature* and *The Writing of the Disaster* as some of the most important work on Blanchot in English thus far. [Jason D. Fichtel]

Edward Desautels. *Flicker in the Porthole Glass.* Mammoth, 2002. 277 pp. Paper: $17.95.

Edward Desautels's intriguing first novel offers a disturbing—and eerily riveting—account of the dilemma posed by our cultural addiction to film, how we have been given new license to disregard the heft of the real world and relish the sturdy pleasure-prison of the movie house. Jack Ruineux, a projectionist in a run-down Philadelphia movie theater and a struggling writer pounding out on his ancient Royal typewriter an enthralling word-picture of late-century urban streetlife, is trapped in the tension between projections, the ones that flicker by him at work and his own fictional persona, which he types into reality as he endures the long hours in the booth. That fictional projection embodies what Ruineux fears he will become: a decrepit old man living out his closing days amid the roaches and stench of a flophouse in Philadelphia (itself a city that participates effortlessly in two tenses simultaneously). The riveting "recollections" of Ruineux's fictional projection create the novel's difficult tension: Ruineux, a young man nevertheless already in ruins who resists confronting the difficult upbringing that has left him with such diminished expectations and who prefers writing in a sort of creepy fast-forward about the burned-out ends of this doppelganger's lost life. Counterpoised against Ruineux's internal shadowshow of crossed projections is the tonic offered by the vibrant Jasmine: the generous benediction of the sweet press of the real and of imperfect love as a way out of the narrowed dead ends and awful loneliness of Ruineux's imagination. Although the deft handling of such cross-narratives is compelling and the handling of cinema metaphors striking, the achievement here is Desautels's prose, an aural event both jagged and elegant, assaultive and inviting, that moves with the clipped, dangerous, urgent kinesis of hard bop jazz. [Joseph Dewey]

Jorge Volpi. *In Search of Klingsor*. Trans. Kristina Cordero. Scribner, 2002. 414 pp. $26.00.

In Search of Klingsor revolves around Francis Bacon, a young American physicist sent to Germany in the aftermath of World War II to investigate inconsistencies in the Nuremberg hearings. While reading the transcripts, he stumbles upon a reference to "Klingsor," a mysterious personage who apparently controlled all of the scientific funding during the Nazi reign. Bacon becomes obsessed with finding Klingsor and enlists the help of a mathematician named Gustav Links. They visit a number of the great scientific figures of the twentieth century in an attempt to uncover Klingsor's real identity. This novel does have a number of "spy story" elements, but it's a mistake to dismiss this book as merely a thriller, and readers looking for something in that vein will end up very disappointed. To get a structural idea of how the thriller genre is subverted, one simply has to look at how the Klingsor storyline is introduced. The first mention of Klingsor occurs on page thirty-six, setting up what is believed to be the main plot of the book. After this, though, the reader is presented with one hundred pages of only tangentially relevant background material on Bacon, which, more importantly, is told through a series of hypotheses and disquisitions that attempt to demonstrate the interaction between scientific theories and life. This interplay of essay and art points to what Volpi is really up to in this book. As a member of the "Crack" group—a handful of young Mexican writers who have renounced American neorealism and magical realism in favor of the literary experiments of Fuentes and Cortázar—Volpi is much more concerned with the form the novel takes than with relating an action-packed story. The novel's overall structure develops out of three disparate sections, and along with the subtle shifts that alter the course of the narration this is the most interesting aspect of the book. Overall, this is an impressive and playful English-language debut from an author likely to become one of Mexico's premier writers. [Chad W. Post]

Karin Boye. *Kallocain*. Trans. Gustaf Lannestock. Intro. Richard B. Vowles. Univ. of Wisconsin Press, 2002. 193 pp. Paper: $17.95.

The world is more like it is now than it ever was before, Dwight Eisenhower said late in his second term as president, and if that were less apparent when Swedish poet Karin Boye published *Kallocain* in 1940, shortly before her suicide, it has become more and more true with each successive publication of the novel in English in 1966, 1985, and 2002. This time *Kallocain* reads as if it were today's news, not something written sixty years ago. *Kallocain* is the memoir of chemist Leo Kall, written in prison, and, like *1984*, documents the control of a totalitarian state over its citizens. Kall had helped support the state through his invention of a drug, kallocain, which caused those injected with it to reveal their innermost thoughts. However, his success only increases his insecurity. It leads him to betray both his colleague and his wife, and he comes to understand that his life had not only been destructive but also indifferent. (His imprisonment under the new rulers, he notes, is little different from his freedom in the previous regime.) Boye had joined the international worker movement Clarté and in 1928 made a trip to Russia. She was disillusioned by what she saw and further disillusioned by a trip to Germany in 1932. Neither the East nor the West offered any possibility of human life, and *Kallocain* became the work, she wrote her publisher, that she had to do. Peter Weiss gives it a place of importance in *The Aesthetics of Resistance* as an exemplary act of resistance. "She anticipated all this destructive energy of the super powers," he says, "which have rendered the individual human being totally powerless." The longer we live today, the more Boye's *Kallocain* or Marina Tsetaeva's *The Ratcatcher* seem like texts of our time. [Robert Buckeye]

Nazim Hikmet. *Human Landscapes from My Country: An Epic Novel in Verse*. Trans. Randy Blasing and Mutlu Konuk. Foreword Edward Hirsch. Persea, 2002. 466 pp. $39.95.

Hikmet's massive twentieth-century epic dramatizes in poetic dialogue several extended episodes of a people's fervent struggle for liberty. The poet's sharply etched representative scenes from Turkish life under and in resistance to late Ottoman rule, alternately pathetic, impassioned, and poignantly humorous, illuminate generations of long-suppressed, frustrated aspirations. Restlessly awaiting freedom's eventual triumph over political oppression, poverty, and ignorance, Hasan Shevket, Mustafa the poet, the political prisoner Halil, and many other memorable dramatis personae relentlessly assail the ponderous machinery of tyranny. In a stirring cavalcade celebrating humble, ordinary people's yearning and ardor, the words and deeds of these partisans-in-spite-of-themselves celebrate their ceaseless, uphill struggle for liberty. Hikmet's poetic line is terse, staccato, conversational in its deceptive informality, while rhythmical variation and repetition create a narrative ebb and flow punctuated by moments of epiphany as someone finds his role, another his voice, to combat centuries of peonage. Hikmet's unabashed communist politics, for which he languished in prison or exile most of his adult life, are reflected in vignettes of idealized "Ivans" of soldierly valor and of real-life heroes, "Tanya" the teenaged Russian revolutionary and the Nazi-martyred journalist Gabriel Peri. Still, the poet's most profound sympathies lie with the poor man striving to sustain himself and his family in pursuit of a fleeting happiness. Living out prolonged confinement for political activities, dreaming of his wife and child as blindness threatens and days become years, unbowed Halil recalls the poet's own situation, a cynosure of what an entire culture was forced to endure. Ultimately Hikmet's art suggests a spaciousness, a grandeur in the details of poor people seeking just to breathe while events portend an invidious recurrence of suffering for love, ambition, misfortune—for living. Finally available complete in English, Hikmet's hauntingly eloquent masterpiece never flags. [Michael Pinker]

Murray Bail. *Camouflage*. Farrar, Straus & Giroux, 2002. 195 pp. $20.00.

Australian writer Murray Bail is mainly noted as a novelist, but he's also produced a small body of short fiction that's at last available in the U.S. *Camouflage* assembles fourteen stories (eleven more than the UK edition with the same title, be warned), comprising a tidy overview of his career. It's hard to tell which of the pieces are of recent vintage, first because the publisher provides no provenances, but more importantly because they're all equally fresh and equally timeless. Whatever setting Bail depicts, whether it be a suburban backyard, a competitive office, or a reverent museum, he subtly defamiliarizes it, always making it seem new and often rendering it positively uncanny. His style is flexible enough to paint perfect verbal portraits and to experiment with formal boundaries, sometimes in the same paragraph. His prose is economical, almost terse at times, suggestive far beyond what it makes explicit. While there's no mistaking Bail's voice, several other authors sprang to mind as I read these stories— Penelope Fitzgerald for her compression of ideas, Steven Millhauser for his dreaminess, Robert Coover for his innovation—and what they all have in common is their confident mastery. Like them, Bail is an assured writer in perfect command, able to achieve any effect he might wish. He can be sedate or shocking by turns, and is frequently funny in either mode, but the most prevalent tone in this volume is one of detached melancholy, as when he writes, "She sat at my kitchen table one afternoon and wept uncontrollably. How can words, particularly 'wept uncontrollably,' convey her sadness (her self-pity)? Philosophers other than myself have discussed the inadequacy of words." Whatever truth there may be in the discussions of those philosophers, there's no inadequacy in *Camouflage*. [James Crossley]

Dave Eggers. *You Shall Know Our Velocity*. McSweeney's, 2002. 371 pp. $22.00.

Y.S.K.O.V.'s narrative—two guys attempt to travel the world, giving away thousands of guiltily gotten dollars to whomever they decide deserves or needs it—begins on the cover, continues onto the inside front, and proceeds without a break until the final page. This urgency, literal and thematic, is countered by the narrator's spiritual impotence: he wants "every option, simultaneously," but we soon realize that he wouldn't know what to do with those options were they available to him. He's like one of Mark

Pauline's self-destructing machines, the frames of which are too weak for the strength of their motors: his heart is big beyond his ability to follow through, a will with no way, and he tends to end up flopping around in helpless, indecisive fury. (His name is Will, not incidentally.) Eggers's first novel is both sort of slight—it's basically a Road Novel; there've been a few—and startlingly earnest and profound. With *A Heartbreaking Work etc.* Eggers pushed snarkiness to the limit of readers' endurance. It was fun, but relentless, and left you feeling a little like you'd been spoken down to. Here he moves to something more heartfelt, wrestling with sincerity in a complicated and pitiless world. Will, bearing an uncanny verbal and characteristic resemblance to the Eggers of *Heartbreaking,* isn't recoiling from modernity so much as he's stumbling from it, overwhelmed, driving the multiplicity-of-truths concept further by accepting all truths simultaneously. Throw in some comfortable-white-American-male guilt and the consequence is a man so stunned by modern discord that he can function only in fits. When the guys, following whims, ask airline agents to suggest destinations, the agents respond by asking them where they want to go. They don't know; they want to be told. Their velocity is that of flux: they writhe in place. [Tim Feeney]

Jean-Philippe Toussaint. *Faire l'amour.* Les Éditions de Minuit, 2002. 179 pp. €13.00.

The first sentence of Jean-Philippe Toussaint's latest novel offers a scene that is chilling enough for anyone: "I had filled a flask with hydrochloric acid, and I always carried it with me, thinking that one day I would throw it in somebody's face." The narrator of this tale, anonymous like Toussaint's other protagonists, doesn't have anyone particular in mind. But the principal candidate would seem to be Marie, his companion of seven years. He and Marie are falling out of love, violently and ineluctably. For her part, Marie opines that one day he will throw the acid in his own face; and the narrator is forced to admit that this is not beyond the realm of possibility. Chekhov once suggested that if there is a shotgun on the wall in act 1, it had better go off in act 3, and this shotgun will be fired, too—but not quite in the direction we might have expected.

Faire l'amour (Making Love) is Toussaint's seventh book for the Editions de Minuit, in a career inaugurated in 1985 with the quirky and splendid novel *La Salle de bain* (The Bathroom). This tale is darker than any he has told in the past. The absurdist qualities that Toussaint has always put on display in his writing are present here, but they are considerably leavened by the grimness of the problem with which the narrator and Marie grapple. The story is set in Tokyo, where Marie, a fashion designer, has been invited to exhibit her latest collection. For good or for ill, the narrator has come along for the ride. It is a Tokyo beset by cold, by snow, and by darkness, both literal and spiritual. Jet-lagged and ill, abstracted from the banality of their everyday life in Paris and the anesthetic habits of the quotidian, living for once face-to-face, these two people are forced to come to terms with the fact that neither loves the other in the way that they once did: "We loved each other," says the narrator, "but we could no longer bear to be with each other." The earthquakes that recur with regularity during their stay in Tokyo serve only to remind this couple of the seismic nature of their own relationship. Catastrophe comes in many different shapes, of course, and Toussaint speculates incisively on how people react to disaster, whether that disaster be natural or personal. Love is a telluric force, he argues. If the earth moves when people make love, it can move just as powerfully when love is unmade, too. [Warren Motte]

Sam Shepard. *Great Dream of Heaven*. Knopf, 2002. 142 pp. $20.00.

Although these startling stories demonstrate Shepard's obsessive themes—the broken family, the search for salvation, the edge of hysteria—they should be read as innovative. Shepard is indeed a writer who can employ his talent in various genres. "The Remedy Man," which introduces the collection, is told by a young narrator who is fascinated by a horse trainer. The trainer, unlike his own father, is able to do things properly—to fix chaos. There are parallel relationships—Shepard is always interested in duets of violence. (Look, for example, at *True West,* which details the "crossing" of brothers.) Although Shepard is at his best in his portrayal of the father-son relationships represented here, he is able to capture a strange, hysterical perspective, which changes suddenly in all of the stories: "I could see the horse's eyeball roll back and catch me perched above him. I could see everything turned around, from his perspective." "Blinking Eye" is another wonderful story. The woman, carrying her mother's cremated ashes, tries to be careful while she drives toward her destination. Suddenly she sees a hawk diving down at her window: "The hawk suddenly goes completely berserk and busts out of its sweatshirt bondage, shrieking like a banshee." The surrealistic turns and counterturns—again, swirling perspectives!—force us to accept that there is no stability of vision, no ordered reality. The driver, the hawk, the mother (in ashes), seem to merge so that it is impossible to see clearly. These lines convey the hysterical movement: "Her face is coated with ashes. She can feel them clinging to her lips as she runs her tongue across them. Her mother tastes like salt." "Remedy Man" becomes horse becomes youthful narrator. Hawk and mother and daughter are thrust together. Is it any wonder that we are terrified by Shepard's stories of explosive change? [Irving Malin]

Blaise Cendrars. *To the End of the World*. Trans. Alan Brown. Peter Owen/Dufour Editions, 2002. 253 pp. Paper: $19.95.

Blaise Cendrars (1887-1961) had a stimulating and askew view of the world, developed by his life as an adventurer, as a filmmaker, and as a soldier in the First World War, in which he lost an arm. Though a modernist

poet and novelist, he stands outside all isms. His economical style and poetic eye are in service to an extravagant imagination. *To the End of the
World* (1956) is a roman à clef set in the post-WWII Parisian theater scene.
The opening pages are typically Cendrarian, merging violent sex with war
atrocities and physical sickness. Sentences propelled by strong verbs create
an intense and rich oratorical flow, while the characters, depicted first as
ordinary beings, are soon converted, in a natural progression, into larger-
than-life creations. One of the seemingly paradoxical delights of Cendrars
is that when he references historical events or inserts real people (in this
novel, Mallarmé, George Moore, Dégas), the reader can barely refrain from
interrogating what's presented. When Cendrars includes himself, as he
does here (and as he did more explicitly in *Moravagine,* from 1926, well
translated by Alan Brown in 1968), he deliberately invites investigation of
the novel's veracity. On that last point, this edition lets one down somewhat. Advertised as part of the book is an introduction by Margaret
Crosland, but it is missing. It appeared in the 1991 hardcover and, while
brief, helpfully described the novel's setting. Additionally, the translation,
from 1966, is too dated and too British for such a singular stylist. Yet
Cendrars in English is hard to find, so every edition is welcome. His oeuvre
runs to several volumes in French. It would benefit from a North American
publisher dedicated to bringing Cendrars's complete works to English readers in a contemporary language and manner. [Jeff Bursey]

Victor Beilis. *"The Rehabilitation of Freud" and "Bakhtin and Others."*
Trans., intro., and afterword Richard Grose. Other Press, 2002. 127 pp.
$20.00.

I'm just a casual reader of Russian literature, and yet even I can see
that something remarkable was happening in the last years of the Soviet regime. Last year saw into English Leonid Tsypkin's extraordinary
book *Summer in Baden-Baden,* which counterposed a retelling of
Dostoyevsky's period at the resort city with the narrator's visit to the
Dostoyevsky museum in St. Petersburg. This year sees the publication in
one volume of two novellas by Victor Beilis, one of which, *Bakhtin and
Others,* is clearly a comic masterpiece. It tells the fictional tale of the literary theorist M. M. Bakhtin, who, in the effort to finish an essay on the
rules governing the relationship between author and character, rents a
room in a dacha owned by a family—an unfaithful wife, a tyrannical
grandfather, a kleptomaniac teenager—whose problems so absorb
Bakhtin's attention that he cannot pull himself away from the domestic
drama long enough to write about the author's struggle to separate himself from the characters he has created out of himself. For all of the ironies
and philosophical play, *Bakhtin and Others* develops characters of flesh
and blood. In *The Rehabilitation of Freud* the characters never quite overcome the ideas they embody. The central figure, Volodya, is a person so
obsessed with and so self-conscious of his incestuous desires for his

mother that he cannot form a relationship with any woman and ends up unconsciously committing suicide. But a true Freudian reading would suggest that although Volodya *thinks* his problem is his love for mother, that obsession is a reaction-formation to cover up his anger and his more dangerous desire for his father. Richard Grose translates these difficult works into graceful, idiomatic English. I wait for more of Beilis to make it into English. [David Bergman]

Gary Lutz. *Stories in the Worst Way*. 3ʳᵈ Bed, 2002. 152 pp. Paper: $8.00.

There is no finer writer of sentences than Gary Lutz; his sentences are both original and sublime. In "Waking Hours," a story about a divorced middle-aged man who is often on the road, the protagonist describes his apartment: "My life was cartoned off in three rooms and bath, one of several dozen lives banked above a side street. I convinced myself that there were hours midway through the night when the walls slurred over and became membranes, allowing seepages and exchanges from unit to unit." With sentences like these, Lutz accomplishes two things. First, he forces his readers to slow down and relish the movement within each sentence. Second, his sentences force readers to reexamine the ordinary moments, the routine habits, of daily life. Throughout the collection, the first sentence often establishes the ethical inquiry of the story. "Slops" begins: "Because I had colitis, I divided much of my between-class time among seventeen carefully chosen faculty restrooms, never following the same itinerary two days in a row, using a pocket notebook to keep track." At a fundamental level, Lutz demonstrates that we understand the world through language. And, thankfully, Lutz is a careful observer. "Devotions," a story whose protagonist has had a series of wives, begins, "From time to time I show up in myself just long enough for people to know they are not in the room alone," and ends, "What was wrong was very simple. Sometimes her life and mine fell on the same day." *Stories in the Worst Way* is one of the finest short-story collections of the last decade. 3ʳᵈ Bed is to be commended for reprinting the collection, first published in 1996 by Knopf. [Alan Tinkler]

Jerome Charyn. *The Isaac Quartet: Blue Eyes, Marilyn the Wild, The Education of Patrick Silver, Secret Isaac*. Four Walls Eight Windows, 2002. 610 pp. $35.00.

Jerome Charyn is a writer of extraordinary power, one of America's great originals. His supercharged language pushes itself and readers almost to the point of hysteria, each sentence carrying more pure narrative drive, more fascination and surprise, than multiple pages of other writers. Sentence after sentence rolls from his hand like fate's own dice, each a perfect small chapter, gnomic, expansive: beautiful and grotesque at the same time. Wanting always to "find the magic," Charyn has little interest in the discarded husks of daily life. ("I am not interested in impersonation, I am interested in hallucination.") His work ranges widely—from the satire of *Tar Baby* to the loose magic realism of *War Cries over Avenue C* and *The Paradise Man*, from sui generis "conjured autobiographies" such as *The Catfish Man* and *Pinocchio's Nose* to what may well be the ultimate novel of paranoia, *Death of a Tango King*—but at the center of it all there's an essential Charyn. That Charyn, a moralist in some crucial way, wants simultaneously to bear true witness, to dance on reality's bones, and to write endlessly re-readable books. Profound ambition here, and talent to match. It was in these four proto-mysteries, first published in 1974 through 1978, that Charyn hammered out, on the anvil of a seemingly commercial fiction, both a vision of America and a style that struggles to convey that vision in all its sensory variegation, all its physical and emotional bludgeoning, all its unforgiving duplicities. [James Sallis]

Juan Goytisolo. *State of Siege*. Trans. Helen Lane. City Lights, 2002. 155 pp. Paper: $13.95.

Juan Goytisolo's career has moved in an ever-widening circle of cultural excavation and exploration of literary form, becoming more enmeshed in his recurrent themes of exile, war, and Spain's suppressed Moorish cultural history. The latest reverberation of these motifs, *State of Siege*, combines them with Goytisolo's more recent thematic interest in the Arab world and is a well-crafted, dexterous novel whose slimness belies its reach. Like his mentor Jean Genet, Goytisolo is an exacting writer, eliciting the most meaning possible from his words to the advantage and delight of his reader. Set during the siege of Sarajevo, *State of Siege* provides the reader with the building blocks of a story, an assortment of texts centered on a mystery: the corpse of a Spanish visitor has disappeared, leaving behind writings signed with the initials J. G. These and various other texts involved in the mystery compose the novel—J. G.'s stories and homoerotic poems; the investigating major's reports; descriptions of dreams that J. G. sent to a government functionary before his death; and the explanations given by a hotel employee and his cohorts. The reader joins various characters in trying to construct the "real" events from parallel texts that never coalesce, and in doing so walks a tightrope between literature and war, concepts that are closely tied in the world Goytisolo creates. The book explores the power of language in a war-torn city: it is both the prime target of the besiegers, who aim to wipe out the city's collective memory, and the only weapon of the besieged, who fight their loss of freedom through humor and erudition. By creating an uneasy tension between the book and its components, Goytisolo exposes the most basic quality of consciousness that both feeds on and creates literature, the part that spawns violence and madness, humor and language. [Megan A. McDowell]

A. M. Homes. *Things You Should Know*. HarperCollins, 2002. 213 pp. $23.95.

Many of the characters in A. M. Homes's latest collection of stories are look-ing for something, often something they seem unable to name. This wanting can reach spectacular heights, and so it's no real surprise to find that the resulting tension is what tends to sustain the stories' narrative tide. This said, even the most ordinary of constructs has the potential to turn foreign or foreboding under Homes's fictive care. Like a soggy paper left to dry in the sun, the borders of these stories curl, Homes's characters and their workaday lives left warped. For Homes's fans, the landscapes of these fictions will be happily familiar: a hyperreal *now,* a suburban Gothic full of menace, where sprinkler systems and shady lanes offer little relief from the pain and dys-function in their midst. Familiar too will be the shaky couples unable to con-nect (with each other or their children or their immigrant help), the sex-addled adolescents, and the aging parents who grow more alien each day. That's not to say that these stories are merely derivative of ones past. Rather, *Things You Should Know* possesses a mature polish and, in many places, a disturbing emotional punch that speaks of Homes at the very top of her game. As for the characters, they seek, in essence, a sense of self; a search usually bungled by a desire to belong. When Homes is going strong, these di-oramas of angst are works of wonderful simplicity and keen detail, where perspective is always slightly askew. Take, for example, the tightly wound woman who's "killed" (dropped) a favorite plant: "I can't bear it. I need to be reminded of beauty," she moans, until her teenaged daughter soberly clari-fies that the thing's "not dead . . . It's just upside down." Such exchanges are Homes's forte and, in this collection, rarely disappoint. [Stacey Gottlieb]

Jeff VanderMeer and Forrest Aguirre, eds. *Leviathan 3: Libri quosdam ad sciéntiam, álios ad insaniam deduxére.* Ministry of Whimsy, 2002. 468 pp. Paper: $21.95.

This third installment in the *Leviathan* anthology series bills itself as a showcase of "fantastical fiction." But to get a sense of this anthology, it's more useful to note that the oxymoron of the publisher's name comes from Orwell's *1984* than it is to think of the occult or big-bosomed space heroines. In seeing how many ways the bounds of the "real" can be stretched, the an-thology also reaffirms how uncategorizable literature can be when prac-ticed as a freewheeling art-form. Borges is clearly an important influence in the editorial selection, while the anthology's Latin subtitle serves as an Umberto Eco-esque riddle whose significance really does emerge, as the in-troduction says it will, while readers wander the "libraries" that make up this book. Along the way, the anthology presents consistently strong work by some twenty authors, including exemplary short works by Michael Moorcock and Tamar Yellin. Lance Olsen's "Village of the Mermaids," a lineated meditation on time coming apart during the disintegration of an airliner, lays bare the pensive substrate of most of his fiction. "The Progenitor," a language-intense story by Brian Evenson, is almost a cubist painting in words, the disjunctions Evenson creates between his and normal vocabulary-usage underscoring the consequences of the unthinking acceptance of legacies. Likewise, the poetic lyricism of Rikki Ducornet's prose is enough to seduce a reader through "Buz," even if her descriptions of an imaginary land by that name didn't offer the insights that they do on their own. Jeffrey Ford's "The Weight of Words," a story about a man who has discovered a means to convey meaning through the physicality of written language, is both philosophical and funny: a story that, like *Leviathan 3* itself, is a potent antidote to the quotidian thinking (and writing) that infuses much of mainstream life. [Steve Tomasula]

Frederic Tuten. *The Green Hour*. Norton, 2002. 265 pp. $24.95.

Frederic Tuten has already given us an ultra-experimental collage-novel (*The Adventures of Mao on the Long March,* 1971), a telescoped historical biography (*Tallien: A Brief Romance,* 1988), a political novel populated by comic-book characters (*Tintin in the New World,* 1993), and a time-warp tribute to an iconic artist (*Van Gogh's Bad Café,* 1997)—an acrobatic oeuvre by any standard. *The Green Hour,* Tuten's most conventional book to date, is written without recourse to the jaw-dropping juxtapositions that give such piquancy to the earlier work. It is a love story narrated in the third person from the viewpoint of a female protagonist, Dominique, an American art-historian who has shifted focus from the nightmare world of Goya to the neoclassical idealism of Poussin, and who is unable to choose between two lovers: the lefty vagabond, political activist, and bohemian Rex (all passion, no commitment) and the cultivated entrepreneur Eric (millionaire, much more sensible choice). Wealth, Tuten reminds us, is the prerequisite of the artistic high. "[Money] lifted you like a balloon above the earth, where human sadness and its blighted landscape vanished, leaving visible from that height and silence only the earth's ravishing contours, shapes, colors and forms." This novel will tickle academics on either side of the gulf of incomprehension that separates graying "formalists" from politically engaged new-model scholars. It is also a brave exercise in character imagination, strong on the psychological nuances of infatuation. Even as Tuten employs mellow narrative techniques to evoke, for once, his own time and milieu (New York academia, with sojourns in Paris and Madrid), he keeps sinuous faith with his key concern: the necessity of art. A novel by Frederic Tuten is always an event and a new departure. [Philip Landon]

José Carlos Somoza. *The Athenian Murders.* Trans. Sonia Soto. Farrar, Straus & Giroux, 2002. 262 pp. $24.00.

John Gardner once referred to the novel as a "vivid and continuous dream." José Carlos Somoza explores the more unsettling implications of this statement in *The Athenian Murders.* Somoza's novel takes the form of a translated ancient Greek manuscript centered on the mysterious death of Tramachus, a promising student at Plato's Academy in Athens. When Tramachus's bloody body is recovered from the city's outskirts, authorities at first suspect an attack by wolves. But Heracles Pontor, known as the Decipherer of Enigmas, is not convinced. Heracles, an ancient analogue of Poe's C. Auguste Dupin, embarks on his own investigation, which leads from the placid gardens of the Academy to the decadent artistic and religious underground of Athens. While this mystery unfolds, a parallel narrative develops in the form of the translator's footnotes to the text. The translator believes that *The Athenian Murders* is an "eidetic text" containing words and images that are meant to convey a secret message to readers. As the translation proceeds, the translator begins to see references to himself within the story that cause him to question not only his own perceptions of reality but the nature of reality itself. It is now commonplace to see language as a problematic way of articulating experience, but Somoza's complex narrative evokes this idea with eerie plausibility as the translator confronts the disturbing sense that language is the *only* reality. Both writing and reading become dangerous acts that test the limits of understanding. The thrill of this novel comes from both its ingeniously structured mystery plot and the larger questions it raises about what constitutes knowledge and experience. Language itself becomes a central character whose tenuous yet oppressive power is vividly rendered, albeit only fictional. Or is it? [Pedro Ponce]

Robert Walser. *Selected Stories.* Trans. Christopher Middleton, et al. New York Review Books, 2002. 196 pp. Paper: $12.95.

Robert Walser's short prose fills fourteen volumes, ten of which he published before permanently entering the sanatorium in which he spent the final twenty-three years of his life (later telling a friend that he was there not "to write, but to be mad"). *Selected Stories,* which reprints the 1982 Farrar, Straus & Giroux collection (same title, same translations, same preface, same everything), contains forty-two pieces written between 1907 and 1929—just a few years before the author's 1933 retreat from the world. Prior to his career in mental illness, Walser had been a prolific feuilletonist and contributor to magazines, a butler, an eccentric among the artistes of Berlin, and the often penniless former employee of one employer or another. Admired by Franz Kafka, Christian Morgenstern, and Hermann Hesse, Walser's work has been described by his translator Christopher Middleton as "sketches, soliloquies, improvisations, arabesques, and capriccios," as "miniature impressions, gossipings, entertainments, anecdotes, parables." Walser himself saw his prose pieces as fragments of a never-ending novel, "a variously sliced-up or torn-apart book about myself." However classified, these pieces have been sliced from one interesting melon, a mind unlike anyone else's; one, in Middleton's words again, of "perfect and serene oddity." Whether Walser is conjuring the precocious daughter of a Berlin art dealer or imagining the German writer Heinrich von Kleist on vacation, knocking off a mock job application or meditating on women's trousers, soaring in a balloon above the things that torment him or taking "a little ramble" through the splendidly ordinary mountains, the narrator is likely to sound "a little worn out, raddled, squashed, downtrodden" ("Nervous"). He invariably seems a "small, pale, timid, weak, elegant, silly little fellow" who, when doing his little dance of words, nevertheless manages to forget that he is "nothing but a happy floating-in-the-air" ("Helbling's Story"). [Brooke Horvath]

Gao Xingjian. *One Man's Bible*. Trans. Mabel Lee. HarperCollins, 2002. 464 pp. $26.95.

Gao Xingjian's newly translated novel is a fictionalization of his life during China's political upheaval in the 1960s and seventies. Readers with little or no knowledge of the Cultural Revolution will find *One Man's Bible* bewildering and possibly nonsensical, as Gao never offers any historical background. The absence of any explanation for the warring Mao factions, the public disavowal of loving parents by their children, and the mindless bloodshed that all defined the era hint that the author finds it incomprehensible himself. Through his fictionalized experience, Gao seeks to transform the futility and massive human waste of Mao's hyperpolitical nightmare into a personal manifesto for living well—the bible of the novel's title. Gao's nameless narrator moves from a first-person voice to a second- and a third-, and these narrative variations are inconsistent and unpredictable. This narrative blending conveys the schizophrenia of the Cultural Revolution, during which the narrator had to articulate beliefs that were not his own in order to survive, all the while preserving his own thoughts and moral integrity deep in his mind. This practice led to an intense personal philosophy wherein the narrator became his own God and disciple, a defiant solution to the political turmoil that threatened to physically and mentally squash him. Oddly enough, the novel's premise is that the narrator is relating his experience of the Cultural Revolution to his lover in near present-day Hong Kong in between lovemaking sessions. Even though Gao's intense eroticism makes a strange bedfellow for the revelations concerning China's bitter past, this unique pairing gives the book a tenderness and desperation it might otherwise lack. Gao's ability to detach himself from the political fervor of the Cultural Revolution enabled him to endure and later give his country its first Nobel Prize winner in letters. [Jason Picone]

Stephen Dixon. *I*. McSweeney's, 2002. 338 pages. $18.00.

Characteristically enough for a book published by McSweeney's, Stephen Dixon's fascinating new novel, *I.,* begins on the cover. There, an "I" and an accompanying period have been cut into the cloth and cardboard, through which we see an I-shaped section of a sketch beneath: a man's eye centering the book and with an expression one might describe as "blank." Upon opening the novel, we discover that the sketch is of the author himself, the expression, seen now in full, replete with anxiety. Far from a mere promotional gimmick, this visual pun proves the book's major concern, as the novel forces us to question the author lying behind the narrative I/eye—" 'I am not I.,' he's tempted to say"—the degree to which the first-person pronoun is always shorthand for something that cannot be entirely represented. The novel is broken into nineteen highly unified chapters, each of which could stand as its own story, in which readers encounter a middle-aged writer caring for his daughters and a wife with a debilitating disease. Beyond this, there is little narrative arc, but rather a series of dense, third-person monologues in which "I." appears as an abbreviation. But the real triumph of Dixon's work is the emotional power generated by close attention to the specificities of the protagonist's interaction with his wife and family, as well as the meditations upon an anger "I." struggles to understand. The author brings us in close contact with a situation that, in a lesser writer's hands, could so easily have turned sentimental but in Dixon's becomes a moving examination of the tensions between art and life, between private and public responsibility, between the "I" that so readily reveals itself and the "I." that remains, even to itself, a mystery. [Aaron Gwyn]

Lynn Crawford. *Simply Separate People.* Black Square/Hammer, 2002. 183 pp. Paper: $14.00.

Lynn Crawford is the sort of writer who is very difficult to pin down; each book feels at once entirely hers but at the same time not like the others. Her first book was a collection of odd, sometimes oblique stories that were compared to the early fiction of John Hawkes. Her second, *Blow,* was a sort of surreal fairy-tale about the people who live at the base of the imaginary Mount Anf. Her latest, the novel *Simply Separate People,* exchanges the overt strangeness of these first two for a quieter, realistic, yet nevertheless quirky story. The book is narrated by four women, their voices alternating, as they reveal themselves and others. At first seemingly disconnected strangers, it soon becomes clear that all are tied together in unexpected ways. Physh, who narrates the most sections, is a woman who has lost her family in an accident. She and her boyfriend DR (who has also lost his family) are trying to reach a point of stability. Physh takes a dogsitting job, which leads her to meet a woman running a gas station whom she refers to as Pumper, to a seamstress, and finally to a woman who runs a preschool. Each has her story, each has her quirks and obsessions. Crawford carefully balances the intensity and oddness of their private lives with a good portion of humor. Pumper's boyfriend, for instance, stops sleeping with her, instead taking midnight walks where he has pseudosexual experiences with a tree. What is remarkable is Crawford's ability to integrate the outlandish with a complex narrative structure in such a way as to create a work that appeals both on the level of story and aesthetically. *Simply Separate People* is Crawford's most ambitious and most fully realized book. Taken together with her earlier books, it shows her to be a varied and consummate writer. [Brian Evenson]

Mikhail Epstein. *Cries in the New Wilderness: From the Files of the Moscow Institute of Atheism.* Trans. and intro. Eve Adler. Paul Dry Books, 2002. 236 pp. Paper: $15.95.

Cries in the New Wilderness does not read like a novel. It purports to reprint an obscure 1985 research study in Soviet political sociology, *The New Sectarianism,* edited by Professor Raissa O. Gubaydulina of the former Institute of Atheism, along with selected reviews, selections from Gubaydulina's literary archives, and a tribute to the late professor. Yet in doing so, Mikhail Epstein takes on more than state-sponsored scholarship. Allegedly the official counterpart of samizdat, Gubaydulina's "Reference Manual" examines numerous species of native religious enthusiasm, the contemporary fringe of faith. Her contributors have sifted classified intelligence, so the story goes, sorting and distributing distinctive subspecies among so-called Everyday, Philistine, Nationalist, Atheist, Doomsday, and Literary sects. Passages from sources identified only by authors' initials glorify the peculiar dogmas and devotions of, among others, Bloodbrothers, Sinnerists, and Steppies. Yet the absurdity of these avant-garde sects' "religio-mystical" practices undercuts their legitimacy, despite the fulminations of a careful cross-section of reviewers. If such niche denominations portray a desperate hunger for faith, especially among the intelligentsia, they can be taken only half-seriously. The joke is on Epstein's doughty Marxist-Leninist editor, alert to the dangers to materialism but unable to stem the tide. Efforts by Gubaydulina and her cohort to obliterate all worship but to the State became passé in Russia and elsewhere. Still, whether descanting on the glories of spilt blood, the sacrificial necessity of sin, or the irresistible allure of open spaces, these imagined sectarians may indeed represent a yearning for spiritual succor that continues to haunt the land. If so, Mikhail Epstein, literary critic and cultural theoretician, here takes aim not only at social scientific research but also the insufficiency of traditional religious practices to satisfy a rising generation. And his aim, if not his manner, seems true. [Michael Pinker]

Eckhard Gerdes. *Cistern Tawdry.* Fugue State, 2003. Unpaginated. Paper: $18.00.

"Language connects. To disconnect, language must be discarded. Freedom cannot result from socialization—only indebtedness can. If you learn a lan-

guage." Except that the characters in *Cistern Tawdry* keep connecting, even
as they die and split into other selves, even as their language appears to be
unraveling: "you think you can refrain from meaningful communication?
Impossible!" With multiple disruptions of continuity, *Cistern Tawdry* is a
story that creates meaning through visuality, fragmentation, collage, witty
wordplay, and humor, as well as narration. Although the text at first appears
daunting, Gerdes provides encouragement to readers in the "Editor's Foreword," where he offers explanations and interpretations of the first several
primary visual pages. Potential readers who continue on where the "Editor's
Foreword" leaves off will find themselves pleasantly enmeshed in the story of
Cistern Tawdry, a writer trapped in the midst of an unfulfilling job and failing marriage. After a night of drinking, he comes home to discover that his
wife has left him and taken their children with her. Cistern commits suicide,
and his soul splits into multiple pieces and personalities. The second half of
the book follows these parts in their heroic quest to reunite and return to the
earth. Any text requires the engagement of the reader in order to make
meaning. *Cistern Tawdry* highlights this aspect of reader interaction by presenting a text refreshingly unlike those we are used to interpreting—it demands active engagement on the part of the reader. Sometimes this
engagement requires effort as we attempt to decode unfamiliar signs, but it
is always delightful and surprising. [Lorraine Graham]

Christian Oster. *Dans le train*. Les Éditions de Minuit, 2002. 159 pp. €11.90.

The narrator of Christian Oster's ninth novel, *Dans le train* (In the Train),
is a man with a train to catch. Frank likes taking trains—any train at all; it
doesn't matter to him. More particularly, he takes trains in order to meet
women, hoping eventually to find one who might agree to spend the rest of
her life with him. Perhaps it's something about the rhythm of the train that
inspires Frank: I *think* I can, I *think* I can. . . . Anne, for her part, is taking
a train from Paris to Gournon in order to bed a novelist who happens to be
on a book tour there. But of course after Frank meets her on the train, his
plans for Anne are quite different.

Solitary and lonesome like many of Oster's protagonists, Frank is a very
diffident hero at best. He is plagued with an acute consciousness of his own
shortcomings as a social being. He is likewise cursed with an introspective
spirit, and the coldly critical gaze he casts on the least of his actions is the
source of a great deal of comedy in this novel. For despite his best intentions, Frank is no Lothario. The courtship he pays to Anne is a slavish,
stumbling one; and the likelihood of Frank crossing the finish line seems
dim. Yet he is nothing if not steadfast. Patient, true, and sincere in his love,
hope springs eternal in Frank's benighted breast. Undoubtedly, once in a
very blue moon, the world rewards human qualities such as those.

Oster plays maddeningly (and most delightfully) on those very qualities
in his novel, trifling with his reader's patience, straining his reader's cred-
ibility, testing his reader's semiotic desire. He hopes that we will take
Frank's quest upon ourselves, making it our own. It's a stretch, though, as
Oster himself is the first to realize. Frank is not like us—or so we would

dearly like to believe. His quest is a classic one nonetheless; and the travel topos in which it is cast is equally classic. Surely, *Dans le train* is not the *Odyssey,* nor *The Canterbury Tales,* nor yet *Don Quixote.* But it borrows elements from all of them, reconfiguring them in parodic fashion. What results from that process is a novel that is much like Frank himself. *Dans le train* argues that romance, whether it be the passion or the literary genre, is not entirely dead in our culture; that both stories and journeys respond to fundamental human needs; that the ordinary upon examination can prove to be extraordinary; and that every dog—however abysmally cynical we may be about such things—must at last have his day. [Warren Motte]

Ismail Kadare. *Spring Flowers, Spring Frost.* Trans. from the French of Jusuf Vrioni by David Bellos. Arcade, 2002. 182 pp. $23.95.

In Ismail Kadare's latest novel, Albania awakes from the isolation and terror it experienced under communist dictatorship. But this awakening is bittersweet. With all of the benefits of joining the modern European order come unforeseen problems: taxes, bank robberies, and the rebirth of the *kanun,* an ancient system of blood-debt and revenge that perpetuates an endless cycle of violence. Within this Albania we follow Mark Gurabardhi, a painter and minor governmental functionary, as he ponders the mysteries in his own life: his missing friend Zeb, the murder of his boss, the visit of his girlfriend's mysterious uncle and her subsequent disappearance, and the location of a secret archive of files used as blackmail during the communist era. Between the chapters that tell this story are a series of "counter-chapters" in which the writing breaks free from the restraints of naturalism and where Kadare shows his virtuosity as novelist and poet. The counter-chapters take diverse forms—folk tale, Greek myth, dream, and prose poem—but each is handled with masterful skill. Kadare's retelling of the Tantalus myth has Bulgakov's fantastic absurdity; it portrays the Ministry of Death as a vast bureaucracy with its endless forms and hierarchies. Zeus is a totalitarian dictator, employing spies and interrogating Tantalus behind closed doors in the "Great Prison," burying his crime under state-sponsored propaganda. In another scene of interrogation, the iceberg that sank the *Titanic* confesses, offering as a defense a meditation upon the divide between those born of heat and those born of ice, a boundary never to be crossed. This bizarrely touching meditation encapsules the eerie tone of the novel; it is as odd as it is elegiac, yet resists descending into bathos. [Matthew L. McAlpin]

Thomas Colchie, ed. *A Whistler in the Nightworld: Short Fiction from the Latin Americas.* Plume, 2002. 410 pp. Paper: $16.00.

As Thomas Colchie points out in his introduction to *A Whistler in the Nightworld,* one of the defining characteristics of new Latin American literature is its diverse, international nature. It is no longer possible to pigeonhole Latin American writing as falling under the influence of the "boom." And "magical realism" doesn't work any better. Actually, in the case of this anthology, there is a distinct, and intentional, lack of "magical realists." Instead these writers are very cosmopolitan and worldly. The subjects and styles of the stories range widely, from Pedro Juan Gutiérrez's darkly lyrical depiction of an afternoon in Havana trying to scam two tourists and then almost witnessing a shooting while waiting in line for a bottle of rum, to Mayra Montero's account of a man forced to recall a disturbing event from his youth that included the family's chauffeur splitting his head open in the gallery, to Edmundo Paz-Soldán's story of an eccentric crossword-puzzle maker who includes the name of a woman he is obsessed with in all of his puzzles. Two of the more interesting stories are by Ignacio Padilla and Jorge Volpi, both members of the "Crack" group. Volpi's "Ars Poetica" is a hysterical story that opens, "I'll begin the story with a statement of principles: I am a character and I am prepared to speak (badly) of the author of the books in which I appear." "Ars Poetica" demonstrates the influence world literatures have on one another, since it is obviously more in line with Flann O'Brien's *At Swim-Two-Birds* and Gilbert Sorrentino's *Mulligan Stew* than most Latin American authors (although Juan Onetti does come to mind). I wish only that other members of the "Crack" group had been included. [Chad W. Post]

Joe Ashby Porter. *Touch Wood*. Turtle Point, 2002. 192 pages. Paper: $15.95.

The ten stories in Joe Ashby Porter's fifth volume of fiction, *Touch Wood*, read like storybook fables, Gothic fantasy, eighteenth-century travel-journals, picaresque tales of disguise, and equatorial magical realism, with a contemporary American inflection. The collection is a curio box of fictions, opening with "A Man Wanted to Buy a Cat," which with its shopkeeper characters and snowy village setting has an air of a Hans Christian Andersen tale, and closing with the titular story, in which story folds in upon story like a Möbius strip. Porter's prose has a charmed quality, comprised as it is of subtle syncopation, incantatory syntax, and bracing diction, which even in the simplest descriptive passages can transport: "Nothing much here under the power lines humming in the lucency — bottle caps and such oddments, scraps, bones, ribbons and what not strewn among clumps of old wild dead grass and some green sprouting through, but little refuse." His prose is often tinctured with near-ludicrous imagery — "The cat groomed his wrist with its tiny rough tongue down into the palm, along the destiny line still welted from carpal tunnel surgery" — suggesting a suffusive wryness reminiscent of Tom Robbins. Ranging from eight to fifty-three pages in length, the stories compensate for their lack of traditional narrative shape with an organic narrative drift, confirming what the narrator of "Icehouse Burgess" remarks about his own tale, that "here . . . other aims rule" — making the stories like so much tinder readily kindled into a burning glow. [Peter Donahue]

Carol Emshwiller. *The Mount*. Small Beer, 2002. 232 pp. Paper: $16.00.

While science fiction has, since its inception as a genre, generally been dominated by commercial publishing houses and the demands of that popular market, there have always been active, scattered small presses bringing out the "other" science fiction—without them, we wouldn't have *The Demolished Man* or *Dune,* classics in the field that were originally small-press titles. Carol Emshwiller has been writing fantasy, speculative, and science fiction for many years; she has a dedicated cult following and has been an influence on a number of today's top writers. Unfortunately, as reality would have it, a cult writer is not often attractive to the conglomerates. Brooklyn-based Small Beer Press, formed a couple of years ago and putting out noteworthy titles, has stepped in to fill that hole by simultaneously publishing two new Emshwillers: *Report to the Men's Club,* a collection, and a novel, *The Mount*. The latter is an alien-invasion yarn, but not like any alien-invasion story I've ever read, and certainly not the kind you'll soon see Steven Spielberg turn into a TV miniseries. It took me about thirty pages to figure out who was narrating the narrative—my one complaint— but the title should have given it away sooner. While a quirky novel, it is very easy to fall into the rhythm of Emshwiller's poetic and smooth sentences and run with the flow. It'll be interesting to watch what other unique titles Small Beer Press will issue in the future. [Michael Hemmingson]

Yann Martel. *Life of Pi*. Harcourt, 2002. 319 pp. $25.00.

This ultra-linear novel begins with, and not after, an author's note from which a word is used to summarize travel in India: "bamboozle"—soon put to use at a train station when a clerk claims, "There is no bamboozlement here." *Publisher's Weekly* revealed the bamboozlement of their reviewer by referring to Martel's "captivating honesty about the genesis of his story." Martel lifted the idea for this novel from one by Moacyr Scliar about a Jewish zookeeper who ends up in a lifeboat with a panther. Now we have Pi, an Indian teenager on a lifeboat with a Bengal tiger named Richard Parker. Martel doles out name-play like chunks of hyena for the reader to chew on—comic relief from the cultish deluge of detail and gory animal behavior. Early in the story, during a youthful phase of comparative-theology samplings, Pi is bemused by Christianity's singular story. "Humanity sins but it is God's Son who pays the price?" He tries to imagine his father, a zookeeper without a religious bone in his body, feeding him to the lions to atone for their sins. Martel's brand of verbal alchemy loosens our grip on belief, allowing faith to pop up like any good mirage worth its salt. When Pi rules out killing the tiger in favor of taming him, a reciprocal relationship evolves. A bit of a MacGyver of the high seas, Pi relies on earthbound lessons (including the danger of anthropomorphism) to survive 227 days of staring Richard Parker down. Once back on dry land, two officials from the shipping company arrive to obtain information from Pi, who accepts the cookies they offer, collecting enough of them to miraculously offer them back to these disbelievers, who graciously accept and go forth to chronicle their findings as "unparalleled in the history of shipwrecks." Do I believe in God after hearing Pi's story? I believe everyone has a story to illuminate faith, and each of these stories is the best. [Jean Smith]

Greg Boyd. *The Double (Doppelangelgänger)*. Leaping Dog, 2002. 136 pp. Paper: $14.95.

The Double is a book about a reader named Jeff. One of the books he reads is a collection of odd stories (in one, a giant phallus is delivered to a church; in another, a woman shaves her head to piss off her boyfriend), the other a collection of fairy tales written by a woman he meets in the course of his misadventures. Jeff is also his book's narrator, and the tale he tells is about how a man who looks like him is ruining his life by impersonating him, causing him to lose his job, apartment, girlfriend, identity. Between disasters, Jeff reproduces in appendices and footnotes the twenty stories he reads. What Jeff's story means is anybody's guess, despite a small smorgasbord of proffered possibilities (Jeff and his double are halves of a split personality; one is the other's "guardian angel"; one is the product of the other's fiction-infected imagination). To understand Jeff's story, readers are encouraged to connect it to those Jeff reads and passes along, but how these gloss what is going on is equally anybody's guess. What is clear is how much of Jeff's life story consists of what he reads (more than half of the book) and how little of what he reads proves in any way helpful to him. Like a lot of people, Jeff is living an odd, crisis-riddled life filled with peculiar stories that fail to help make sense of it. But Jeff isn't even trying to find instruction or truth. Rather, his reading kills time and proves a pleasant distraction—not unlike the afternoon when I read *The Double* and for a few hours forgot, more or less, how disenchanted with the world outside its pages I was. That, at any rate, is my story. [Brooke Horvath]

Arthur Phillips. *Prague*. Random House, 2002. 367 pp. $24.95.

Prague opens with its main characters not in Prague but in Budapest, seated at a bar and playing a game called "Sincerity," in which players make true and false statements and are then rewarded points for detecting lies and successfully concealing their own. These players are of the new "Lost Generation"—young foreigners (in this case, four Americans and a Canadian) living in Europe in the early 1990s. Nothing in the novel actually happens in Prague, and instead we watch these characters go about trying to find their identity and purpose in the streets of Budapest, all the while suspecting that in Prague things are far more authentic. The novel unfolds as these characters' lives intertwine, and throughout there are some very fine moments.

For example, John Price, an American journalist who has followed his brother overseas, writes a newspaper column in which he perhaps too closely captures the attitude of his generation of Soviet Studies majors and youth who get their knowledge of the Cold War from "CIA techno-thriller novels." Another character, Mark Payton, is in Budapest working on his doctoral dissertation on the history of nostalgia, and the discussion of how coffeehouses came to be the centers for artistic production is so good I can almost recommend the novel on the basis of this scene alone. Phillips himself comes with quite a pedigree—as the dust jacket notes, he has been many things in his life, perhaps most impressively a five-time *Jeopardy* champion. I highlight this qualification because, at times, *Prague* reads as if its sole purpose is to illustrate the copious knowledge of its author. A section entitled "The Horváth Kiadó," which describes the entire history of a publishing house, bogs the novel down and seems only to serve as Phillips's extended attempt to prove his ability to create detailed history. But despite this, the novel is an entertaining read. Phillips possesses an extremely keen eye for detail, and the humor that pervades the novel works every time. [Jason D. Fichtel]

Dawn Raffel. *Carrying the Body.* Scribner, 2002. 126 pp. $18.00.

Like the gem at its center, *Carrying the Body* is a hard, sharp, multifaceted thing. The novel describes the return of a prodigal daughter, Elise, son in tow, to her parents' house, where her sister, called only Auntie, is taking care of their father, whose health fails daily after the death of Mother. Raffel uses this trope to its full effect. The house without Mother, or Father for that matter, falls into disrepair, and the characters move about it like specters, encountering each other almost by accident and repeating conversations and gestures with constricted formality. This kind of Existential Metaphor could be overwrought and terrible, but Raffel has a light touch and tempers it by creating in Auntie a pitch-perfect passive caretaker bubbling with resentment. She voices her discontent only when alone, but infuses her polite conversation with frustration and anger to the point of cutting herself off much of the time. In this house certain things must not be said, and the burden of the unsaid is as heavy as the titular body. Raffel shoots all of this through a modernist prism, carving the story into small chapters that jump in space and time. The love for which Elise left is recounted slowly through the whole book, as is Auntie's telling to Elise's son the story of the Three Little Pigs, which reflects, increasingly, the chaos of the house and her own frustration. Certain things—just what did happen to Mother?—are repressed right out of the book, leaving the reader to feel the empty spaces the characters presumably feel. And this is Raffel's strategy. The reader feels Auntie's exasperation with the child's repetitive banter, feels the claustrophobia of the house, and wonders, like Elise and Auntie, what is wrong with the father. Raffel sets a high mark for herself and, for the most part, meets it with exquisite prose and a keen unflinching eye for the subtleties of familial disintegration. [Gregory Howard]

Mark Costello. *Big If*. Norton, 2002. 315 pp. $24.95.

In *Big If* Mark Costello, probably most familiar to readers of this journal
as co-author with David Foster Wallace of *Signifying Rappers,* offers a
slice of contemporary America in which image and reality cavort in an
increasingly complex and uncertain dance. The main characters, Vi and
Jens Apslund, are introduced as children of the seventies, the offspring
of a father, an insurance claims adjuster, who questioned in his own
quiet, Republican, New England way the claims of absolute truth and determinate reality. Crossing out the *God* in *In God We Trust* on his money,
then replacing it with *Us,* Apslund *père* cast his vote for chance and con-
tingency. Adult Jens, a computer wiz, becomes a programmer for BigIf,
an online game set in a postapocalyptic Southwest in which players try
to work their way past mutant monsters to the Pacific. Vi becomes a Secret Service agent assigned to the detail protecting the vice president,
who, à la Al Gore, is running for president. Both Apslunds are in the uncomfortable business of creating simulations of reality while keeping
death at bay. Jens tries to sell his bosses on a program to make the shadows in BigIf more realistic, while they want a new monster, Todd, a Col-
umbine-esque adolescent killer. Vi and her team are responsible not only
for protecting the VP but also for making his morning jogs and coffee
klatches appear normal, despite the mammoth disruptions in traffic,
business, and lives they occasion. There's a wealth of smart, funny, and
cleverly drawn character sketches and takes on contemporary society
here, though one wishes that it all came together more completely—too
much is left up in the air, and there seems to be very little payoff for such
an elaborate setup. *Big If* is better enjoyed in its parts than as a whole.
[Robert L. McLaughlin]

Gabe Hudson. *Dear Mr. President*. Knopf, 2002. 155 pp. $19.00.

Although Hudson has been influenced by the war novels of Vonnegut and
Heller, he is not a mere imitator. His first collection is a remarkable weapon;
he fights war—however it may be defined—with metaphor and hallucination. He moves swiftly; he attacks patriotic clichés. Hudson creates a world
in which bodies turn into parts, minds overwhelm official speech. The narrator of "Cross Dresser," who is in the mental ward of a VA hospital, makes a
fashion statement: instead of an official uniform, he says, "I tape my penis
down between my legs and put on a pair of flowered panties. I put on one of
my mom's dresses and too much lipstick and eyeliner and admire myself in
the big mirror in the living room." (Hudson laughs at masculinity in many
stories.) In "Dear Mr. President" the narrator writes to President Bush to
explain his transformation. He sees that he is losing parts of his body (and
mind) and gaining new ones: "I figure if you can get an ear or a mouth, then
it's possible to get a set of wings. And, of course, if I had wings I could fly out
to my mother-in-law's house in Seattle, and I know that if Mrs. Laverne
looked up in the sky and saw me flying with my new wings, she would get

over the ear and mouth and nose thing. Who could turn down a man with wings?" Hudson deliberately destroys the logic of hierarchy. He knows that war is not so much a matter of transcripts, briefs, registered documents—a paper world—as a wired (weird) machine inhabited by mentally challenged visions and disintegrating bones. [Irving Malin]

Rela Mazali. *Maps of Women's Goings and Stayings.* Stanford Univ. Press, 2001. 382 pp. Paper: $24.95.

Maps of Women's Goings and Stayings is an in-depth examination of the metaphorical and literal meanings of "a woman's place." The author takes a strongly feminist position in delineating these concepts: she relates the restriction of women's movements to their intellectual containment, due to cultural definitions of space. Mazali examines the processes of "footbinding and mindbinding" to demonstrate how women have been "kept in place" by their cultures. Through interviews with both real and imagined women, the book explores a number of societies, showing how in each one, starting in childhood, the woman "habituates the glass corridors through which she must learn to move." The story travels in time as well as place, going back in history to the journal of a female Marco Polo, supposedly written in the thirteenth century. At the heart of the book lies the complex process of authenticating the manuscript, which requires scientific and linguistic investigations, and reveals the intense emotional involvement of the historian. What is strikingly original about *Maps of Women's Goings and Stayings* is its integration of fiction, scholarly research, and ethnographic interviewing. The interviews are transcribed with all the halts and hesitations of each individual speaker in an attempt to provide a faithful recording of authentic speech patterns. References to scholarly works are included within the body of the text, and a chapter called "Housekeys"—placed in the middle of the book, rather than at the end—gives bibliographic details. Mazali seems to have invented a feminist methodology, one in which scholarly references are abundant but easily accessible to the lay reader. [Leslie Cohen]

Martine Desjardins. *Fairy Ring.* Trans. Fred A. Reed and David Homel. Talon, 2001. 223 pp. Paper: $14.95.

In *Fairy Ring,* an epistolary novel set in 1895 Nova Scotia, Clara Weiss, the beleaguered wife of botanist Edmond, suffers from a malaise necessitating a "sleep cure," while the man who pines for her, Captain Ian Ryder, languishes amid frozen waters, trapped and abandoned by his crew during an abortive journey to the North Pole. Not coincidentally, Freud's *Studies in Hysteria* was published in 1895 and, although never explicitly referenced, provides a backdrop for Clara's woes and a disconcerting justification for Edmond's actions. While Ian is at sea, Edmond and Clara take up residence on Ian's isolated coastal estate, leaving Clara vulnerable to her husband's chilling ministrations. Edmond's attempts to penetrate Clara, both psychically and physically, precipitate some of the novel's most startling and grotesque images. While Edmond wields a veterinary speculum, Clara bitterly observes, "In the most isolated houses, the cruelest and vilest acts can be committed in secrecy and with impunity." The indignities Clara suffers at her husband's hands and with the cooperation of the medical establishment reveal some of the intrinsic sadism of the Victorian age and the capriciousness inherent in definitions of normalcy. Unfortunately, Clara's observation that "human beings always risk becoming attached to that which enchains them" proves prescient, and the novel effectively conveys the inescapable power of the ideologies permeating a particular place and time. [Rhonda M. Nicol]

———

John Yau. *My Heart Is That Eternal Rose Tattoo.* Black Sparrow, 2001. 165 pp. Paper: $17.95.

My Heart Is That Eternal Rose Tattoo appeared almost simultaneously with Yau's *Borrowed Love Poems,* but while that latter book declares its affiliation to poetry in its title, *My Heart*'s affiliations are harder to figure out. Indeed, *My Heart* offers sixty-three pieces of prose, ranging in length from a single sentence to eleven pages. At moments these remind one of the prose poetry found in Yau's *Radiant Silhouette* and *Forbidden Entries,* but at others they drift closer toward narrative, recalling Lydia Davis's short shorts. What is interesting is the range of these pieces, the way that each of the six sections of this short book takes a different approach to notions of what prose is or can be. In one section, for instance, elusive prose snippets seem to accumulate from piece to piece into something larger for the section as a whole. Another section contains only one piece with a clear and very direct narrative. Still others pursue various complex negotiations between genres. In the first section in particular, Yau pursues strategies that recall the innovative prose of Jason Schwartz's *A German Picturesque* or Ben Marcus's *The Age of Wire and String* without being beholden to either. Taken as a whole, *My Heart Is That Eternal Rose Tattoo* serves as an effective *esquisse* on the history of prose, with Yau gleefully straddling genres in all possible ways. [Brian Evenson]

———

Christine Brooke-Rose. *Invisible Author: Last Essays.* Ohio State Univ. Press, 2002. 206 pp. $45.00.

Brooke-Rose takes her title from her experience as a writer; while she has a small group of faithful readers, she reflects on the unhappy idea that nobody seems to have noticed the self-imposed constraints within which she has attempted to work, e.g., the elimination of the verb *to be* in *Between*. This book consists of six previously published sections and three added chapters, a structured self-analysis. In it we meet the shrewdly acute intelligence and sensitive assiduity of a longtime innovator. She gives a brief history of narrative criticism, unveils the composing mind of an ingenious writer, and moves the critic's attention away from the "story" to the devices, especially linguistic, that keep narrative alive. We might associate her with Roussel or Oulipo writers (Perec) as she analyzes the challenges and sense of verbal play that generate her fiction. Immersed in structuralism and theory, she applies the same incisiveness to critical problems as she has to those of narrative. The core of the work details her response to Alain Robbe-Grillet and his use of the "paradoxical" present tense, a challenge she has mastered. Having developed a strong interest in if not an obsession with the grammatical aspects of narrative structure, she writes close analyses of several of her works, e.g., *Thru,* and those of other critics and novelists, the most interesting of which examines Mark Danielewski's *House of Leaves*. Her reading ranges broadly and cuts deeply; her insistence on her invisibility, the problems of an "experimenter" increased by gender bias, strikes one as doubly unfortunate. Greater exposure to the fiction and criticism of Christine Brooke-Rose would benefit us all. [Richard J. Murphy]

Paul Auster. *The Red Notebook*. New Directions, 2002. 103 pp. Paper: $10.95.

A recently divorced man recalls his first (and only) true love, a woman he met some twenty years before; three days later she calls him, and they are reunited. A woman doesn't have the money for an operation her cat desperately needs. While waiting at a stoplight, she's hit from behind. The cost of the repairs is exactly the amount she needs for the operation. Two friends, one the author's sister-in-law, both of whom have studied Chinese in Taipei, discover that they have family living on the same street in New York City. As the conversation progresses, they realize that their families not only inhabit the same apartment building, but live on the same floor. These and more comprise the "chain of anecdotes" compiled in *The Red Notebook*. Auster, the author of ten novels, most recently *The Book of Illusions,* has been fascinated throughout his writing life with unlikely coincidence and the odd ways in which fate brings people together, and this collection is no exception. These are preoccupations of anyone interested in creating a coherent narrative out of the chaos of life. Indeed, there would be no literature without the urge to organize chance events into narrative. But Auster is more interested in the capriciousness of fate than most. He has said elsewhere that for him the story is primary; that a sentence, no matter how good, falls to the wayside if it isn't necessary to the story. His clear, lucid prose attests to this conviction, as does the somewhat detached tone with which he suggests that stories are found and not created. There's a quiet sadness to these stories, a sense that the identities we claim for ourselves are always vulnerable to the vagaries of chance, more fragile than we'd like to believe, but also much more fascinating. [Valerie Ellis]

Mario Vargas Llosa. *Letters to a Young Novelist*. Trans. Natasha Wimmer. Farrar, Straus & Giroux, 2002. 136 pp. $17.00.

In the introduction to Rilke's *Letters to a Young Poet,* the young poet in question, Franz Xaver Kappus, gives a summary of the history of his brief correspondence with Rilke. In a beautifully written passage, Kappus writes, "I found myself writing a covering letter in which I unreservedly laid bare my heart as never before and never since to any second human being," and concludes the introduction by writing, "Only the ten letters are important that follow here, important for an understanding of the world in which Rainer Maria Rilke lived and worked, and important too for many growing and evolving spirits of today and tomorrow. And where a great and unique man speaks, small men should keep silence." And then, in the spirit of postmodern fiction, we have Vargas Llosa's *Letters to a Young Novelist.* Unlike Rilke's *Letters,* Vargas Llosa's *Letters* have no re-cipient. Or should I say, all of us readers are the "recipient," since the "let-ters" are clearly meant not to be letters to a young novelist at all but to be Vargas Llosa's Lessons in Literature. Actually, they're not letters at all, but both literary criticism (i.e., would a young novelist know what *epigones* means?) and a primer (i.e., a chapter devoted to knowing who your narrator is). Vargas Llosa has taken Rilke's letters to a genuinely and nonfictionally young poet (whose introduction reads more like *Mon coeur mis à nu* than a standard introduction) and by fictionalizing the re-cipient and the reason for the correspondence in the first place has cre-ated a kind of parody. Under the persiflage of letters to a young novelist, Vargas Llosa gives us his take on writers and writing, much of which is a bit superficial but which, at times, gives new insight into the creative pro-cess. [Mark Axelrod]

Paul Metcalf. *From Quarry Road: Uncollected Essays and Reviews of Paul Metcalf.* Ed. and intro. Robert Buckeye. Preface Jonathan Will-iams. Amandla (Box 431, East Middlebury, VT 05740), 2002. 100 pages. $20.00.

Metcalf lived on Quarry Road (in Chester, Massachusetts), and the name seems to have suited him well. In pursuit of literary game and during the mining of his subjects, he reveals himself to have been both quarrelsome and querulous. His query for quarry led him to his great-grandfather Herman Melville, to Dickinson, Reznikoff, Lucien Freud, Pound, Olson, Williams, Dahlberg (there is much about Dahlberg, who bagged one of his ex-wives, says Metcalf, "by convincing her that he was the reincarnation of Herman Melville, and she must marry him to save American litera-ture"), and to Todd Moore, a poet Metcalf seems to have great affinity for. Actually, what most of these writers have in common is the fact that they were all notorious cranks. Even more appealing than the astuteness of ob-servation in Metcalf's essays and reviews is the underlying crankiness that pervades them: "Gil [Sorrentino] is a fine critic . . . but I just can't read his own work. Zukovsky I don't have the patience for . . . I find it very dull. I've seen fragments of [Douglas] Woolf's novel . . . sounds to me like he's not really growing . . . I used to like Bronk, but he begins to wear thin . . . As I get older and crankier, I find myself with diminishing tolerance for people who play games with language." His crankiness is amusing. It was an inspired wellspring for Metcalf, who retired from Cambridge, moved to the Berkshires, and became a farmer. His death in 1999 has left us with one less literary crank whose turn was not really up. I am glad that Robert Buckeye has mined Metcalf's reviews and letters for this material—it really provides an endearing introduction to Metcalf the crank, Metcalf the critic who nonetheless comes across with affection for his subjects, Metcalf the crotchety old farmer-poet whom one just can't help but embrace. [Eckhard Gerdes]

Joseph Tabbi. *Cognitive Fictions*. Univ. of Minnesota Press, 2002. 166 pp. Paper: $17.95.

Like Tabbi's first book, *Postmodern Sublime: Technology and American Writing from Mailer to Cyberpunk*, *Cognitive Fictions* is an interdisciplinary project, building its argument at the crossroads of fiction and postmodern studies, systems and electronic media theory, and cognitive science. The critic is here in distinguished company: Brian McHale, for postmodern fiction criticism and "fictional (possible) worlds" theory, and in relation to the latter, Thomas Pavel, Marie-Laure Ryan, and David Herman, who have made significant contributions to narratology and cognitive science; also N. Katherine Hayles, John Johnston, Silvio Gaggi, and Scott Bukatman, for systems theory, cyberculture, hypertext, and "mediality" in relation to postmodern/cyberpunk prose. But Tabbi's book is, to my knowledge, the first to approach recent American fiction from a cognitive-science angle. The approach is systematic and focuses on relevant authors: Thomas Pynchon, Richard Powers, Paul Auster, David Markson, Harry Mathews, and others. There are some usual suspects on this list, but also names that speak to Tabbi's interests in more electronically oriented avant-pop/experimental writers, some of whom have found a hospitable forum in Tabbi's cool *electronic book review*. Any conspicuous—unavoidable—absences? Maybe DeLillo (*White Noise, Underworld*), who is mentioned but not analyzed? More important, I find Tabbi's discussion of post-1980 American "cognitive fictions" persuasive, well articulated, showing elegantly how contemporary fiction acts out the systemic workings of cognition. The critic lays out the homologies obtaining among mind, literary works, the media, and the reader's own cognitive apparatus as texts rise and are processed mentally in our media-saturated world. Breaking new ground, *Cognitive Fiction* makes a strong case for the cognitional materiality of writing and reading. [Christian Moraru]

Joseph Dewey. *Understanding Richard Powers*. Univ. of South Carolina Press, 2002. 176 pp. $29.95.

In this excellent introduction to the work of Richard Powers, Joseph Dewey resolutely describes the author of *The Gold Bug Variations* and seven other "big novels of ideas" as being torn between two all-American impulses, "Emersonian engagement and Dickinsonesque withdrawal." In what at first sight looks like a reductive effort to neatly structure the novels under scrutiny, Dewey assigns the odd-numbered books—*Three Farmers on Their Way to a Dance* (1985), *The Gold Bug Variations* (1991), and *Galatea 2.2* (1995)—to engagement, and the even-numbered ones—*Prisoner's Dilemma* (1988), *Operation Wandering Soul* (1993), and *Gain* (1998)—to withdrawal. Powers's seventh novel, *Plowing the Dark* (2000), then assumes the status of a "summary text," combining the two inclinations with the contrapuntal refinement so typical of its author. Dewey's great strength resides in his ability to make a convincing case for the dialectic development around which he has organized his book. Thus *Dilemma* contains a "counterargument" to *Three Farmers* by showing that an energetic imagination (as displayed and seemingly commended by Powers in the first novel) can lead to isolation, and *Wandering Soul* embodies a pessimistic vision that seems to undermine the "ascendant premise" of *Gold Bug*. Dewey is nicely informative about each novel and manages to provide encompassing readings. While his interpretation of *Gold Bug* perhaps does not meet the expectations raised by this extraordinary work, and while his rhetoric is occasionally overcome by his desire to prove the humanistic concerns at the root of Powers's work, Dewey's book is by far the best overview treatment around. If Powers was serious when he confirmed via E-mail Dewey's view of *Plowing* as a capstone, Powers readers may be in for a real treat with *The Time of Our Singing* (2003). [Luc Herman]

Mark Royden Winchell. *"Too Good to Be True": The Life and Work of Leslie Fiedler*. Univ. of Missouri Press, 2002. 366 pp. $39.95.

Asked to name the most influential American literary critic of the past half-century, one could reasonably reply: "Leslie Fiedler, alas." Fiedler, because of his trenchant, prolific, innovative work in American studies, feminist criticism, science fiction, queer theory, ethnic literature, and popular culture. Alas, because Fiedler the young gadfly was an irritant and, still feisty in his eighties, now seems to some an embarrassment. He described himself as having gone from "the status of *enfant terrible* to that of 'dirty old man' without passing through a decent maturity." Mark Royden Winchell, author of a book on Donald Davidson, characterizes Fiedler, the first to apply the term "postmodern" to literature, as the sorcerer's apprentice, an innocent who summoned up forces that have since flooded the culture. Winchell conceives Fiedler's career as the arc of four overlapping identities: postwar Jewish intellectual, pioneering myth-critic, interpreter of Americana, and obituarist of the canon and literature. While respectful of Fiedler's fiction, especially his novellas, Winchell locates his greatest achievement in his works of literary anthropology, especially *An End to Innocence, The Return of the Vanishing American,* and, particularly, *Love and Death in the American Novel*. Because Fiedler altered critical discourse as much through his provocative, personal style as his ideas, biography is a crucial—as well as vibrant—way to approach his legacy. Relying on extensive interviews with his subject, Winchell presents a sympathetic portrait of an exuberant outsider who, from perches in Missoula and Buffalo, launched assaults on academic conventions. It was during a Fulbright in Rome that Fiedler, a specialist in the Renaissance, first found himself conscripted as cicerone to his own native literature. Despite minor errata, Winchell is a lively guide to a prodigal lover and professional amateur. [Steven G. Kellman]

Books Received

Acker, Kathy. *Essential Acker: The Selected Writings of Kathy Acker.* Ed. Amy Scholder and Dennis Cooper. Intro. Jeanette Winterson. Grove, 2002. Paper: $15.00. (F)

——. *"Rip-Off Red, Girl Detective" and "The Burning Bombing of America: The Destruction of the U.S."* Grove, 2002. Paper: $14.00. (F)

Alcalay, Ammiel. *From the Warring Factions.* Beyond Baroque, 2002. Paper: $12.00. (F)

Ali, Thalassa. *A Singular Hostage.* Bantam, 2002. Paper: $13.95. (F)

Arvin, Nick. *In the Electric Eden.* Penguin, 2003. Paper: $14.00. (F)

Ascher/Straus. *ABC Street.* Green Integer, 2002. Paper: $10.95. (F)

Ashbery, John. *Chinese Whispers.* Farrar, Straus & Giroux, 2002. $22.00. (P)

Auster, Paul, and Sam Messer. *The Story of My Typewriter.* Distributed Art Publishers, 2002. $17.95. (NF)

Bail, Murray. *Holden's Performance.* Picador USA, 2002. Paper: $14.00. (F)

Bailie, Grant. *Cloud 8.* Ig Publishing, 2002. Paper: $14.95. (F)

Barreca, Regina, ed. *Don't Tell Mama! The Penguin Book of Italian American Writing.* Penguin, 2002. Paper: $16.00. (F, NF, P)

Bastin, Nina. *Queneau's Fictional Worlds.* Peter Lang, 2002. Paper: $43.95. (NF)

Bedford, Sybille. *Aldous Huxley: A Biography.* Ivan R. Dee, 2002. Paper: $24.95. (NF)

Bellow, Saul. *Collected Stories.* Ed. Janis Bellow. Intro. James Wood. Penguin, 2002. Paper: $15.00. (F)

Bennett, Bruce. *Australian Short Fiction: A History.* Univ. of Queensland Press, 2002. Paper: $27.00. (NF)

Berrada, Mohammed. *Fugitive Light.* Trans. Issa J. Boullata. Foreword Michael Beard. Syracuse Univ. Press, 2002. $24.95. (F)

Blauner, Laurie. *Somebody.* Black Heron, 2003. $22.95. (F)

Boulé, Jean-Pierre. *HIV Stories: The Archaeology of AIDS Writing in France, 1985-1988.* Liverpool Univ. Press, 2002. Paper: £17.95. (NF)

Bowles, Paul. *Collected Stories & Later Writings.* Library of America, 2002. $40.00. (F)

——. *The Sheltering Sky, Let It Come Down, The Spider's House.* Library of America, 2002. $35.00. (F)

Boyd, William. *Any Human Heart.* Knopf, 2003. $26.00. (F)

Breuer, Lee. *La Divina Caricatura.* Green Integer, 2002. Paper: $14.95. (F)

Brownstein, Gabriel. *The Curious Case of Benjamin Button, Apt. 3W*. Norton, 2002. $23.95. (F)

Bundy, Alison, and Keith and Rosmarie Waldrop, eds. *One Score More: The Second Twenty Years of Burning Deck, 1982-2002*. Burning Deck, 2002. Paper: $15.00. (F, NF, P)

Bunge, Nancy, ed. *Conversations with Clarence Major*. Univ. Press of Mississippi, 2002. Paper: $18.00. (NF)

Byatt, A. S. *A Whistling Woman*. Knopf, 2002. $26.00. (F)

Cady, Jack. *Ghosts of Yesterday*. Night Shade, 2003. Paper: $15.00. (F)

Camilleri, Andrea. *The Shape of Water*. Trans. Stephen Sartarelli. Penguin, 2002. Paper: $5.99. (F)

Caradec, François. *Raymond Roussel*. Trans. Ian Monk. Atlas, 2002. Paper: $24.95. (NF)

Chan, David Marshall. *Goblin Fruit*. Context Books, 2003. $21.95. (F)

Chee, Alexander. *Edinburgh*. Picador USA, 2002. Paper: $13.00. (F)

Clark, Nancy. *The Hills at Home*. Pantheon, 2003. $25.00. (F)

Coetzee, J. M. *Stranger Shores: Literary Essays 1986-1999*. Penguin, 2002. Paper: $15.00. (NF)

Connelly, Joe. *Crumbtown*. Knopf, 2003. $23.00. (F)

Conte, Joseph. *Design & Debris: A Chaotics of Postmodern American Fiction*. Univ. of Alabama Press, 2002. $60.00. (NF)

Cooney, Ellen. *The White Palazzo*. Coffee House, 2002. Paper: $14.00. (F)

Coover, Robert. *The Adventures of Lucky Pierre: Director's Cut*. Grove, 2002. $24.00. (F)

Correas de Zapata, Celia, ed. *Short Stories by Latin American Women: The Magic and the Real*. Foreword Isabel Allende. Modern Library, 2003. Paper: $12.95. (F)

Crombie, Deborah. *And Justice There Is None*. Bantam, 2002. $23.95. (F)

Daudet, Alphonse. *In the Land of Pain*. Ed. and trans. Julian Barnes. Knopf, 2003. $18.00. (NF)

DeLillo, Don. *Cosmopolis*. Scribner, 2003. $25.00. (F)

Dewey, Joseph, Steven G. Kellman, and Irving Malin, eds. *Underwords: Perspectives on Don DeLillo's "Underworld."* Univ. of Delaware Press, 2002. $39.50. (NF)

Disend, Michael. *Stomping the Goyim*. Green Integer, 2002. Paper: $12.95. (F)

Djaout, Tahar. *The Watchers*. Trans. Marjolijn de Jager. Ruminator, 2002. $23.00. (F)

Dorfman, Ariel. *In Case of Fire in a Foreign Land: New and Collected Poems from Two Languages*. Trans. Edith Grossman and the author. Duke Univ. Press, 2002. Paper: $15.95. (P)

——. *Widows.* Trans. Stephen Kessler. Seven Stories, 2002. Paper: $12.95. (F)

Driscoll, Rob. *American Holidays.* 1st Books, 2002. Paper: $11.50. (F)

Duncker, Patricia. *The Deadly Space Between.* Ecco, 2002. $23.95. (F)

Eggers, Paul. *How the Water Feels.* Southern Methodist Univ. Press, 2002. $19.95. (F)

Evenson, Brian. *Dark Property.* Black Square, 2002. Paper: $14.00. (F)

Fauchereau, Serge. *Complete Fiction.* Trans. Ron Padgett and John Ashbery. Black Square, 2002. Paper: $14.00. (F)

Firan, Carmen. *The Farce.* Trans. Doru Motz. Ed. Bruce Benderson. Spuyten Duyvil, 2003. Paper: $10.00. (F)

Fleming, Bruce. *Kigali, Rwanda.* Six Gallery, 2002. Paper: $14.95. (F)

——. *A Structure Opera.* Six Gallery, 2002. Paper: $12.95. (F)

Foos, Laurie. *Bingo under the Crucifix.* Coffee House, 2002. Paper: $14.00. (F)

Franzen, Jonathan. *How to Be Alone: Essays.* Farrar, Straus & Giroux, 2002. $24.00. (NF)

Friedman, Susan Stanford, ed. *Analyzing Freud: Letters of H.D., Bryher, and Their Circle.* New Directions, 2002. $39.95. (NF)

Fusselman, Amy. *The Pharmacist's Mate.* Penguin, 2002. Paper: $11.00. (F)

Gale, Kate, and Charles Rammelkamp, eds. *Fake-City Syndrome: American Cultural Essays.* Red Hen, 2002. Paper: $29.95. (NF)

Gauch, Sigfrid. *Traces of My Father.* Trans. William Radice. Preface Antony Copley. Northwestern Univ. Press, 2002. Paper: $17.95. (F)

Gay, William. *I Hate to See That Evening Sun Go Down.* Free Press, 2002. $24.00. (F)

George, Elizabeth. *I, Richard.* Bantam, 2002. $21.95. (F)

Gibson, Miles. *Mr Romance.* Do-Not Press/Dufour, 2002. Paper: $14.95. (F)

Giono, Jean. *The Solitude of Compassion.* Trans. Edward Ford. Foreword Henry Miller. Seven Stories, 2002. Paper: $15.00. (F)

Glancy, Diane. *Designs of the Night Sky.* Univ. of Nebraska Press, 2002. $24.95. (F)

——. *Stone Heart: A Novel of Sacajawea.* Overlook, 2003. $21.95. (F)

Gordimer, Nadine. *The Pickup.* Penguin, 2002. Paper: $14.00. (F)

Gray, Alasdair. *Lanark: A Life in Four Books.* 4 vols. Canongate, 2002. £35.00. (F)

Green, Angela. *Cassandra's Disk.* Peter Owen/Dufour, 2002. Paper: $21.95. (F)

Grynberg, Henryk. *Drohobycz, Drohobycz and Other Stories: True Tales from the Holocaust and Life After.* Trans. Alicia Nitecki. Ed. Theodosia Robertson. Penguin, 2002. Paper: $14.00. (F, NF)

Gudding, Gabriel. *A Defense of Poetry.* Univ. of Pittsburgh Press, 2002. Paper: $12.95. (P)

Gunderson, Joanna. *The Field.* Red Dust, 1998. Paper: $10.95. (P)

——. *Kaleidoscope 1969.* Spuyten Duyvil, 2001. Paper: $12.00. (F)

Haeger, Diane. *My Dearest Cecelia.* St. Martin's, 2003. $24.95. (F)

Harris-Lopez, Trudier. *South of Tradition: Essays on African American Literature.* Univ. of Georgia Press, 2002. $24.95. (NF)

Harrison, M. John. *Things that Never Happen.* Intro. China Miéville. Night Shade, 2003. Paper: $15.00. (F)

Hecker, Robert L. *The Greatest Summer Job in the Whole, Wide World.* Silk Label, 2000. Paper: $14.99. (F)

Herrmann, Michael. *Breakfastinfur.* Fremantle Arts Centre Press, 2002. Paper: $20.95. (F)

Hill, Leslie. *Bataille, Klossowski, Blanchot: Writing at the Limit.* Oxford Univ. Press, 2001. $74.00. (NF)

Hirsch, Edward. *Lay Back the Darkness.* Knopf, 2003. $23.00. (P)

Hirschman, Jack, ed. *Art of the Line: Essays by Artists about the Point Where Their Art and Activism Meet.* Curbstone, 2002. Paper: $18.95. (NF)

Hofmann, Michael. *Behind the Lines: Pieces on Writing and Pictures.* Faber and Faber, 2002. $26.00. (NF)

Horne, Alistair. *Seven Ages of Paris.* Knopf, 2002. $35.00. (NF)

Howell, Brian. *The Dance of Geometry.* Toby, 2002. $19.95. (F)

Hudson, W. H. *The Purple Land.* Intro. Ilan Stavans. Illus. Keith Henderson. Univ. of Wisconsin Press, 2002. Paper: $19.95. (F)

Iyer, Pico. *Abandon: A Romance.* Knopf, 2003. $24.00. (F)

Jones, Lisa. *Up.* Sticky Press, 2002. Paper: $12.95. (F)

Joyce, Michael. *Liam's Going.* McPherson, 2002. $22.00. (F)

Karlin, Wayne. *The Wished-For Country.* Curbstone, 2002. Paper: $16.95. (F)

Keillor, Garrison. *Lake Wobegon Summer 1956.* Penguin, 2002. Paper: $14.00. (F)

Keun, Irmgard. *The Artificial Silk Girl.* Trans. Kathis von Ankm. Intro. Maria Tatar. Other Press, 2002. $22.00. (F)

King, Martha. *Separate Parts (Six Memory Pieces).* Avec, 2002. Paper: $10.00. (F)

Kinzie, Mary. *Drift.* Knopf, 2003. $23.00. (P)

Kitchen, Judith. *The House on Eccles Road.* Graywolf, 2002. $22.00. (F)

Knode, Helen. *The Ticket Out.* Harcourt, 2003. $24.00. (F)

Koch, Kenneth. *A Possible World.* Knopf, 2002. $24.00. (P)

— —. *Sun Out: Selected Poems 1952-54.* Knopf, 2002. $25.00. (P)

Krapp, John. *An Aesthetics of Morality: Pedagogic Voice and Moral Dialogue in Mann, Camus, Conrad, and Dostoevsky.* Univ. of South Carolina Press, 2002. $34.95. (NF)

Lear, Edward. *The Complete Verse and Other Nonsense.* Ed. Vivien Noakes. Penguin, 2002. Paper: $16.00. (P)

Leggett, John. *A Daring Young Man: A Biography of William Saroyan.* Knopf, 2002. $30.00. (NF)

Levertov, Denise. *Selected Poems.* New Directions, 2002. $24.95. (P)

Leviant, Curt. *"Ladies and Gentlemen, the Original Music of the Hebrew Alphabet" and "Weekend in Mustara": Two Novellas.* Univ. of Wisconsin Press, 2002. $21.95. (F)

Lodge, David. *Thinks . . . .* Penguin, 2002. Paper: $14.00. (F)

López, Diana. *Sofia's Saints.* Bilingual Press, 2002. Paper: $14.00. (F)

MacLaverty, Bernard. *The Anatomy School.* Norton, 2002. $25.95. (F)

Maraini, Dacia. *Darkness.* Trans. Martha King. Steerforth, 2002. $21.00. (F)

Marías, Javier. *When I Was Mortal.* Trans. Margaret Jull Costa. New Directions, 2002. Paper: $14.95. (F)

Maso, Carole. *Beauty Is Convulsive: The Passion of Frida Kahlo.* Counterpoint, 2002. $24.00. (P)

Matsuoka, Takashi. *Cloud of Sparrows.* Delacorte, 2002. $24.95. (F)

McCracken, Elizabeth. *Niagara Falls All Over Again.* Delta, 2002. Paper: $12.95. (F)

McDermott, Alice. *Child of My Heart.* Farrar, Straus & Giroux, 2002. $23.00. (F)

McElroy, Joseph. *Actress in the House.* Overlook, 2003. $26.95. (F)

McManus, John. *Born on a Train.* Picador, 2003. Paper: $14.00. (F)

Mills, Magnus. *The Scheme for Full Employment.* Picador USA, 2002. $19.00. (F)

Mistry, Rohinton. *Family Matters.* Knopf, 2002. $26.00. (F)

Mobilio, Albert. *Me with Animal Towering.* Black Square/Hammer, 2002. Paper: $14.00. (P)

Monfort, Nick, and Wiliam Gillespie. *2002: A Palindrome Story in 2002 Words.* Illus. Shelley Jackson. Spineless, 2002. Paper: $16.00. (F)

Morris, Leslie, and Karen Remmler, eds. *Contemporary Jewish Writing in Germany: An Anthology.* Univ. of Nebraska Press, 2002. $60.00. (F)

Mulisch, Harry. *The Procedure.* Trans. Paul Vincent. Penguin, 2002. Paper: $14.00. (F)

Myers, B. R. *A Reader's Manifesto: An Attack on the Growing Pretentiousness in American Literary Prose.* Melville House, 2002. Paper: $9.95. (NF)

Nel, Philip. *The Avant-Garde and American Postmodernity: Small Incisive Shocks.* Univ. Press of Mississippi, 2002. $45.00. (NF)

Nevils, René Pol, and Deborah George Hardy. *Ignatius Rising: The Life of John Kennedy Toole.* Louisiana State Univ. Press, 2002. $24.95. (NF)

Noyes, Tom. *Behold Faith and Other Stories.* Dufour, 2002. Paper: $14.95. (F)

Oates, Joyce Carol, ed. *Best New American Voices 2003.* John Kulka and Natalie Danford, series eds. Harcourt, 2002. Paper: $14.00. (F)

Olson, Kirby. *Gregory Corso: Doubting Thomist.* Southern Illinois Univ. Press, 2002. $40.00. (NF)

Orgel, Stephen, and A. R. Braunmuller, eds. *The Complete Pelican Shakespeare.* Penguin, 2002. $65.00. (F)

Oster, Christian. *A Cleaning Woman.* Trans. Mark Polizzotti. Other Press, 2003. $20.00. (F)

The Oulipo. *Winter Journeys.* Trans. Ian Monk, Harry Mathews, and John Sturrock. Atlas, 2001. Paper: £15.00. (F)

Parisi, Joseph, and Stephen Young, eds. *The "Poetry" Anthology, 1912-2002: Ninety Years of America's Most Distinguished Verse Magazine.* Ivan R. Dee, 2002. $29.95. (P)

Pearson, Allison. *I Don't Know How She Does It: The Life of Kate Reddy, Working Mother.* Knopf, 2002. $23.00. (F)

Perry, Grayson. *Cycle of Violence.* Atlas, 2002. Paper: $18.00. (F)

Pessoa, Fernando. *The Book of Disquiet.* Ed. and trans. Richard Zenith. Penguin, 2002. Paper: $15.00. (F)

Philip, Leila. *A Family Place.* Penguin, 2002. Paper: $14.00. (F)

Phillips, Robert. *News about People You Know.* Texas Review Press, 2002. Paper: $18.95. (F)

Piercy, Marge. *Colors Passing Through Us.* Knopf, 2003. $23.00. (P)

Pontiggia, Giuseppe. *Born Twice.* Trans. Oonagh Stransky. Knopf, 2002. $23.00. (F)

Powell, JB. *The Republic.* Livingston, 2002. Paper: $14.95. (F)

Price, Richard. *Samaritan.* Knopf, 2003. $25.00. (F)

Prior, Lily. *Nectar.* Ecco, 2002. $23.95. (F)

Pye, Michael. *The Pieces from Berlin.* Knopf, 2003. $24.00. (F)

Renek, Nava. *Spiritland.* Spuyten Duyvil, 2002. Paper: $13.00. (F)

Restrepo, Laura. *The Dark Bride.* Trans. Stephen A. Lytle. Ecco, 2002. $24.95. (F)

Rice, Anne. *Blackwood Farm.* Knopf, 2002. $26.95. (F)

Roiphe, Katie. *Still She Haunts Me.* Delta, 2002. Paper: $12.95. (F)

Rollyson, Carl. *Reading Susan Sontag: A Critical Introduction to Her Work.* Ivan R. Dee, 2002. Paper: $14.95. (NF)

Rulfo, Juan. *Pedro Páramo.* Photos Josephine Sacabo. Trans. Margaret Sayers Peden. Univ. of Texas Press, 2002. $35.00. (F)

Sandemose, Aksel. *The Werewolf.* Trans. Gustaf Lannestock. Intro. Harald S. Næss. Univ. of Wisconsin Press, 2002. Paper: $24.95. (F)

Schickler, David. *Kissing in Manhattan.* Delta, 2002. Paper: $12.95. (F)

Schieber, Ava Kadishson. *Soundless Roar: Stories, Poems, and Drawings.* Preface Phyllis Lassner. Northwestern Univ. Press, 2002. $29.95. (F)

Scott, Gail. *Spare Parts, Plus Two.* Coach House, 2002. Paper: $15.95. (F)

Scott, Joanna. *Tourmaline.* Little, Brown, 2002. $23.95. (F)

Searcy, David. *Last Things.* Viking, 2002. $24.95. (F)

Semilian, Julian. *A Spy in Amnesia.* Spuyten Duyvil, 2003. Paper: $14.95. (F)

Seveigny, Genevieve. *A Half-Dozen Eclairs: Travel in the Guise of Letters.* Texture, 2003. Paper: $10.00. (F)

Shalev, Zeruya. *Husband and Wife.* Trans. Dalya Bilu. Grove, 2002. $24.00. (F)

Singleton, George. *The Half-Mammals of Dixie.* Algonquin Books of Chapel Hill, 2002. $22.95. (F)

Siratori, Kenji. *Blood Electric.* Creation, 2002. Paper: $14.95. (F)

Sisman, Adam. *Boswell's Presumptuous Task: The Making of the Life of Dr. Johnson.* Penguin, 2002. Paper: $15.00. (NF)

Slavitt, David R. *Aspects of the Novel: A Novel.* Catbird, 2003. $20.00. (F)

Smith, Zadie. *The Autograph Man.* Random House, 2002. $24.95. (F)

Steinbeck, Thomas. *Down to a Soundless Sea.* Ballantine, 2002. $24.95. (F)

Stern, Richard. *What Is What Was.* Univ. of Chicago Press, 2002. Paper: $18.00. (F, NF, P)

Surman, Susan. *Sacha: The Dog Who Made It to the Palace.* Silk Label, 2002. Paper: $9.99. (F)

Swartz, Mark. *Instant Karma.* City Lights, 2002. Paper: $11.95. (F)

Swartz, Richard. *A House in Istria.* Trans. Anna Paterson. New Directions, 2002. $23.95. (F)

Tartt, Donna. *The Little Friend.* Knopf, 2002. $26.00. (F)

Tawada, Yoko. *Where Europe Begins.* Trans. Susan Bernofsky and Yumi Selden. Preface Wim Wenders. New Directions, 2002. $23.95. (F)

Tellermann, Esther. *Mental Ground.* Burning Deck, 2002. Paper: $10.00. (P)

Timm, Uwe. *Morenga.* Trans. Breon Mitchell. New Directions, 2003. $25.95. (F)

Tomalin, Claire. *Samuel Pepys: The Unequalled Self.* Knopf, 2002. $30.00. (NF)

Ulin, David L., ed. *Writing Los Angeles: A Literary Anthology.* Library of America, 2002. $40.00. (F, NF)

Vachss, Andrew. *Only Child.* Knopf, 2002. $24.00. (F)

Valenzuela, Luisa. *Black Novel with Argentines.* Trans. Tony Talbot. Latin American Literary Review Press, 2002. Paper: $17.95. (F)

Vassilikos, Vassilis. *The Few Things I Know about Glafkos Thrassakis.* Trans. Karen Emmerich. Seven Stories, 2002. $24.95. (F)

Weinstein, Miriam, ed. *Prophets & Dreamers: A Selection of Great Yiddish Literature.* Steerforth, 2002. Paper: $14.00. (F)

Wells, Kellie. *Compression Scars.* Univ. of Georgia Press, 2002. $24.95. (F)

Welsh, Irvine. *Porno.* Norton, 2002. $24.95. (F)

West, A. B. *Wakenight Emporium.* FC2, 2002. Paper: $10.95. (F)

West, Paul. *Cheops: A Cupboard for the Sun.* New Directions, 2002. $25.95. (F)

——. *Oxford Days: An Inclination.* British American Publishing, 2002. $24.95. (NF)

Willett, Jincy. *Jenny and the Jaws of Life.* Foreword David Sedaris. Dunne/St. Martin's, 2002. Paper: $12.95. (F)

Williams, Miller. *The Lives of Kelvin Fletcher: Stories Mostly Short.* Univ. of Georgia Press, 2002. $24.95. (F)

Williams, N. D. *Ah, Mikhail, O Fidel!* Xlibris, 2002. Paper: $26.99. (F)

Yi, In-hwa. *Everlasting Empire.* Trans. Yu Young-nan. Intro. Don Baker. EastBridge, 2002. Paper: No price given. (F)

Young, Kevin. *Jelly Roll.* Knopf, 2003. $24.00. (P)

Zabytko, Irene. *When Luba Leaves Home.* Algonquin Books of Chapel Hill, 2003. $22.95. (F)

Zafris, Nancy. *The Metal Shredders.* Blue Hen/Putnam, 2002. $24.95. (F)

Contributors

DAVID ANDREWS lectures on American literature and writing at the University of Illinois at Chicago. His essays have appeared in a number of collections and journals, including the *Review of Contemporary Fiction,* the *Chicago Review, Film Criticism, Nabokov Studies, Leviathan,* etc. His book *Aestheticism, Nabokov, and "Lolita"* appeared in 1999. Currently, Andrews is an associate editor at *Bridge.*

KEVIN ALEXANDER BOON is an Assistant Professor at Penn State, Mont Alto, where he teaches film, writing, and literature. He is the author and editor of a number of books, most recently *Absolute Zero* and *At Millennium's End.* His book on the human genome project is due out this year, and he is currently at work on *Static Texts and Moving Pictures: The Screenplay as Literary Object* for University of Texas Press. Much of his scholarship deals with the relationship between technology and Western culture.

MIRIAM FUCHS, Associate Professor of English at the University of Hawaii and Associate Editor of *Biography,* publishes in the fields of life writing and modern literature. She edited *Marguerite Young, Our Darling: Tributes and Essays* (Dalkey Archive Press, 1994) and co-edited with Ellen G. Friedman *Breaking the Sequence: Women's Experimental Literature* (Princeton Univ. Press, 1989). Her book *The Text Is Myself: Women's Life Writing and Catastrophe* is forthcoming (Univ. of Wisconsin Press, 2003).

TYRUS MILLER is Associate Professor of Literature at the University of California, Santa Cruz. He is the author of *Late Modernism: Politics, Fiction, and the Arts between the World Wars* and is completing a manuscript entitled *Afterlives of the Readymade: Perspective and Delay in Avant-Garde Aesthetics.* Currently, he is director of the University of California study center in Budapest, Hungary.

STACEY OLSTER is Professor of English at the State University of New York at Stony Brook. Author of *Reminiscence and Re-Creation in Contemporary American Fiction* (Cambridge), Olster's new book, *The Trash Phenomenon: Contemporary Literature, Popular*

Culture, Nation (University of Georgia Press), will be released in 2003. Her many articles have appeared in *Modern Fiction Studies, Critique, Critical Inquiry, Studies in the Novel,* and *Michigan Quarterly Review.*

JOSEPH TABBI is Associate Professor of English at the University of Illinois at Chicago. He is the author of *Postmodern Sublime* and *Cognitive Fictions* and editor of William Gaddis's posthumous novel, *Agapē Agape* and his collected nonfiction, *The Rush for Second Place.* He also edits *ebr,* the *electronic eook review.* His articles on contemporary American literature have appeared in many different forums.

The Iowa Review

The

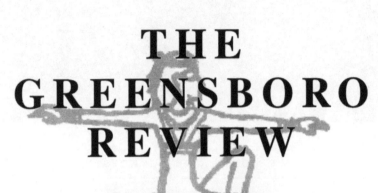

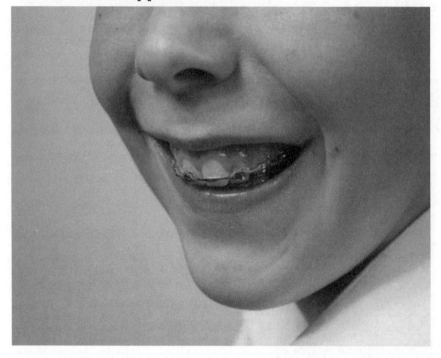
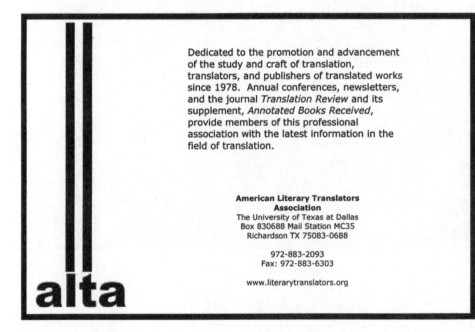

Missions of Interdependence
A Literary Directory
ASNEL Papers 6

Edited by Gerhard Stilz

Amsterdam/New York, NY 2002. XVII,424 pp.
(Cross/Cultures 58)
ISBN: 90-420-1429-6   € 90,-/US$ 90.-
ISBN: 90-420-1419-9   € 43,-/US$ 43.-

At the beginning of the twenty-first century it is necessary to combine into a productive programme the striving for individual emancipation and the social practice of humanism, in order to help the world survive both the ancient pitfalls of particularist terrorism and the levelling tendencies of cultural indifference engendered by the renewed imperialist arrogance of hegemonial global capital.

In this book, thirty-five scholars address and negotiate, in a spirit of learning and understanding, an exemplary variety of intercultural splits and fissures that have opened up in the English-speaking world. Their methodology can be seen to constitute a seminal field of intellectual signposts. They point out ways and means of responsibly assessing colonial predicaments and postcolonial developments in six regions shaped in the past by the British Empire and still associated today through their allegiance to the idea of a Commonwealth of Nations. They show how a new ethic of literary self-assertion, interpretative mediation and critical responsiveness can remove the deeply ingrained prejudices, silences and taboos established by discrimination against race, class and gender.

USA/Canada: One Rockefeller Plaza, Ste. 1420, New York, NY 10020,
Tel. (212) 265-6360, Call toll-free (U.S. only) 1-800-225-3998,
Fax (212) 265-6402
All other countries: Tijnmuiden 7, 1046 AK Amsterdam, The Netherlands.
Tel. ++ 31 (0)20 611 48 21, Fax ++ 31 (0)20 447 29 79
Orders-queries@rodopi.nl   www.rodopi.nl

*S*tudies in *T*wentieth *C*entury *L*iterature

Volume 27, No. 1 (Winter, 2003)

Contributors include:

Malva E. Filer
Jennifer Forrest
Pamela A. Genova
Kimberly Healey
Jutta Ittner
Gerald M. Macklin
Anjali Prabhu

Volume 27, No. 2 (Summer, 2003)

Contributors include:

Susan Carvalho
Laurie Corbin
Scott Macdonald Frame
Raphaël Lambert
Jill LeRoy-Frazier
Eric P. Levy
Laura McLary
Caroline Rupprecht

Silvia Sauter, Editor
Kansas State University
Eisenhower 104
Manhattan, KS 66506-1003
Submissions in: Spanish and Russian

Jordan Stump, Editor
University of Nebraska
PO Box 880318
Lincoln, NE 68588-0318
Submissions in: French and German

Please check our Web site for subscription and other information:

http://www.ksu.edu/stcl/index.html

Dalkey Archive Press

New and Forthcoming Releases

Passages
  by Ann Quin

Chapel Road
  by Louis Paul Boon

Fables of the Novel:
French Fiction since 1990
  by Warren Motte

The Case of the Persevering Maltese:
Collected Essays
  by Harry Mathews

Bad News of the Heart
  by Douglas Glover

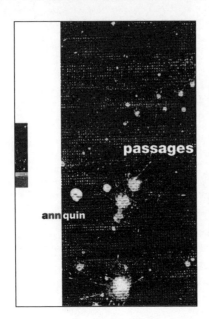

Passages

Ann Quin

British Literature Series
Novel
$12.95 / paper
ISBN: 1-56478-279-4

A book of voices, of landscapes, of seasons, and the passing of time, Ann Quin's finely wrought novels reflects the multiplicity of meanings of the word "passages." Two characters—a woman in search of her brother and the woman's lover in search of himself—travel the Mediterranean landscape trapped in a hopeless relationship.

Mirroring the schizophrenic nature of the characters, the text is broken up into alternating sections of narrative and diary entries. The lyrical nature of the prose counters this fragmentation, as resonances develop amid "cut-up" dreams and fantasies in a fashion similar to a musical composition.

"Ann Quin works over a small area with the finest of tools. . . . Every page, every word gives evidence of her care and workmanship."
—New York Times

"Quin has this talent for throwing off ripples of association . . . her best quality, her subconscious quality."—Alan Burns

—— *Now Available* ——

Dalkey Archive Press

Chapel Road

Louis Paul Boon
Translated by Adrienne Dixon

Netherlandic Literature Series
Novel
$14.95 / paper
ISBN: 1-56478-285-9

> "*Chapel Road* is one long, exuberant flow of language. . . . Boon's people not only breathe, but like Céline's they urinate, defecate, blow their noses in their palms, and make love, or what passes for it, in ditches."
> —*Nation*

Chapel Road is the story of the author L. P. boon, who continues his "illegal writing" (writing without form or function) of the novel "Chapel Road" amid cynical reflections on the work in progress, theories about art, and hilarious anecdotes of Belgian life supplied by his colorful group of friends. Beyond that, a retelling of the myth of Reynard the fox and Isengrinus the wolf constitutes a third storyline, one that underscores the greed, stupidity, hypocrisy, pride and lust motivating the other characters of the book.

Despite Boon's claim that *Chapel Road* is "a pool, a sea, a chaos," this is a meticulously structured novel—one of the most formally inventive works of twentieth-century Flemish literature.

"Chapel Road is one long, exuberant flow of language. . . . Boon's people not only breathe, but like Céline's they urinate, defecate, blow their noses in their palms, and make love, or what passes for it, in ditches. . . . Chapel Road deserves to be read, for if Louis Paul Boon cannot get the whole world into a book, he does manage to encompass much of it."—Nation

—— *Now Available* ——

Fables of the Novel:
French Fiction since 1990

Warren Motte

French Literature Series
Literary Criticism
$19.95 / paper
ISBN: 1-56478-283-2

$49.95 / cloth
ISBN: 1-56478-284-0

Readers of the contemporary novel in France are witnessing the most astonishing reinvigoration of French narrative prose since the New Novel of the 1950s. In the last few years, bold, innovative, and richly compelling novels have been written by a variety of young writers. These texts question traditional strategies of character, plot, theme, and message; and they demand new strategies of reading, too. Choosing ten novels published during the 1990s as examples of that trend, Warren Motte traces the resurgence of the novel in France. He argues that each of the novels under consideration, quite apart from what other story it tells, presents a fable of the novel that deals with the genre's possibilities, limitations, and future as a cultural form.

Warren Motte is a Professor of French and Comparative Literature at the University of Colorado. He is the author of *The Poetics of Experiment: A Study of the Work of Georges Perec, Questioning Edmond Jabés, Playtexts: Ludics in Contemporary Literature,* and *Small Worlds,* and editor of *Oulipo: A Primer of Potential Literature.* He also edited a recent issue of *SubStance* dedicated to the work of Jacques Jouet and is a contributing editor to *CONTEXT* magazine.

—— *Now Available* ——

Dalkey Archive Press

The Case of the Persevering Maltese: Collected Essays

Harry Mathews

American Literature Series
Essays
$14.95 / paper
ISBN: 1-56478-288-3

A companion to last season's *The Human Country: New and Collected Stories,* this volume contains all of Harry Mathews's nonfiction. These astonishing essays cover a wide range of literary topics, including discussions of complex musical forms and Oulipian techniques, to insightful commentaries on the works of Lewis Carroll, Raymond Roussel, Italo Calvino, Joseph McElroy, and Georges Perec. Throughout the collection Mathews carefully examines the relationship between form and literature in a lucid, intimate voice, arguing with intelligence, grace and humor for the importance of artifice.

Harry Mathews is the author of over a dozen books, including the novels *Cigarettes, The Journalist, The Conversions,* and *Tlooth.* In fall 2002, he, along with Trevor Winkfield (the cover artist for both this book and *The Human Country*), was awarded the prestigious Ordre des Arts et des Lettres by the French government.

—— *Available in April 2003* ——

Bad News of the Heart

Douglas Glover

Canadian Literature Series-
Short Stories
$13.95 / paper
ISBN: 1-56478-286-7

A seeing eye dog leads a blind man into a frozen river, a southern Baptist loses his memory and finds true love in Bel Air, an obese dot.com executive has "anorgasmic" latex sex with her CEO, and a homeless man in New York creates an intellectual universe based on Post-it notes stuck to the inside of his cardboard box shelter— Douglas Glover's stories are wildly inventive, deadpan comedies of our universal human catastrophe. They are sly, demanding and wise—stories about language, desire and love (in a very dark place). The humor veers from the wry and sardonic to the salacious, mordant and playful. And always there are moments of such stark emotional intimacy that the reader slides, almost without noticing, from laughter to lament.

"Glover's style is crisp and precise, his observations chillingly perceptive and satirically biting."—Vancouver Sun

"A very nervy writer, the kind who does not play safe and shoots at whatever moon he allows himself to aim at."—Toronto Star

——— *Available in April 2003* ———